# Lionheart

# Also by Douglas Boyd

Histories:
*April Queen, Eleanor of Aquitaine*
*Voices from the Dark Years*
*The French Foreign Legion*
*The Kremlin Conspiracy*
*Blood in the Snow, Blood on the Grass*
*De Gaulle: The Man Who Defied Six US Presidents*
*Normandy in the Time of Darkness*
*The Other First World War*
*Daughters of the KGB*

Novels:
*The Eagle and the Snake*
*The Honour and the Glory*
*The Truth and the Lies*
*The Virgin and the Fool*
*The Fiddler and the Ferret*

# Lionheart

## THE TRUE STORY OF ENGLAND'S
## CRUSADER KING

## DOUGLAS BOYD

**To the memory of
Ehud Netzer,
1936–2010**

*Archaeologist extraordinaire
and friend sorely missed*

First published 2014
This edition published 2015

The History Press
The Mill, Brimscombe Port
Stroud, Gloucestershire, GL5 2QG
www.thehistorypress.co.uk

British Library Cataloguing in Publication Data.
A catalogue record for this book is available from the British Library.

ISBN 978 0 7509 6364 0

Typesetting and origination by The History Press
Printed and bound in Great Britain by TJ International Ltd

# Contents

# Acknowledgements

My thanks are due to four archaeologists and maritime historians who have been extraordinarily generous with their help in tracing the movements of a long-dead English king and gave permission for my use of their copyrighted material published in academic papers and books: Professor John H. Pryor of the Centre for Medieval Studies at the University of Sydney, NSW; and Professor Emeritus Sarah Arenson and Dr Ruthy Gertwagen of the University of Haifa. The late Professor Emeritus Ehud Netzer of the Hebrew University of Jerusalem and Dvorah Netzer not only shared much knowledge with me, but also extended warm welcome and hospitality on my visits to Israel.

Professor Friedrich Heer of the University of Vienna used Jacob Burckhardt's light to illuminate some dark periods of history for me; my Gascon friends Nathalie and Eric Roulet opened my eyes and ears to Occitan as a living language; Eric Chaplain of Princi Neguer publishing house in Pau lent precious source material in that and other languages; fellow author and horsewoman Ann Hyland gave valuable equestrian advice; Jennifer Weller, a wonderful artist, took time out to draw maps and seals; Tuvia Amit helped with details of Arsuf/Apollonia; La Société des Amis du Vieux Chinon authorised me to photograph the unique fresco in the Chapelle Ste-Radegonde; my former comrades-in-arms John Anderson and Colin Priston researched the massacre at York and Hodierna Nutrix, the mystery woman in King Richard's life; the staffs of La Bibliothèque Nationale de France and its online resource *Gallica*, of the British Library and of the Bibliothèque Municipale de Bordeaux made available much source material; that doyen of literary translators, Miguel Castro Mata threw new light on the crusader fleets' stopovers in Portugal; and my partner Atarah Ben-Tovim was an enthusiastic companion following Richard I's travels on both sides of the Channel, in Sicily and the Levant.

Lastly, although chronologically first, I acknowledge my debt to two great teachers, Latinist William McCulloch and George Trotman, an inspiring teacher of French and Spanish, both sometime of Simon Langton School for Boys, Canterbury. Together, they unleashed my passion for linguistics, without which this book, drawn from sources in eight medieval and modern languages, would not have been written.

At The History Press, my thanks go to commissioning editor Mark Beynon, project editor Rebecca Newton, proofreader Emma Wiggin, designer Jemma Cox and cover designer Martin Latham. For this second edition, I thank editor Naomi Reynolds and proofreader Alwyn Harris.

With so much expert support, it goes without saying that any errors are mine.

# Introduction

In the twenty-first century, despite all the tools of enquiry at their disposal, western journalists creating 'history as it happens' overwhelmingly endorse hand-outs from the Pentagon and Downing Street, so that British and American wars are presented as democratic actions undertaken for humanitarian reasons and fought with due respect for human life and protection of non-combatants, even when the government handouts are known by many of those journalists to be patently false, and incontrovertible evidence of war crimes exists. Anyone believing differently need only watch John Pilger's 2010 documentary *The War You Don't See*, which includes shattering admissions of this practice by well-known journalists and elected politicians, government officials and service personnel admitting their morally and legally unacceptable actions during the Iraq War of 2003–11.

History as a record of the past can also be misleading. Living two and a half millennia ago, Herodotus was later dubbed by Cicero 'the father of history' because he was the first person to attempt recording the past methodically. His investigation into the origins of the Greco–Persian wars gave us the word we use today: *istoria*, meaning 'learning by enquiry'. That is the business of historians, of the present or the past.

The first Roman historian to write in Latin was Cato the Elder in the second century BCE. To him, the point of recording the past was to prove the superiority of the Roman race and way of life, and his successors continued to present the Romans always as the good guys and all Rome's wars as just. So, almost from the beginning, history was perverted from Herodotus' open-minded spirit of enquiry by what we today call 'spin', varying from the ethnically biased Roman accounts to the nineteenth-century view of German historian Leopold von Ranke that history should demonstrate a divine plan, with the hand of God manifest in the deeds of men, even when this meant snipping the pieces of time's jigsaw to fit. Ranke's contemporary, the Swiss historian Jacob Burckhardt, disagreed, holding that *all* events should be recorded, whether or not they seem to fit any divine or other plan. However, the teaching of history in Britain's universities followed the Protestant school of Ranke, thanks largely to the great classical scholar Bishop William Stubbs of Oxford. This Christian spin on the teaching and study of history at British universities – and therefore British schools – lasted into the second half of the twentieth century.

To Stubbs, King Richard I of England should have been seen as a heroic figure because he led the Third Crusade with the intention of reconquering Jerusalem from the Saracen. In fact, Stubbs' opinion was that Richard was '… a bad ruler; his energy, or rather his restlessness, his love of war and his genius for it, effectively disqualified him from being a peaceful one; his utter want of political common sense from being a prudent one.' Stubbs' considered opinion was that Richard was 'a man of blood, whose crimes were those of one whom long use of warfare had made too familiar with slaughter … and a vicious man'. [1]

Sir Steven Runciman, another respected historian of the crusades, summed up the two sides of Richard's character: 'He was a bad son, a bad husband and a bad king, but a gallant and splendid soldier.'[2] Richard spent his entire adult life in warfare and consistently displayed supreme physical courage, but *gallant* and *splendid* are not adjectives one would use today.

When writing of the past, it is a responsibility of historians to consult contemporary sources whenever possible, but also to weight them according to their authors' relationship with the subjects of whom and the issues of which they wrote, and to take into account the political and religious pressures on the chroniclers.

In my biography of Richard the Lionheart's mother – that extraordinary woman, Eleanor of Aquitaine, who was the target of calumnies and slanders in her own lifetime and afterwards – it was vital to bear in mind that the contemporary sources in Latin were written by celibate and misogynistic monks. Even St Bernard of Clairvaux, the wise founder of the Cistercian Order, could not bear to look upon his own sister in her nun's robes. In addition to their aversion to all women as the perceived cause of men's lust, the chroniclers owed a political loyalty to either Eleanor's French husband King Louis VII, whom she divorced, or England's King Henry II, who locked her up for a decade and a half after she raised their sons in rebellion against him. The chroniclers were thus extremely unlikely to be objective about this major player on the European stage, and their comments on her must be assessed with that in mind.

Similarly, when evaluating King Richard I, it is necessary to examine closely the enduring legend of this 'parfit gentil knight' and noble Christian monarch who selflessly abandoned his kingdom in 1190 to risk all in performing his religious duty to liberate the Holy Land from the Saracen. In fact, the legend originated as a PR campaign orchestrated by Queen Eleanor to blackmail the citizens of the Plantagenet Empire into stumping up the enormous ransom demanded for his release from an imprisonment that was all of his own making and had nothing to do with religion.

The motto of Hitler's propaganda minister Josef Goebbels – that a big lie will succeed where a smaller one may be questioned – was already understood by Eleanor and used by her, for Richard was held prisoner not by the Saracen enemy in the Holy Land, but by the ruler of the Holy Roman Empire, Henry VI Hohenstaufen. He had not been captured fighting heroically in battle, but while slinking homewards incognito at the end of his pointless crusade which cost tens of thousands of lives on both sides, leaving an undying legacy of hatred in the Muslim world, where *malik Rik* is still a name with which to frighten disobedient little boys. Although the Church protected the persons and property of crusaders during their absence from their homelands, even the pope did little to protect this English king from Hohenstaufen and his vassal Duke Leopold of Austria, one of many European fellow crusaders humiliated and alienated by Richard's arrogance during the abortive Third Crusade.

As Bishop Stubbs knew well, Richard had spent his whole life shedding blood, not tactically and face-to-face with a more or less equally matched enemy, but strategically, by slaughtering defenceless peasant men, women and children, laying waste their fields and cutting down their orchards to bring starvation to the survivors, thus depriving a noble enemy of the support base for his unproductive way of life. It was, to use a modern expression, total war. Because of the enormous suffering thus inflicted on millions of innocent people, the Church pronounced the slaughter of farm animals and the destruction of agricultural implements in war to be a sin. Although professedly devout on occasion, Richard was not deterred by this interdiction.

Edward Gibbon held that history was 'little more than the register of the crimes, follies and misfortunes of mankind'. No other single life better illustrates that judgement than the life of King Richard I. This, then, is the story, *warts and all*, of a man born to parents of unsurpassed intelligence, wealth and achievements and whose birthright raised him to worldwide fame, yet who died in agony, 'naked as he came into this world'.

*Douglas Boyd*
*South West France, 2014*

## NOTES

1.  W. Stubbs, ed., *Itinerarium Peregrinorum et Gesta Regis Ricardi*, Rolls Series (1864), pp. 17, 21, 27.
2.  Quoted in S. Runciman, *A History of the Crusades* (Cambridge: CUP, 1954), Vol 3, p. 75.

# Part 1:

# The Education of a Prince

# To Eleanor, a Son

illions of modern people believe that the relative positions of the constellations at the moment of their birth, as seen with the naked eye from this planet, affect their character and influence the entire course of their lives. It is therefore hardly surprising that astrology was considered a serious science in the twelfth century, several centuries before superstition was gradually replaced by scientific knowledge in the Enlightenment. In what then seemed a proof that astrology was an important and reliable science, during the night of 8 September 1157, two male infants were born in England, 40 miles apart.

The royal palace known as 'the King's Houses', later called Beaumont Palace and eventually demolished, stood near the site of Oxford's Worcester College. A commemorative plaque on the north side of Beaumont Street records its existence and the fact that two kings of England were born there: Richard I and his younger brother John. The palace had been built by their great-grandfather Henry I outside the north gate of Oxford city because it was a comfortable ride from there to his hunting tower at Woodstock.

In the *nova aula* or royal apartments of the palace on that night the most famous woman of her time gave birth to her third son by the man she had married as Count Henry of

Anjou – and who, thanks in large part to her wealth and political acumen, had since become King Henry II of England. Her name was Eleanor of Aquitaine. In addition to being queen of England, she was also duchess of Normandy and Aquitaine and countess of Anjou and Poitou. Because infant mortality was rife at the time and long after, the newborn prince was speedily christened Richard, and would live to become England's most enduringly famous king.

On the same September night when he was born at Oxford, a woman previously unknown to history with the fashionable northern French name of Hodierna or Audierne[1] also gave birth to a son, in St Albans. Hodierna's son was given the name Alexander and grew up to be among the foremost philosopher-scientists of his time, Alexander of Neckham.[2]

Noblewomen did not normally breastfeed their children; it was their custom to bind the breasts tightly after a birth so that they would not acquire the natural curves of peasant mothers. In 1157 it would certainly have been considered inappropriate for the Queen of England to suckle her child, even had Eleanor not insisted on accompanying her husband on his ceaseless travels to impose his authority and his new laws throughout the Plantagenet Empire on both sides of the Channel. Possible candidates for the honour of nursing Eleanor's newborn son included many women who had recently given birth, but Hodierna was chosen, probably on the advice of an astrologer to whom it seemed particularly auspicious that he should be raised on the milk of a woman who had delivered a child on the same night the new prince was born.

Shortly after the birth, Eleanor left her newborn son with her servants in the comfort and safety of the palace and resumed her itinerant lifestyle that lasted until the court settled briefly at Lincoln for Christmas. Only then could her ladies' servants unpack from travelling chests and leather sacks the finery in which their mistresses dressed for the festival. After this, Henry began a twelve-month tour of the kingdom that took in

3,000 miles of travel along roads that had not been repaired since the Romans left eight centuries before – a trip on which Eleanor accompanied him for much of the time.

The queen's itinerant lifestyle precluding prolonged childcare, Hodierna was installed in the King's Houses, bringing her own son with her and breastfeeding both him and Eleanor's newborn, with Prince Richard having the privilege of the right breast, thought to produce richer milk. Living in the royal apartments, Hodierna's relationship with the other members of the household reflected her importance in that age of high infant mortality. To be appointed wet nurse to a prince was both a very high honour and a heavy responsibility: should the royal infant die a cot death, for example, she would be accused of over-lying him. Should he die of some childhood infection outside her control, there too she would be held to account.

It was customary for infants to be breastfed until 2 years old or possibly older, to avoid any possibility of tuberculosis from imbibing cow's milk – a connection that was known even in this time of little understanding of infection. Thereafter, her duties for the young Prince Richard included all his toilet needs, dressing him and preparing all his food, even masticating meat and placing it in his mouth until he was able to chew for himself. Throughout his early years she would stay close to him, picking him up when he fell, comforting him and caring for him if and when he contracted childhood ailments. She was, in short, the source of all that complex of affection and caring that today is labelled 'maternal'.[3] Throughout his life, Richard would visit and care for Hodierna as the woman for whom he felt most affection, in much the same way that many middle-class Englishmen in the twentieth century felt affection for the nannies who brought them up until they were sent away to boarding school. Thirty-three years after his birth at Oxford Richard allotted the annual rent of £7 10s from a house at Rowdon, between Chippenham and Bath, 'to Hodierna *nutrix*', meaning, Hodierna the wet nurse.

Hodierna and her charges lived in the most privileged stratum of Anglo-Norman society, in which 200 families related in easily traceable degree owned half the country. Beneath them toiled the native Anglo-Saxons, few of whom rose to greatness in the cruel occupation that was a slow genocide, with native males being displaced or killed and their more desirable females taken as concubines and wives by their new overlords. Traces of the racial/class divide of this time still exist in the bastard Germanic-Romance language that became modern English. For the live animals herded, tended, milked and slaughtered by the natives, we still use their Anglo-Saxon names like *sheep, calf, cow* and *swine*. For the meat on the table, which only the French-speaking over-lords were allowed to eat, we use the French equivalents: *mutton, veal, beef* and *pork*. Not surprisingly, Prince Richard was to grow up regarding the English as a race of serfs who spoke a barbarous tongue he never learned and who existed only to serve their mas-ters – in his case, once he came to power, as a source of finance.

Eleanor was a remote mother, appearing at intervals and then departing for months at a time on her travels in England and on the Continent. But such was her commanding presence and so tantalising were her arrivals and departures that Richard was never able to outgrow his bond with her. To these two women, then, Hodierna who mothered him and Queen Eleanor who super-vised his education and upbringing in the tradition of her native Aquitaine – of which she was determined he would one day be duke, if not king of England too – Richard remained close all his life. They and his sisters were, in fact, the only women in his life.

Geraldus Cambrensis, or Gerald of Wales, archdeacon of Brecon, a contemporary of Richard, wrote a treatise entitled *De Principis Instructione – On the Education of a Prince –* to illustrate the inculcation of the virtues a monarch should have. Richard's upbringing was far from that ideal.

In the fifteen years of her marriage to Louis VII of France, Eleanor had produced only two daughters..Her failure to give him a son and heir had been the key to the annulment that freed her to marry Henry of Anjou. In the five years so far spent with Henry she had done her queenly duty in providing him with a daughter, Princess Matilda, and three sons, one of whom had died. After Richard, Eleanor was to bear the princes Geoffrey and John and the princesses Eleanor and Joanna. For a royal couple to beget so many offspring was unusual, for it could lead to a repeat of the situation after the death of William the Norman, whose ten children fought over the realm he had acquired by defeating the last Saxon ruler, King Harold Godwinson, at the Battle of Hastings in 1066. Since neither Henry nor Eleanor was stupid, it seems that their purpose in begetting so many offspring was to marry them off to unite the rulers of the whole of Western Europe in a web of common family relationships dominated by ... Henry and Eleanor.[4]

A great-grandson of the Conqueror, Henry was an even more frequently absent parent than the queen. There is no record that he bore any affection for his children. In January 1163 he returned to England after an absence of four and a half years, briefly crossing paths with Eleanor and Richard, who departed in the other direction some weeks later. All the evidence points to Henry having regarded his daughters as political tools to be used in marriage alliances with other royal European families. As for his four surviving sons, he refused the easy way out, which was to make one into a churchman, to reduce the internecine rivalry by that son's consequent ineligibility to exercise royal power. He did, however, appoint his bastard son Geoffrey to be bishop of Lincoln and later archbishop of York.

Richard and the three other legitimate sons were tormented by Henry throughout their childhood, adolescence and adult lives. He would first promise something to one of them and then give it to another, only to take it away when it pleased him to do so and give it to a third. It was a technique he used with allies, vassals and enemies too, having learned it from his mother the Empress Matilda.[5] Life, she taught her son, was like venery: always show the bait to the hawk, but take it away again before the bird can bite in order to keep it hungry and anxious to please.[6] In the protracted bloody civil war against her cousin Stephen of Blois for the throne of England, Matilda's policy had alienated so many allies that she had only narrowly escaped back to France with her life. While the life-is-like-venery approach could thus not be said to have worked for her, Henry used this manipulative technique throughout his life, outwitting enemies and allies alike, but succeeded in making enemies of his own sons.

Richard's mother was by her own birthright countess of Poitou, which by tradition also made her duchess of the thirteen counties that made up the immense duchy of Aquitaine. Since her only brother's death she had been raised for this task, and had been, in the words of her first modern biographer Amy Kelly, accustomed to travel with the peripatetic household of her father Duke William X:

> ... from the foothills of the Pyrenees to the River Loire on those long *chevauchées* made necessary by the ducal business of overlooking intriguing vassals and presumptuous clergy, and carrying law and justice to the remoter corners of creation. She knew ... the scarped heights where the baronial strongholds loomed above their clustering hamlets [of mud and straw huts]. She knew the red-roofed towns and the traffic of each one; here a lazar house, there a hostel thronging with pilgrims returning from Saint James [of Compostela] or the shrines of the pious Limousin. Melle she knew, where there was a ducal mint, and Blaye where, in the glow of forges, armourers repaired their travelling gear and Maillezais where her aunt, the Abbess Agnes, never failed to halt the ducal progress for a largess.[7]

In her childhood, at the end of each day's long ride this privileged heiress of a duke was deferred to by the assembled castellans, bishops, abbots, merchants, troubadours and hangers-on who constituted the ducal court going about its programme of feudal business. This headstrong, intelligent and beautiful girl born to the corridors of power grew up to be the only queen ever to sit on the thrones of both France and England. Becoming duchess when she was just 15 years old, after her father died on pilgrimage to Santiago de Compostela, she married Prince Louis Capet two weeks before he succeeded his father as king of France and took the title Louis VII, making his teenage bride the queen of France.

Eleanor defied the papal interdiction on women travelling with the Second Crusade 'except for decent washerwomen'[8] and accompanied Louis and the French army on the long march overland to the Holy Land, fighting the influence over her husband of the crusade's bishops and his own chaplain. By divorcing Louis VII after the crusade to marry Henry of Anjou, she changed the balance of power in Western Europe.

The divorce had been arranged by negotiation between Louis' bishops and her vassal, Archbishop Geoffroy of Bordeaux. The more worldly of Louis Capet's churchmen, like Archbishop Suger of St Denis, who had also served the late King Louis VI as chancellor, were reluctant to see the taxes of her immense dowry of Aquitaine and Poitou lost to the royal purse. They also considered it dangerous that one-third of France would revert to her personal control in the absence of a husband. Against that, the more pious of Louis' prelates, like Abbot Bernard of Clairvaux, quoted from the Sermon on the Mount, when Christ said that an eye that sinned should be plucked out and thrown away, for it was better to lose a hand or eye than for the whole body to be cast into hellfire. These bishops agonised over the state of the king's soul and wanted him separated as swiftly as possible from 'the whore of Aquitaine', suspected of gross misconduct including an affair with her uncle Raymond of Toulouse during her stay in the Holy Land while on the pointless Second Crusade with Louis. They saw a divorce as the only way to save Louis' soul from further sin by removing from his bed – not that they often slept together – the obstreperous consort who had briefly weaned him away from the influence of the Church, for high office in which he had been raised until called to supreme temporal office by the accidental death of his older brother.

In March 1152 the archbishop of Sens, who had presided over the condemnation of the teacher Peter Abelard, castrated in punishment for his scandalously illicit sexual relationship with his adolescent pupil Heloïse, convened the most important churchmen and lay nobles of Louis' territory at the castle of Beaugency, between Orleans and Blois. Louis, with charity rare among royalty, refused to accuse his queen of anything that might be prejudicial to her and decreed that the marriage be dissolved on the grounds of consanguinity alone. Being a woman, Eleanor was not allowed to speak. Her advocate, Archbishop Geoffroy of Bordeaux, who had negotiated her marriage to Louis fifteen years earlier, stipulated the return of her dowry lands in the same condition as at the time of the marriage, in consideration of which she would remain a faithful vassal of King Louis. After arrangements were agreed for an audit to ensure that this condition was observed, Eleanor was free – at the price of a recent unwanted pregnancy forced on her by the pope and the loss of her two daughters by Louis, who remained the property of their father.

Eleanor departed from Beaugency in a cortège of her vassals, the richest woman in the world by far but a potential prey for any noble with the nerve and force to kidnap and forcibly marry her. This nearly happened twice in the next few days during the journey home to her own lands. Near Blois, 16-year-old Geoffrey Plantagenet attempted an ambush that failed.[9] On the Loire crossing at Tours another ambush by Thibault of Blois, son of the count of Champagne, likewise failed when Eleanor's route was changed at the last minute.

Once safely installed in her own quarters in the Tour Maubergeonne of the comital palace at Poitiers, 30-year-old Eleanor lost no time in repudiating all the charters appertaining to her lands that she had been obliged to sign with Louis. Taking stock of her situation, she had no illusions. Her position was the same as it had been fifteen years earlier after inheriting title to the duchy of Aquitaine on her father's death. So rich an heiress, while unmarried and therefore unprotected by a

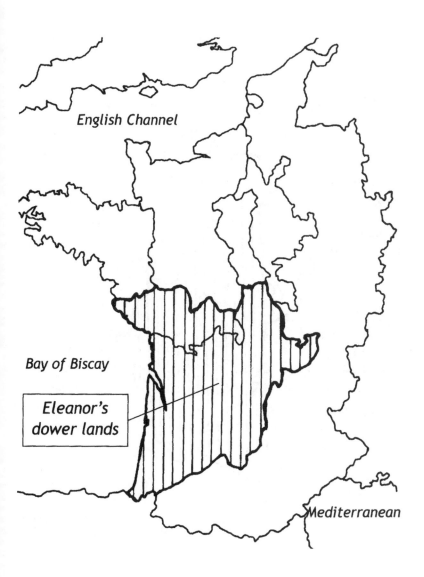

English Channel

Bay of Biscay

Eleanor's
dower lands

Mediterranean

Twelfth-century France showing Eleanor's territorial inheritance

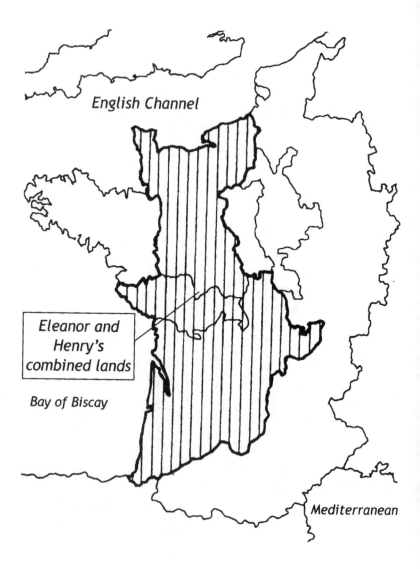

English Channel

Eleanor and
Henry's
combined lands

Bay of Biscay

Mediterranean

Eleanor and Henry's combined lands

father or husband, was constantly at risk of having her territory invaded, and being obliged to wed the invader. Although just released from a marriage that had bored her for years, she had therefore swiftly to remarry a powerful noble, whose territories added to hers would make the couple a force to be reckoned with. Her choice was dictated not by love, but *realpolitik*. It fell on a neighbour whom she had met at the Capetian court when he and his father came to do homage to King Louis.

On 6 April Geoffrey Plantagenet's older brother, the 19-year-old Count Henry of Anjou, whose county abutted on the northern border of Poitou, announced to his assembled vassals that he was going to marry the 30-year-old ex-wife of his overlord Louis Capet. He had previously sought the hand of one of Louis VII's daughters, but abandoned that suit for Eleanor's far richer dowry.[10] Feudal custom demanded that two vassals of Louis must request his approval to their match, but this was something that neither Henry nor Eleanor had any intention of doing. They also chose to ignore the even closer ties of consanguinity between themselves than those which had justified Eleanor's canonical repudiation by Louis Capet. In addition, Henry ignored a new slander being circulated to blacken the name of the woman who had rejected the king of France: that she had slept with Henry's own womanising father, Geoffrey the Fair.

Negotiations on Eleanor's behalf were again conducted by Archbishop Geoffroy of Bordeaux. On 18 May 1152 in the grandeur of Poitiers Cathedral, which lies a short walk from the comital palace, the knot was tied with due ceremony[11] amid excitement and apprehension among their vassals, for the refusal of the two spouses to seek Louis' approval constituted grounds for his military intervention, should he be able to assemble a sufficiently powerful army to come and punish them.

Through his mother Empress Matilda – so called by virtue of her first marriage to the German Holy Roman Emperor Henry V – Count Henry was also duke of Normandy and overlord of Maine and Touraine. Allying Eleanor's lands to his made him the

most powerful man in France. Together, they controlled more
than half the country, which was far more than poor Louis Capet
could claim as his own domain. The icing on the cake for Henry
was that the acquisition of Eleanor's dower lands also increased
immeasurably his chances of recovering what the Empress
Matilda regarded as part of her birthright: the disputed kingdom
of England. For that, Henry of Anjou surely owed his new wife a
debt of lifelong gratitude. Did Eleanor know that Henry's gratitude never lasted? She can hardly have guessed then that, two
decades later, he would be her implacable enemy, against whom
she would raise their adult sons in armed rebellion.

Louis' advisers counselled him to summon Henry of Anjou to
Paris to answer to a charge of treason for marrying without his
suzerain's consent. Although Eleanor was equally guilty, the king
refused then or at any other time to make any move against his
ex-wife. Since Henry showed no sign of putting in an appearance
to be judged, Louis gathered together a host, partly by pardoning vassals like Robert of Dreux, who had joined a coalition of
usurping nobles while Louis was absent in the Holy Land on
crusade. Others, like Thibault V de Blois, were bribed – in his case
by betrothal to Eleanor's 2-year-old second daughter by Louis.
Her other daughter abandoned in Paris, 7-year-old Aelith, had
just been married to Count Henry I of Champagne, enlisting
him and his vassals to the royal cause by bringing to the House
of Champagne the child bride's tenuous claim to her mother's
duchy of Aquitaine.

Normally, the Church would have supported Louis in his
intention to punish Henry and Eleanor, but the French prelates
and the pope were too busy playing another political game to
get involved in this squabble: Pope Eugenius III had instructed
Archbishop Theobald of Canterbury not to crown Eustace
of Boulogne as the future successor to his father Stephen of
Blois on the throne of England. Henry of Anjou's recent marriage thus made him the strongest contender for the throne of
England after Stephen's death. On Midsummer Day, a little over

one month after the May wedding and in the hope of weakening Henry's position in the competition for the crown of England, Stephen also sent a contingent to join Louis' forces invading the Plantagenet possessions. The motives of the other members of Louis' coalition, like young Geoffrey of Anjou, were simpler: to grab and hold on to whatever part of Henry and Eleanor's territories they could conquer and occupy. There was indeed so much territory at stake that each could easily have acquired a county or two for himself, if victorious.

## NOTES

1. Latin adjective *hodierna*, meaning 'of today'.
2. Also spelled Necham and Nequam. The latter, being Latin for 'worthless', was possibly a play on words, or a comparison with his more famous milk-brother.
3. See, inter alia, F. and J. Gies, *Marriage and the Family in the Middle Ages* (New York: Hudson and Row, 1987), pp. 176–203.
4. See at greater length D. Boyd, *Eleanor, April Queen of Aquitaine* (Stroud: The History Press, 2011), pp. 179–82.
5. Originally christened Edith and also known as Maud.
6. Walter Map, ed. M. Rhodes James, *De Nugis Curialium* (Cambridge: Cambridge University Press, 2010), p. 238.
7. A. Kelly, *Eleanor of Aquitaine and the Four Kings* (Cambridge, MA: Harvard University Press, 1981), pp. 6–7 (abridged by the author).
8. W. Stubbs, *Roger of Howden Chronica*, Vol 2, p. 335.
9. A. Richard, *Histoire des Comtes de Poitou* (Paris: Picard, 1903), Vol 2, p. 108.
10. Kelly, *Eleanor of Aquitaine*, p. 193.
11. William of Newburgh, *Historia Rerum Anglicarum*, ed. R. Howlett in *Chronicles of the Reigns of Stephen, Henry II and Richard I*, Rolls Series 82 (London: Longmans, 1884), Vol 1, p. 93.

# 2

# Duke to King, Duchess to Queen

I t seemed, briefly, that Henry had been caught unawares because he was heavily involved with preparations to invade England and reclaim the kingdom lost by his mother in the protracted civil war against Stephen of Blois – a time of strife in which, it was said, 'Christ and his angels slept' while the country was ravaged by Stephen's Flemish mercenaries and even the palace of Westminster was turned into a dosshouse. In fact, Henry had been preparing for Louis' move ever since the council of war on 6 April. The speed and savagery with which he now led his forces to lay waste Robert of Dreux's lands caused the Church to beg for a truce, a chance Louis leaped at after falling psychosomatically ill. Ignoring both, Henry rode south with his customary speed to capture the castle of Montsoreau from a castellan who supported his brother Geoffrey. One by one, his other enemies fled the field, leaving Eleanor and her husband the strongest force in France and in a stronger position to invade England the following year.

They spent that autumn *en chevauchée* – literally riding the length and breadth of her lands together to impress on every vassal, both lay and religious (for an abbot was required like any other baron to lead his contingent of armed men in the field in support of his overlord) that the new duke would ruthlessly crush any attempts at secession during his absence the following year when Henry intended invading England. Just one example was needed to impress all the other vassals. It came when the couple arrived at Limoges for Henry's coronation as duke and were at first greeted with acclamation by the populace and the abbot and his community. Following feudal custom, Henry demanded accommodation and food for his retinue but the abbot of Limoges refused, pleading that the custom only covered a modest ducal party lodged within the walls, whereas Henry's retinue, expanded by many of his vassals and vavasours who had come to witness the ceremony, was encamped outside them. It is probable that the dispute had more to do with the numbers involved than where exactly they were sleeping but, when fighting erupted between his soldiery and the resentful townsfolk, Henry ordered that they and the abbot be taught a lesson. The newly built bridge across the River Vienne was torn down, as were the recently rebuilt city walls,[1] making Duke Henry's point that his retinue was no longer 'without the walls' which no longer existed, and therefore should be fed.

Once crowned duke of Aquitaine, he was deterred from further punitive action in the Limousin by news from England that his mother's erstwhile supporters in England were now prepared to support his claim to the throne of England. To them he was known as Henry fitz-Empress, meaning 'son of the Empress'. Others called him by the sobriquet Curtmantle, from his habit of wearing a short cloak, which, although offering less protection from the weather than a long one, allowed quicker reactions in the saddle. It was a sartorial expression of his pragmatic nature and impatience. The chronicler Peter of Blois observed that Henry could ride in one day the distance others would cover in four or five; as Louis' supporters had found out, his speed of attack was to become legendary.

Instead of waiting for milder weather, Henry now insisted on braving the winter gales by crossing the Channel with a small army of mercenaries transported in a fleet of twenty-six vessels from the little port at Barfleur in the lee of the Cotentin Peninsula on 8 January 1153.[2] In a series of marches, counter-marches and skirmishes without any major battle, he and Stephen manoeuvred for advantage, with Henry and his supporters controlling the south-west, the Midlands and much of northern England, while Stephen held the more valuable south and east. The biggest confrontation seemed likely to happen on the River Thames at Wallingford, where the castle had been besieged by Stephen for months, but the barons on both sides were more in favour of a settlement, allowing the bishops to arrange a truce, during which Henry and Stephen met face-to-face.

A few days after Eleanor gave birth to his first son in August 1153, Henry learned that King Stephen's son Eustace of Boulogne had choked to death during a meal. In the hope of avoiding another protracted civil war, the grieving king of England agreed to name Henry his successor to the detriment of his surviving son, William, and this succession was confirmed by treaty negotiated by Archbishop Theobald of Canterbury and witnessed by fourteen bishops and eleven earls of the realm. Since Stephen was more than thirty years older than Henry, and thus an old man by the standards of the time, it was virtually certain that the young count of Anjou would soon inherit the crown of England without having to fight for it, although hostilities continued in a desultory fashion until November, when the Church arranged the Treaty of Winchester, in which cathedral the reigning king of England exchanged the kiss of peace with Henry of Anjou, who was formally adopted as his son and heir.

Whilst absent in England, he had left his mother's iron hand in control of Normandy and Eleanor ruling their southern continental domains from the comital palace at Angers. The two duchesses' courts could not have been more different. His mother's in Rouen was austere and pious like her; while approving the match politically, Matilda disliked her daughter-in-law as an immoral opportunist, more given to pleasure than prayer. After years in Louis VII's comfortless court on the Île de la Cité in Paris and the months on the road with Henry, Eleanor was determined to enliven her own court in the spirit of her grandfather Duke William IX, inviting troubadours to compose poetry and risqué songs and *jonglars* to sing and entertain her in French and Occitan with songs like 'A la entrada del tens clar' ('At the beginning of spring'):

> Qui donc la vesés dançar e son gent còrs deportar
> ben pogrà dir' de vertat qu'el mond non aja sa par,
> la reina joiosa!

> [He who sees her in the dance, / sees her noble body twist and twirl, / must surely say that in all the world / for beauty there's no equal/ of this joyful queen.]

She also exercised her feudal right as matchmaker, pairing young gallants who met her standards of elegance with suitable young ladies of the court, neither party being able to marry without her consent.[3] For this she was called, in Occitan, the language of southern France, *la reina aurilhosa* or the April Queen – a southern synonym for the Queen of the May in northern countries, where spring comes a month later than in Aquitaine.

Though far away across the Channel, Henry was not without news, or rather gossip, of the goings-on. Eleanor's court attracted troubadours, one of the most famous of whom was Bernat de Ventadorn,[4] who, although low-born of a sergeant-at-arms and a cook, had the talent that enabled him to mix in high society. When he became a little too familiar with his duchess, he was summoned to join her husband's itinerant court in England, as pleasureless as the Empress Matilda's at Rouen. He lamented his exile in verse:

Aissí'm part d'amor e'm recrè.

Mòrt ma per mort li respond

e vau m'en, pos ilh no'm reten,

ciatius en eissilh no sai ont.

[I must leave my love and go away / banished I know not where /
for she does not bid me stay / though this cruel exile I cannot bear.]

Giving birth to Henry's first son, Eleanor expunged the ignominy
of being considered the queen who had produced only daughters
for Louis Capet. The supply of fashionable names for the nobility
was limited, with many a William, Henry and Geoffrey, so the
boy was named William after her father and grandfather and all
the other Williams in her line. He was also given the courtesy
title 'duke of Aquitaine'. Some indication of Eleanor's newfound
independence is to be found in the charters she signed at this
time without mentioning Henry, who was, after all, the titular
duke of Aquitaine by right of marriage. Her vassal Archbishop
Geoffroy proudly declared in Bordeaux that Aquitaine acknowledged her alone as its suzerain.[5]

However, while waiting to inherit the English crown, Henry
returned to France to demonstrate his power by summoning Eleanor and their infant son to live in the ducal palace at
Rouen. In return for a 'fine' of 1,000 silver marks,[6] Louis VII
agreed to cease including the title 'duke of Aquitaine' among his
many others, which he had the right to do under a technicality
of the annulment contract. That canny churchman Archbishop
Geoffroy of Bordeaux sniffed the wind of change and proclaimed
that the master of Aquitaine was now Henry of Anjou.[7] Henry,
for his part, acknowledged his obligation as a vassal of King Louis
in respect of his continental holdings by leading an army to help
him pacify the restless territory of the Vexin, which lay between
Normandy and Louis' domains.

Although the twelfth century lies within the academic field
of medievalists, the near-incessant warfare of the time can only

be understood as the birth pangs of what we call the Middle Ages. European civilisation was in a state of flux, still emerging from the Dark Ages. Everywhere, might was right in this time of perpetual manoeuvre for advantage, each noble, baron or king, whatever the title he had inherited, having only the authority gained by his last confrontation. Alliances were made to be broken; feudal duty had constantly to be reimposed on his vassals by every overlord using fire and sword. Anyone who doubts this has only to see the thousands of castles that pock the face of France, built by barons but also by every local lordling to keep his enemies at bay.

Society was formally divided into three classes, *pugnantes, orantes et laborantes* – those who fought, those who prayed and the nameless many whose toil supported the totally unproductive knightly class. The Church attempted to moderate the worst excesses of this martial chaos, intervening on behalf of the peasants who bore the brunt of each invasion and raid, but was itself on occasion the cause of strife as it manoeuvred for temporal power under successive popes. If this is confusing for the modern reader, it was all the more so for those who lived through this time.

Shortly after Stephen's death on 25 October 1154, messengers from Archbishop Theobald arrived to tell Henry that he was now England's monarch, making Eleanor England's queen. The devout Louis Capet was so discountenanced by this swift turnaround in the fortunes of his former wife that he departed on pilgrimage to Santiago de Compostela. Refusing to ask for safe conduct through her territory, he took a longer route through Catalunya, which also gave him an excuse to visit the Christian courts of northern Spain in search of a new wife.

Within two weeks of hearing the news from Canterbury, Henry assembled an impressive retinue including the most important barons and prelates of Normandy. The Empress Matilda was, diplomatically, not included in the party for fear her presence might alienate the many enemies she had made in England from her son's cause. Eleanor, seven months pregnant, joined the party at

Barfleur, to find herself facing many of the Norman nobility and churchmen who had enjoyed her humiliation on the Second Crusade when she was abducted in disgrace from her uncle's court at Antioch.[8] She would not have been human if she did not savour every minute of their discomfiture in now having to show supreme deference to the queen of England, who was no mere consort, but a duchess and countess in her own right and whose possessions far outweighed theirs.

And there they stayed, in enforced proximity in the little Norman port, while November gales blew in from the Atlantic so violently that no ship could put to sea. In the back of everyone's mind was the tragic loss of the *la Blanche-Nef* or White Ship, in the wreck of which Henry I had lost his heir and his bastard sons when it sank just outside the port in 1120, in an accident said by many to be God's punishment for the sodomy practised by many aboard. By 7 December the patience of Eleanor's husband was exhausted. Determined to be crowned before Christmas so that the coronation could take place before the austerity of Lent, he set out in defiance of the elements in a clinker-built vessel with a high forecastle and raised poop very like the one that had sunk. Even with reefed sails, the ships of his little fleet soon lost contact despite bugle calls and horn lanterns displayed at mastheads during the night. For more than twenty-four hours the human and equine passengers were buffeted by wind and pushed off course by tides. With no compasses then available and clouds obscuring the stars, it seems a miracle that they all made landfall, although in harbours widely separated, on the south coast of England. The royal party landed near Lyndhurst in the New Forest, where King William Rufus had been assassinated under cover of a hunting accident, allowing Henry's grandfather to seize the throne a few days later by locking up his elder brother for life.

Henry and Eleanor rode first to Winchester to secure the treasury of the realm, commandeering fresh horses along the way and acquiring a cortège of Anglo-Norman nobility and clergy eager to demonstrate loyalty to their new overlord. Archbishop

Theobald awaited them at Westminster with the assembled bishops of the realm, but both the abbey and the palace of Westminster had been vandalised by Stephen's mercenaries, forcing the royal party to set up home in the palace of Bermondsey, a low island in the unhealthy malarial marshes south of the River Thames. The coronation on the Sunday before Christmas took place in Westminster Abbey – a mixed scene of pomp and squalor.

The Jersey poet Robert Wace described a banquet that may have been the coronation feast, with beef, pork and game consumed in large quantities, flavoured with herbs and imported spices. To finish, there were stewed and candied fruit, jellies, tarts, waffles and wafers – thin pastries served with sweet white wine – the servers then entertaining the assembly with tumbling, music and dance. There may also have been some wit – all in French, of course – from *joculatores* to raise a belly laugh and perhaps, riskiest of all, a *joculatrix* to make them laugh, although at such a moment political correctness must have been an uneasy line to tread.

The men were clean-shaven; beards were a sign of unfashionable Englishness. Henry's short cloaks set a fashion: men had their long cloaks, favoured by Stephen, cut down to show their political sympathies, and wore their hair shoulder-length; women had longer hair. Both sexes wore furs for warmth in the ill-heated living quarters, where braziers of glowing charcoal exuded carbon monoxide fumes. The city of London was, in chronicler Walter Map's words, a haunt of pimps and whores, though his less squeamish fellow courtier William fitz Stephen thought it a noble city. Most houses were built of wood with thatched roofs; destructive fires ravaged the city repeatedly. But London was big, even for Eleanor who knew Paris and Constantinople: within its walls Paris covered only 25 acres; girdled by London Wall were 326 acres of homes, shops, taverns, cookhouses and the bustling port itself – all, as Richard would later decide, producing taxes for him to spend as he chose. So cramped were living conditions in this vast metropolis that richer citizens were already moving out to live in the meadows around Clerkenwell and St Clement's

Well where wells had water less likely to be polluted by the ubiquitous, stinking cesspits.

Roughly half of England was held as fiefs by the Anglo-Norman barons, the balance belonging to the Crown and the Church. To see things for himself, Henry immediately set off to tour his new possessions while Eleanor prepared for the birth on 28 February 1155 of her second son, named Henry after his father, who was absent in the North at the time, forcibly impressing upon some recalcitrant barons that he was their new master. At Whitsuntide Eleanor moved her *familia* or household into the palace of Westminster, renovated, refurbished and furnished at record speed by men working day and night under the workaholic young Thomas Becket, whose rise to become Henry's chancellor displaced Eleanor from the royal councils. Recommended to the king by Archbishop Theobald of Canterbury as the man most likely to bring the state finances into order after nineteen years of misrule, Becket forfeited sleep as a good courtier must, sharing not only the king's working hours but also his leisure pursuits of horses, hawks and hounds or a game of chess or some learned discourse late into the night. Almost the only waking hours they were separated were during Henry's womanising, which Becket refused to share.[9]

At Westminster, Eleanor found herself responsible for raising not only her own young sons but also Henry's bastard Geoffrey by his Saxon mistress Ykenai until he was old enough to be sent off to be educated for high ecclesiastical office in the schools of Northampton. That old gossip Walter Map spitefully labelled Geoffrey's mother *meretrix* – a prostitute[10] – but Henry's paranoia would never have let him take an interest in a mistress' child of doubtful paternity.

There was little privacy in the modern sense of the word, whether at Westminster or on the road with Henry. It was then thought aberrant to wish to be alone – except in hermits, among whom it was considered a sign of their piety. When travelling, the court slept in one great hall, with a solar at one end, so that all could see who was with whom and why. In September Eleanor moved to Winchester, which had been the capital of Saxon England, while Henry took time off to hunt in the nearby New Forest where, as in all the forests, it was forbidden for the hungry Anglo-Saxon inhabitants to seek food or even collect firewood.

By the Christmas court of 1155, held at Winchester, Eleanor was pregnant again and shortly to be abandoned by Henry when he crossed to France to placate Louis Capet and declare a brief war on his brother Geoffrey for daring to claim that an oath sworn by Henry on their father's deathbed should be honoured, giving him territory of his own to govern. While Eleanor held no writ of regency, that did not stop her travelling the country in great pomp and style, furnishing her temporary lodgings with tapestries and favourite furniture, issuing charters over her own seal and arranging marriages that ensured the spouses owed her loyalty. In June she was back at Winchester for the birth of a daughter, christened Matilda in honour of her formidable grandmother, an event closely followed by the death of Prince William.

She lost little time in grieving, travelling to France to be present when Henry was in her lands. The cartulary of the important abbey of La Sauve, lying east of Bordeaux, records their visit with a glittering retinue that included 'Thomas of London'[11] who constantly had Henry's ear. So busy was Henry with punishing anyone who flouted his ducal authority, and razing their fortifications when the mood took him, that it was rumoured his speed in operations must be due to his use of widespread treachery. At some point in their separate progresses back to the North, Eleanor must have met up with her husband, for she was pregnant again when she returned to England in February 1157 – this time with the son who would be her favourite.

## NOTES

1. A. Richard, *Histoire*, Vol 2, p. 114.
2. Ibid, p. 113.
3. For a fuller account of Eleanor's court, see Boyd, *Eleanor*, pp. 137–9.
4. Also sometimes called Bernard de Ventadour.
5. A. Richard, *Histoire*, Vol 2, p. 116.
6. A mark was equivalent to one-third of an English pound.
7. A. Richard, *Histoire*, Vol 2, p. 116.
8. For greater detail see Boyd, *Eleanor*, p. 136.
9. William fitz Stephen, *Life of Becket*, ed. J.C. Robertson, Rolls Series No 67 (London: Longmans, 1875), Vol 3, p. 17.
10. Map, *De Nugis*, pp. 238, 246. His phrase *meretrix quedam publica* more likely expresses Anglo-Norman contempt for an Anglo-Saxon noblewoman.
11. C. de la Ville, *Histoire de l'Abbaye de La Sauve Majeure* (Paris: Méquignon junior and Bordeaux: Th. Lafargue, 1877), p. 177.

# 3

# Court Whores and Confusion

This, then, was the turbulent Plantagenet family into which Richard was born at the palace outside Oxford. The name of the dynasty founded by Henry and Eleanor is said to come from Richard's grandfather Geoffrey the Fair, who wore a sprig of *planta genista* or bright yellow broom – *genêt* in French – in his helmet to make him instantly recognisable in fast-moving equestrian combat.

When the royal family was gathered together for a Christmas or Easter court the sibling rivalry and tensions must have made life hellish for the four princes and three princesses, not least because their father had inherited from his Norse ancestors a tendency to go berserk when angry or thwarted. He would then fall down in a fit, foaming at the mouth and rending his clothes in fury to roll among the rotten reeds that covered the flagstones of whichever palace they were in – reeds that, if not freshly laid, were fouled with food scraps and the excrement of dogs and other animals.

Even family members mysteriously came and went, adding to the children's insecurity. Before Richard's fifth birthday, his elder brother Henry was sent to continue his education in the London house of Chancellor Thomas Becket. This sending away of noble sons to be brought up in another household was not unusual at the time, but Princess Matilda was also sent away young – to

Germany when only 12, having long been betrothed by her father
to Duke Henry of Saxony, known as Henry the Lion. There were
also new additions to the royal family. Henry II's obsession with
alliances would lead him to inveigle Eleanor's first husband Louis
VII of France to hand over two daughters by his second wife:
Princess Marguerite was betrothed to Prince Henry and Princess
Alais was betrothed at the age of 9 to Richard, who had previously been betrothed after the Christmas court of 1158, when
he was only seventeen months old, to Berengaria – a daughter
of the count of Barcelona, not to be confused with Berengaria
of Navarre, to whom he was later married by Eleanor's wiles
during the Third Crusade. For similar political reasons, Alix
of Maurienne was betrothed in infancy to Prince John and
Constance of Brittany was betrothed to Prince Geoffrey.

Marriage was a political tool, as when, in October 1160, Richard's
father stole a march on Louis VII. He ordered Eleanor to bring
Prince Henry from England to Normandy and thence to do
homage to Louis for the duchy of Normandy. With the conniv-
ance of certain papal legates, he then had Prince Henry married in
Neubourg to Louis' daughter Princess Marguerite. The groom was
aged 7 and the bride a mere 3 years old, so this was in direct breach
of the agreement made two years before with Louis: that the marriage would be effected when she reached puberty. The purpose
of the marriage was simply to secure Marguerite's dowry, which
included the strategically important castle of Gisors, on the borders
of Normandy and Louis' domains, and two other important castles.[1]
Work was immediately put in hand to strengthen the fortifications
at Gisors, with the moats deepened and a new curtain wall running
around the castle for 800 metres, protected by eight new towers.

All these young people and still others were treated as
Richard's brothers and sisters by other members of the court. Life
became even more complicated when statuses changed, as when
Richard's second betrothed, Princess Alais Capet, caught King
Henry's roving eye while she was still a young teenager and was
forced to become one of his mistresses.

The royal family had many fortified residences but no fixed home. In those times, kings and the nobility had to be mobile in order to keep their restless vassals frightened into obedience and shows of loyalty, as well as paying up the latest tax demands. The court or *curia* was, then, not a place, but consisted of the king and his courtiers, wherever they might be at a given time, and Henry II's court was even more peripatetic than most. When on the road, its members never knew where they would be sleeping in two nights' time. They were likened by Peter of Blois, who served as Queen Eleanor's secretary and therefore knew Henry's habits well, to the *milites Herlewini* – soldiers in the army of the mythical English King Herla, who 'in endless wandering makes mad marches without stay or rest', any man who dared to fall out of the ranks being 'turned to dust'.[2] The simile was apt because no courtier could afford to be elsewhere when summoned by the king at any hour of the day or night, for those whom Henry had raised high could easily be cast down for a simple misdemeanour or brief absence from the court – the social equivalent of being turned to dust.

Another *curialis* or courtier was Walter Map, who wrote in his work *Courtiers' Gossip*, 'Saint Augustine said, "I am in time and I speak of time, and yet do not know what time is." Similarly I am in the court and I speak of the court, yet do not know what it is.'[3] As though to confuse all his retinue, Henry II would frequently announce an early start next day and then remain in bed, alone or not, until noon. This left the entire retinue of 100 or more men and women dozing beside their harnessed mounts and draught animals since before dawn. Or, he might declare the next day a rest day and then change his mind, to rise early and depart with a small bodyguard in a cloud of dust, leaving scores of riders and wagon-drivers and passengers to perform their toilet and ready themselves in panic, harnessing their animals and following as best they could. Commenting on this, Peter of Blois recorded that the king's latest travel plans were most easily found by 'running to the court whores, for this breed of courtier often knows the palace secrets'.[4]

When travelling to the various family gatherings, such as Christmas and Easter courts, Richard and the other princes and princesses too young to ride a horse were transported, wrapped in furs, with their nurses, inside lumbering barrel-roofed wooden ox-carts with leather curtains that protected them from the rain or cold. These took their place in an expanded retinue of 200-plus guards, courtiers, clerks, household servants, prelates serving as ambassadors in the hope of catching the king's ear, plus merchants and other assorted hangers-on – all of whom literally fought for sleeping space at overnight stops after the best accommodation had been taken by the royal family. The tumultuous life of Henry's court reflected the cataclysmic coming together of Richard's equally strong-willed parents, whose relationship was always turbulent.

When one enters a medieval castle today, the courtyard of the keep is usually empty except for a few other visitors. Not so in Richard's time: as wall plates projecting from the inner walls of the *corps de logis* often testify, lean-tos of one, two and three storeys were erected, taking up much of the space in the courtyard. The din of human voices, horses neighing and dogs barking, the clatter of hooves and clang of wheel rims, plus the hammering of armourers, farriers, wheelwrights and other craftsmen, and all the comings and goings of the court bounced off the stone walls in a ceaseless cacophony, harder on the medieval ear than in modern times when even remote areas of countryside in developed countries are rarely without the noise of road traffic, agricultural machines or aircraft that has raised our aural threshold significantly. With only the privileged able to avail themselves of the long-drop toilets, the stench of human excrement that had to be carried in pots and wooden tubs out of the keep each morning and the animal dung that had to be removed must have made anyone with a sense of smell long to be on the road again, breathing fresh air.

It is possible that Richard found the ceaseless travel and confusion of the court harder to bear than his siblings did. Whether to protect him or for some emotional reason, Eleanor decided early in his childhood to keep him close to her as much as possible, ensuring that he was raised as a future duke of Aquitaine, to become a warrior-poet like her grandfather Duke William IX.[5] Known as William the Troubadour, the latter had famously defied the Church in warfare, treating his vassals in holy orders exactly like all the others and publically flaunting his mistress, known as La Dangerosa and La Maubergeonne. After his second wife retired to a nunnery where his first wife already lived, William bore his mistress' nude portrait on his shield – in return, so he said, for her bearing him in bed. To ensure there was no doubt what that meant, he summed up the situation in his poem *Un vers convinent* in terms that every fellow knight would understand:

> Dos cavalhs ai a me selha ben e gen.
> Bon son e adreg per arms e valen,
> mas no'ls puesc amdos tener
> que l'us l'autre non cossen.

> [I have two purebred horses for my saddle
> fine-spirited and both well trained for battle
> but I can't stable them together
> for neither tolerates the other.]

Many nobles were illiterate, using clerics as secretaries to read and write for them, but Eleanor, literate herself, insisted her favourite be taught to read, write and converse in Latin, northern French and Occitan – the language spoken in the south of France. Richard learned while young to pen a witty *sirventès* or rhyming tribute to a girl's beauty as an academic exercise. Other essential aspects of Richard's education for noble twelfth-century manhood were horsemanship astride a mettlesome, highly bred *destrier* or trained warhorse – the name comes from the custom of the knight's squire riding a palfrey and holding the reins of his master's warhorse in the right hand – and how to wield, on foot and on horseback, the weapons of war, including swords, daggers, lances, axes and the mace.

Fighting with lance in the tactic that would later be called a heavy cavalry charge required split-second timing as the two sides collided. With the kite-shaped shield – the top flattened off for better visibility when held high to protect the face – protecting the knight's left side, the wooden lance, tipped with steel, was held level across the horse's neck, pointing slightly left so that two approaching knights each threatened the other in the same way. The first to strike his opponent generally won by killing, wounding or unhorsing him. Often, the shock of contact head-on, with both opposing knights firmly seated between the high pommel and cantle of their saddles, was such that the wooden shafts of their lances shattered. Many knights were blinded by wooden splinters penetrating their eyes.

The knightly sword at this time was not the elegant, tapering blade of later years and nothing like the elegant rapier of Renaissance times. Although pointed at the tip for stabbing lunges, this was a weapon primarily designed to be brought down onto the adversary or laterally across the body with sufficient force to cleave unarmoured flesh deeply and shatter bones. Practising with it in adolescence and using it regularly in adult life gave the warrior caste a lop-sided appearance from massive over-development of the right shoulder and arm muscles – and almost guaranteed arthritic problems in the right shoulder and arm in later life, if a man lived long enough. The broad blade, strengthened as much as a third of the way from the cross by a longitudinal rib on each side, had a flattened diamond cross-section. Although the hilt was long enough to be held in both hands when the occasion warranted, the twelfth-century sword was usually wielded one-handed, the pommel at the end of the hilt preventing it being easily struck from the wielder's hand.

The armour worn had evolved a little from that depicted on the Norman knights in the Bayeux Tapestry. The *cotte* of mail was shorter, the skirt ending about the knees to protect the thighs from an adversary's sword slash when on horseback, but not so long as to hinder movement on foot, if unhorsed. Mail leggings and spurred boots protected the lower leg and feet, and mail gloves the hands. The headpiece of the *cotte* came up over the mouth to the level of the nose so that, with a conical helmet made from several riveted segments, complete with nasal, only the eyes and part of the cheeks were exposed, which made them a prime target. So many men suffered disfiguring facial wounds there that the new pot-helmet was introduced. This covered the whole head, with a slit to see out of and holes pierced lower down for breathing through and speaking.

It is easy to see why armour was usually donned at the latest prudent moment before combat, and not worn while travelling. So, Richard's training was not just in the use of weapons, but also in developing the stamina and brute force required to do so for hours, wearing full armour in midsummer heat.

The word 'jester' did not originally mean a fool with a quick wit, a bladder and a talent for prat-falls; it was derived from the Latin *gesta*, meaning the deeds of great men in warfare, and described the courtier with a better than good memory who could recount those deeds in detail as entertainment for a noble court. On both sides of his family, Richard was descended from the Norsemen who had settled Normandy by bloody conquest, forcing Charles the Simple, king of the Western Franks, to constitute it a duchy and cede legal title in 911 to its first duke, Rollo the Viking, in return for him paying homage as Charles' vassal.

A Norse boy of earlier generations would have repeatedly heard the sagas of Viking heroes whose manhood was epitomised by their willingness to die on the field of battle. So Richard was entertained again and again with accounts of deeds of prowess in the First Crusade, when Godefroi de Bouillon had leaped from the platform of a Frankish siege tower onto the battlements of Jerusalem and led the way for a handful of knights who hacked their way through living flesh and blood to the Damascus Gate, which they opened to allow the mass of Christian soldiery to pour into the city and massacre every Muslim, Jew and eastern Christian living there. The crusaders' chaplain recorded with sanctimonious delight how the whole Temple platform was awash with blood and bodies of the slain were piled so high that they reached the knee of a mounted knight. Only the richest were saved for ransom, pending which they were used as slave labour to remove and dispose of the thousands of corpses. Five months later, celebrating the Feast of the Nativity in the mosque, renamed *templum domini* by the knights of Christ, all the incense in the Holy Land could not mask the stink of decaying flesh that assailed the nostrils of the worshippers. This was not ancient history, for Richard's own paternal great-grandfather Count Fulk V of Anjou had been crowned King of Jerusalem in 1131 and worn that crown until 1143. The lesson for Richard was that no less would be expected of him when he reached man's estate.

At the Christmas court of 1164, held at Marlbrough, 6-year-old Richard and the other princes and princesses may have been eyewitnesses to one of Henry's famous rages, directed against Thomas Becket. Since being made archbishop by Henry, the former model chancellor had become an increasingly difficult vassal. In particular, he had refused to recognise the Constitutions of Clarendon – a set of laws introduced by Henry to reduce the power of the Church and abolish certain ecclesiastical privileges. Leaving England clandestinely, Becket had, with assistance from Louis VII, reached Rome before Henry's emissaries could get there and enlisted the support of Pope Alexander III in his dispute with the king.

Learning this on Christmas Eve, Henry went literally berserk, after which, whether eyewitnesses or not, the whole court walked softly, fearing to attract the attention of the king until he was in a calmer mood. This was certainly not the case the following day, when Henry invoked the Germanic principle of *Sippenhaft* to banish from the island realm everyone related to Becket, however vaguely. A total of 400 men, women and children, innocent of everything but some connection with the renegade archbishop, were forcibly shipped to Flanders and there abandoned in midwinter, homeless and without money or food, possessing only the clothes they were wearing. Prince Henry, who had been brought up in Becket's household during the years when he was Henry's chancellor, regarded the dispute as one more reason to hate his manipulative father.

## NOTES

1.  A. Richard, *Histoire*, Vol 2, p. 132.
2.  Map, *De Nugis*, pp. 13–15.
3.  Map, *De Nugis*, p. 248.
4.  R. Bartlett, *England under the Norman and Angevin Kings* (Oxford: OUP, 2000), p. 140.
5.  The dukes of Aquitaine were known also by their numbers in the succession to the county of Poitou. For simplicity, only their ducal numbers are used in this book.

# The 15-Year-Old Duke

I t has to be said that Richard and his male siblings were an unlovable lot, judged by any modern standards. Henry II was reputed to have had a mural painted in Windsor Castle representing himself as a dying eagle being attacked by four eaglets. If that is true, it was a remarkable prophecy of the end of his life. A truer visual simile of his attitude as a father would have shown him as a huntsman holding four hounds on intertwined leashes, he curbing them at every turn and them continually snapping and snarling at each other, waiting only for a chance to bite the hand that held them.

Richard's eldest brother, Prince Henry, grew up to be a vain but popular playboy, surrounded by a coterie of flattering admirers attracted by his open-handed generosity when he was in funds, which was never for long. When able to break away from the – to him – boring round of governance with his father's court, his main leisure interest lay in the tournaments. At that time, they were not the ordered ritual they later became, with noble ladies watching two knights charging at each other along separated tracks, each endeavouring to unseat the other with his lance. That was dangerous, but the *mêlée* of the middle twelfth century was far more so, with two teams of heavily armed mounted knights setting upon each other with whatever weapons they liked in a lethal forerunner of tag wrestling. The *mêlée* began on an agreed signal, usually in an open space in or near a town, but continued with pursuers chasing their opponents for miles across the countryside, damaging crops and property and riding down anyone unwise enough to get in their way. An unhorsed knight could expect to be deliberately ridden down, or hacked at with sword, mace or axe until literally clubbed and/or stabbed to death. Limbs and sometimes heads were lost to blows from opponents' swords; limbs and skulls were crushed by maces and shattered by axes. If overwhelmed by one or more opponents, a knight could surrender to save his life, but was then a prisoner with his horse, arms and armour forfeit, and would be released only after payment of a ransom calculated in accordance with his rank and wealth.

The noble troubadour Bertran de Born, joint castellan of the castle of Autafòrt in Périgord, gained most of his wealth from plunder and ransom. He loved the whole tournament scene:

> Bela m'es pressa be blezos
> coberts de teintz vermelhs e blausd'entresens e de gonfanos
> de diversas colors tretaustendas e traps e rics pavilhos tendre
> lanzas frassar, escutz trancar e fendre
> elmes brunitz, e colps donar e prendre …

> [The *mêlée*, with its thousand charms: / shields vermillion and azure / standards, banners, coats of arms / painted in every bright colour, / the pavilions, the stands, the tents, / shattered lances, shields split and bent, / blows given, taken, helmets dented …]

For Young Henry, the *mêlée* was a source of steady income, thanks to having the mightiest warrior in Europe on his team, William the Marshal, who reputedly took 103 knights prisoner in a single year.

At Montmirail on 6 January 1169 Henry II went through the motions of sharing out his empire among his sons. Under this, Eleanor gained permission to cede title to the county of Poitou and duchy of Aquitaine to her favourite son, whereupon

12-year-old Richard performed homage by swearing fidelity to Louis VII. Young Henry, who was married to Louis' daughter Marguerite, did the same for Maine and Anjou, after which Louis gave his consent, as feudal overlord of the continental possessions, to the betrothal of Prince Geoffrey to Countess Constance of Brittany. Geoffrey was smaller in stature than the two eldest princes and of a swarthy complexion. He had the best brain of the four and, since he was unlikely to accede to the throne, would have made a successful cardinal, had his father been prepared to allow him to escape his paternal domination. Having a lawyer's gift for words, Geoffrey was able to make black seem white and could always talk round even those who already had good reason to mistrust him. The son whom Eleanor regarded as the runt of her second litter was John. A full 12 inches shorter than Richard when fully grown, he lacked Geoffrey's intellect, Richard's undoubted courage and Young Henry's popularity. Their father made most use of him to annoy and worry his older brothers by conferring on John gifts and possessions that had been promised to the others – and were later taken away again.

The whole elaborate charade of Montmirail was Henry's way of manoeuvring Louis into handing over 9-year-old Alais Capet, who was now formally betrothed to Richard. Her dowry, the region of central France still known today by its feudal name Berry, lay between Aquitaine and Burgundy and had long been coveted by Henry for strategic reasons. During the meeting at Montmirail, Louis again tried to reconcile Henry and Becket, whom Henry agreed to meet face-to-face for the first time since Becket's furtive departure from Sandwich in a humble rowing boat four years previously. Becket, however, was at his most obstreperous and not even his own counsellors were surprised when Henry stormed away from the meeting, exasperated.[1]

Leaving Prince Henry to keep order in Normandy with William the Marshal's support and counsel, Henry rode south with Richard to reimpose ducal authority on their perpetually squabbling vassals in Poitou and Aquitaine. These months with his father gave Richard a taste for real warfare. Where Henry could be both ruthless and, when the occasion called for it, diplomatic, Richard would always take the violent way out of a problem, although the other side of his complex character included a love of church ritual. When singing in the Mass, he was known to deal a vigorous beating to any monk who was not singing in tune or with sufficient gusto.

During August father and son took a break from the often bloody business of state to go hunting together near Angers. Travelling north afterwards, Henry left Eleanor to guide Richard's first ducal months, an arrangement that suited him well, for he disliked having Eleanor near him more than ever since her menopause had rendered her unable to provide further princes and princesses.

In Bayeux, Henry met papal legates who also urged him to effect a rapprochement with Becket. All this was part of a power struggle between the papacy and the Holy Roman Emperor Frederik I Barbarossa, who wanted to extend his rule of northern Italy all the way south to meet the territory of William II, ruler of the Norman kingdom of the Two Sicilies, to whom Henry had betrothed Princess Joanna. On 18 November 1169 at Saint-Germain-en-Laye, west of Paris, Henry restored Becket's confiscated property in England and asked him to officiate at the coronation of Prince Henry. This was in the nature of an olive branch, extended for reasons of geopolitics, since a coronation did not have to be conducted by the archbishop of Canterbury, the rival archbishops of York having also officiated at coronations since the Norman Conquest. Becket, however, did not grasp the olive branch that could have ended the dispute between Church and Crown there and then. He was by now arguably mad. In addition to the verminous hair shirt he wore, provoking sores all over his body, and the daily flagellations he underwent, Becket had osteomyelitis of the jaw after being locked in the sewers of the monastery at Pontigny with a tooth abscess as self-imposed penance for sexual desires, and had also refused any pain relief during an operation to remove two splinters of bone from his jaw.[2]

As Becket stubbornly, or insanely, pursued the road to martyrdom, Henry's mood was black at the Christmas court in Nantes – a venue decided on to make the point to the Bretons that Geoffrey and his bride Constance of Brittany were truly their count and countess. So much for Geoffrey. Henry had also resolved to have Prince Henry crowned by the archbishop of York in a ceremony copying the Capetian tradition of coronations for a crown prince to ensure an undisputed succession on his father's death. His determination to do this without delay caused him to cross from Barfleur to Portsmouth on 3 March 1170, setting sail against all advice during a gale that sank the largest ship in the royal convoy with the loss of some 400 souls.[3]

When the Plantagenet Empire was apportioned at Montmirail, no provision was made for John – hence his nickname, Jehan sans Terre, or John Lackland in English. His character was not improved by being despatched as an oblate to the abbey of Fontevraud, an experience that made him an atheist with a lifelong detestation of religion and those in holy orders. Convinced that he had been deprived of his rightful share in the family fortunes, he was, and remained, an unloved and unlovable paranoid prince whose ill humour was hardly improved by the knowledge that a day's ride to the south of the cloister in which he languished, Richard was already living the life of a warrior-poet, overtaking his tutors in swordplay, riding the best horses that money could buy and on occasion riding down vassals and peasants who had incited his wrath, for the code of what later was known as chivalry had little place in the twelfth century.

Eleanor had herself flouted feudal protocol, which forbade vassals to marry without their suzerain's consent, when she married Count Henry of Anjou. But in Poitiers she grasped with both hands the traditional right to arrange the marriages of her vassals to her own advantage. Her court had at any time up to sixty marriageable heiresses being courted by at least that number of young knights, all of whom could acquit themselves well with sword or lance, knew how to set a falcon on its prey and could ride a mettlesome *destrier* as though of one flesh with their mount. But that was not enough for the woman who had inherited the duchy of Aquitaine at the age of 15. Her love of elegance also required of them good manners, fashionable attire and the ability to conjure a tune from a lute or turn words into poetry.

What Richard made of the erotic ambiance of his mother's court when not occupied with his knightly training is hard to say. The *gay saber* of the southern civilisation had produced the courts of love, whose canon was that love could not exist between husband and wife[4] and that it had to be sought outside the marriage. Marriage among the nobility was joined for political reasons and love was an unfulfillable dream for the ladies of the court. One anonymous contemporary troubadour expressed the dilemma:

> En un verger, sotz fuelha d'albespí
> tenc la domna son amic còsta sí …
> Bels doucs amics, baisem-nos ieu e vos
> aval els pratz on chanto'ls auzelós.
> Tot o façamen despiech del gilós …

[In an orchard, beneath the hawthorn tree / the lady holds her lover lovingly. / O sweet my friend, let us kiss in bliss / while down in the meadow birds sing this / sweet defiance of my jealous husband …]

The influential future saint Abbot Bernard of Clairvaux criticised the luxury of the court at Poitiers, where the ladies wore floor-length dresses and sleeves so long that they had to be knotted up out of the way for the slightest activity. According to the chronicler Geoffroy du Vigeois, the price of furs and fine cloth doubled in the south-west of France, where even bishops were ashamed to wear the simple clothes of their parents' generation, demanding that their tailors slash the voluminous sleeves of outer garments to reveal the precious material beneath. As to where the material came from, historian Alfred Richard records that in 1172 Richard richly rewarded a Poitevin merchant named Geoffroy

Berland with Eleanor's consent. Probably in return for a loan that was not repaid, Berland was granted an exclusive franchise to rent out stalls to merchants who had the courage and good fortune to cross war-torn France with linen goods from Flanders, French woollen goods, various furs and silk, which they sold to the public at the annual fair marking the end of Lent.[5]

The instruments played at Eleanor's court included recorders in several pitches, transverse flutes, Pan pipes, simple bagpipes, crumhorns and other double-reed wind instruments, the five-stringed lute played with a quill plectrum, harps, the bowed viol and the *rebàb* and *rebec*, two bowed stringed instruments of Moorish origin, the former having a sound board of skin and the latter a sound board of thin wood. Perhaps the strangest looking was the *chifonie*, a viol whose strings were made to vibrate not by a bow but by a cylindrical brush turned by a handle at the bottom of the instrument, rather like a hurdy-gurdy, and therefore capable of producing sustained notes.

This contemporary Occitan song captures the atmosphere in Eleanor's court:

> A l'entrada del tens clar, per jòia recomençar
> e per gelos irritar, vol la reina mostrar
> qu'el es si amorosa. El'a fait pertot mandar
> non sia jusqu'a la mar pucela ni bachelar
> que tuit no vengan dançar en la dança joiosa

[In spring, the queen / worries her husband by showing him / that she still knows what love is. / She summons to her from far and wide / every unwed knight and maid / to join her in the joyous dance.]

Unlike his father, who wore his clothes carelessly, Richard adored dressing up and was happy to pen a verse or two when not engaged in more violent pursuits. The darker side of his character included a greed for gold that would literally be the death of him and a fascination with, and love of, slaughter – whether of animals in the hunt or of his fellow men when given the slightest excuse. For the next twenty years, until he inherited the throne of England, Richard regarded the comital court in Poitiers as his home, inasmuch as anywhere was home to a prince incessantly at war or enjoying the hunt. He already showed a fair resemblance to his father at the time Henry II married Eleanor in 1152, and grew to be well over 6ft tall, heavily built, with a trained warrior's stance, reddish hair and blue eyes. To impress his vassals with her favourite son's bearing and authority, Eleanor summoned them to a plenary court at Niort during Easter 1170, where they were to pay homage to him.

Now 12 years old, he was as at home in the saddle as on his own feet, and considered by his household knights to be a young warrior-poet in the traditions of the long line of counts of Poitou and dukes of Aquitaine.[6] From Niort, the queen travelled with him to Poitiers, where the counts of Poitou were traditionally proclaimed *ex officio* abbot of St Hilaire. Officiating at the ceremony, Archbishop Bertrand of Bordeaux and the bishop of Poitiers presented the young prince with the lance and standard that signified his authority as count of Poitou in an impressive service that ended with a huge procession, in which everyone sang the responses in Latin, hailing him as *princeps egregie!*[7] It was a prophetic moment: in the years to come, they would realise that he was indeed, even for those turbulent times, an egregious prince – a titular abbot who was personally responsible for several thousand violent deaths.

Determined to make the political point that Richard was her son, and therefore in the line of 'native' dukes of Aquitaine and not an incomer like his father, Eleanor then travelled with him in some state to Limoges, where Henry had alienated both clergy and laity after their wedding in 1152. Limoges was, in a sense, two towns jostling for position. There was the city proper with the cathedral, bishop's palace and the workshops where the famous Limoges enamels were produced. There was also the citadel with the abbey of St Martial and the viscount's fortress. Geoffroy du

Vigeois, then a monk at the abbey of St Martial, described how his bishop placed on the finger of the adolescent duke the ring of martyred St Valérie, patron saint of the city, making Richard her symbolic bridegroom, much as a nun was said to marry Christ.[8] The importance of the ring came from a new 'life' of St Valérie having been written, portraying her as the martyr of Limoges. According to this story, Leocadius, Roman procurator of Gaul, was killed in a rebellion of the local tribes in 42 CE, leaving only one daughter, Valeria. The new procurator, referred to as Étienne, was by tradition supposed to marry the girl to signify the continuation of Roman power. He departed to subdue the Bretons, during which time Valeria was converted to Christianity by St Martial. On Étienne's return, she refused to marry him, saying that she already had a husband in Christ. Not unnaturally angered by this, Étienne ordered her to renounce Christianity, but she refused and paid the penalty of death by beheading.

At the root of these moves lay more than just Eleanor's fiercely possessive adoration of her favourite son and her determination to see him holding court in his own right in the ducal palace in Bordeaux. By having Richard swear fealty directly to Louis and formally installing him in this way, she was seeking to make it more difficult for Henry to reverse the restoration of Aquitaine to her bloodline. She next travelled north to Normandy, en route to the coronation of her eldest son, at which her attendance would have been normal but, to spite her for securing Richard's titles, Henry did not invite her to the ceremony in England. It was also a calculated insult to Louis VII that Young Henry's wife Marguerite Capet was not in her husband's entourage when Prince Henry crossed the Channel on 5 June with the bishops of Sées and Bayonne. Knighted by his father soon after arriving in England, he was crowned in Westminster Abbey by Archbishop Roger of York on Sunday 14 June 1170.[9]

To counter the very real danger of an emissary from Becket crossing to England and preventing or complicating Young Henry's coronation, the Norman justiciar Richard fitz Richard of Le Hommet had been ordered to close all Channel ports on the French side. The ruse succeeded brilliantly: Bishop Roger of Worcester was compelled to kick his heels in Dieppe, unable to cross the Channel and excommunicate all those involved in the coronation, as he had been instructed to do by Becket. This did not stop Becket from excommunicating at a distance the bishop of Salisbury and Gilbert Foliot, who had been his rival for the see of Canterbury and was now bishop of London – this for the 'sin' of assisting at the coronation service.

Once crowned, 15-year-old Prince Henry was formally referred to as Henry III or Henry the Young King, with his father designated 'the old king', although only 37 years old. To make Young Henry's kingship official, his father had a seal engraved with which he could issue charters under his own name. Like many another young man born with a solid gold spoon in his mouth, Young Henry was often carried away by his own importance. At the coronation feast, his father, in a typically informal moment, carried in the platter bearing the decorated and stuffed boar's head. The archbishop of York tried to smooth over an inappropriate remark from Young Henry by saying that it was a privilege to be served by a king. Compounding the initial insolence, Young Henry joked that he saw nothing wrong in the son of a count waiting on the son of a king – a deliberately insulting way of reminding Henry II of his comparatively lowly origin.

Insults came in all shapes and sizes. It was ostensibly to avenge the insult to Marguerite that Louis now invaded Normandy, causing Henry II to hasten to a meeting with him at Vendôme on 22 July, when he agreed to crown Marguerite in the near future. Still prepared to resolve the dispute with Becket, Henry authorised Archbishop Rotrou of Rouen to set up yet another meeting with him on 22 July at Fréteval in central France, which was later to be the setting for a momentous encounter between Richard and Louis VII's son Philip Augustus. There, Henry went as far as he could to build a bridge for the exile's return, admitting that the coronation of the Young King had been a mistake and asking Becket to re-crown him in England, together with his wife Marguerite Capet as the Young Queen. The contentious Constitutions of Clarendon were not mentioned.

In an additional effort to prevent his erstwhile chancellor from persuading the pope to place all England under interdict, Henry offered to go on crusade as a penance for his past behaviour[10] and to entrust Young Henry and the country to Becket as regent during his absence. Knowing the king as he did, Becket presumably treated this generous offer as just another of Henry's promises. Henry refused him the kiss of peace, saying he would get that once back in England.

Two weeks later, on 10 August, the old king fell ill in Domfront with a high fever, possibly malaria. Rumours of his imminent death ran throughout Christendom after he dictated a last will and testament confirming the division of power as at Montmirail, with Richard to be duke of Aquitaine, counselled by his mother.[11] Nearly two months passed before he could celebrate his recovery by a pilgrimage of thanksgiving to the shrine at Rocamadour in Quercy.[12] Grateful to still be alive, Henry was in a less rancorous mood than he had been for a long time when he and Eleanor discussed betrothing 8-year-old Princess Eleanor to Alfonso, the 14-year-old King of Castile, because her betrothal to the son of the German emperor had been broken off due to Henry's intriguing with Saxony, Lombardy and Sicily.

What Richard was doing at this time is a mystery. When the monks of St-Aignan near Saintes came to Chinon to complain that the seneschal of Poitou was illegally taxing the salt produced by the community, it was not Richard, but Eleanor acting in his name, who signed the charter confirming the community's ancient privileges and Richard's signature is not among those appended thereto. Similarly, a charter given to a daughter house of Fontevraud Abbey, confirming its right to gather firewood for heating in the forest of Argenson, was given by Eleanor and witnessed by several functionaries, but not signed by Richard, always bored by the minutiae of feudal governance. Even when he did sign charters, prudent beneficiaries ensured that Eleanor confirmed them afterwards.[13]

In October, Becket had another meeting with Henry II near Amboise before making the fatal decision to return to his duties at Canterbury under safe conduct from the king. In seeming contradiction (for he was suffering pain at a level that blocks rational thought), he continued issuing letters of excommunication right up to 30 November, the day before he landed at Sandwich, heavily in debt but bringing with him a library of books and scrolls weighing half a ton and a whole shipload of wine that was hijacked by ill-wishers somewhere between his landing and the arrival in Canterbury on 2 December. If Henry had been expecting gratitude, he was to be disappointed. Becket continued to provoke him by issuing further excommunications of royal officers and refusing to rescind his excommunication of the English bishops.

Summoned like any other vassal to Henry's Christmas court of 1170 at Bures in Normandy to account for her stewardship of the duchy, Eleanor was present when Bishop Gilbert Foliot and two other excommunicated prelates protested about Becket's unmitigated arrogance. Young Henry was holding his own Christmas court at Winchester, but Richard, Geoffrey, John and Princess Joanna were all at Bures, witnesses to what was about to happen. Furious that Becket was still defying him, despite all the concessions he had made, Henry's mood was such that his chamberlain Ranulf de Broc[14] incited four household knights – Hugh de Morville, who had been an itinerant justice in the north of England, Reginald fitz Urse, Richard de Brito and William de Tracy, a former chancellor of Becket – to travel to England and rid the king of his most troublesome vassal.

After the four grim-faced knights arrived in the cathedral precincts at Canterbury, Becket was accused by his own secretary, John of Salisbury, of having brought the situation upon himself. John of Salisbury was unusual in being an Anglo-Saxon who had risen in the hierarchy by sheer intelligence. He had been a pupil of Peter Abelard in Paris and was a very level-headed counsellor, who modestly referred to himself as *Johannes parvus*, or Little John. He pointed out that an archbishop owed a duty to heed his advisers' counsel just as a temporal lord must listen to the advice of his vassals – a duty in which Becket was constantly remiss.[15] When it became obvious that his master was set on a martyr's death, John pointed out that he and the other members of the archiepiscopal household were sinners who were not yet ready to meet their Maker, meaning that 'no one else present *wanted* to die'.[16]

In his eyewitness account of the events on that momentous evening may lie the key to Becket's constant provocations. He had never participated in the king's womanising when close to Henry and was never reported to have indulged in any other sexual activities, so it seems likely that he was a pathological masochist and, once launched on the progression from hair shirt to daily floggings, could not stop escalating the doses of suffering until the final and fatal overdose.

Begged by John of Salisbury and his other household servants to claim sanctuary in the cathedral, Becket refused. He had to be pulled and pushed against his will through a narrow tunnel leading out of the archbishop's palace and into the cathedral via the cloisters. Protesting all the way, Becket made sure the door was left unlocked, so that the pursuing knights could follow him inside. The service of vespers had not yet ended when some of his servants ran through the choir in panic, interrupting the singing. Becket ordered the monks back to their stalls in the choir and attempted to leave the sanctuary and confront the four knights from Normandy and another man who may have been guiding them. In great confusion, Becket and his cross-bearer met the five intruders on the steps leading up to the choir.

The assassination was messily done, with Becket first being beaten and insulted. The knights tried to carry him out of the building, so that they could commit the deed in the cloister, but Becket fell. The cross-bearer thrust the primatial cross out to shield him and had his arm severed at the elbow by a sword-blow.

After many further blows, Becket lay dead, his brains spilling out on the stone steps. When his body was stripped for burial, it showed great emaciation concealed under his many layers of clothing and also tunnels through the flesh of his back, lacerated by the daily floggings, made by the vermin infesting him.

There is a stained-glass window in the cathedral that was made shortly afterwards. In it, the prematurely grey-haired martyr's face is haggard with pain, not blissful as martyrs were conventionally portrayed. Hagiographical accounts of the martyrdom had Becket as a holy man defending his Church from a rapacious monarch. The truth was that neither in his years at the schools of Paris, nor during the twelve years spent in Archbishop Theobald's service before entering that of the king, had Becket shown any inclination to take further orders. Indeed, during his time as Henry's chancellor, he had shown hostility to the Church. During his archbishopric, he had constantly placed it at risk by his reckless personal feuding with Henry. This was in blatant contrast with his predecessor, for Theobald had been a statesmanlike primate, serving both Church and people throughout Stephen's civil war and establishing a good relationship with Henry, whose accession he had done so much to facilitate. Being a shrewd judge of character, Theobald had *not* suggested Becket as his successor.

## NOTES

1. W. Urry, *Thomas Becket: His Last Days* (Thrupp: Sutton, 1999), p. 116.
2. Ibid, p. 118.
3. *Recueil des Historiens des Gaules et de la France*, ed. L. Delisle (Paris: Palmé, 1869–80), Vol 13, pp. 131–2.
4. In Latin, *causa conjugii ab amore non est excusatio recta.*
5. A. Richard, *Histoire*, Vol 2, p. 242.
6. *Recueil*, Vol 13, p. 151: *comes pictavensorum et dux aquitannorum.*
7. A. Richard, *Histoire*, Vol 2, p. 150.
8. There is still extant the *ordo et benedicendum ducem Aquitaniae* said to be the order of service used, but Richard gives this document a later date (*Histoire*, Vol 2, p. 153).

9. Roger of Howden, *Chronica*, ed. W. Stubbs, Rolls Series (London: Longmans, 1867–71), Vol 2, p. 34.
10. Ibid, p. 163.
11. Ibid, p. 155.
12. *Recueil*, Vol 13, p. 143.
13. Richard, A., *Histoire*, Vol 2, pp. 153–4, 161.
14. Bartlett, *England under the Norman and Angevin Kings*, p. 257.
15. Urry, *Thomas Becket*, p. 116.
16. Ibid.

# Part 2:

# A Life of Violence

# 5

# Rebellion and Betrayal

Learning of the assassination while at Argentan on 31 December 1170 or 1 January 1171, Henry fell into an awesome display of contrition that lasted six weeks, during which he protested to Pope Alexander III that he done everything possible to prevent the murder, in which he had played no part. Everyone present at the Christmas court in Argentan, including Eleanor and Richard, must have been aware of these events, after which they returned to Poitiers, where Eleanor acted as her father and grandfather had done, sealing charters in her own name with Richard's appearing secondarily.

At Easter the pope excommunicated the four household knights implicated in Becket's murder, who took refuge at Knaresbrough castle in Yorkshire for the rest of the year. Hugh de Morville was eventually absolved of his guilt after making pilgrimage to the Holy Land. William de Tracy also departed for Outremer after leaving his Devon manor to Canterbury Cathedral, but died on the way. For three and a half centuries, until Henry VIII had Becket's name erased from prayer books and the shrine despoiled in June 1538, Canterbury prospered thanks to Becket's tomb, which was the most important pilgrimage site north of the Channel and gave Geoffrey Chaucer the rationale of his epic *The Canterbury Tales*. The newly elaborated doctrine of transubstantiation held that the True Cross – of which hundreds of fragments were claimed to be genuine – was infinitely divisible by virtue of its sanctity.[1] Similarly, for many years the best-selling souvenirs of a pilgrimage to Canterbury were thousands of small flasks of diluted fruit juice, allegedly the blood spilled at the martyrdom, which pilgrims drank on the spot or took home with them.

Despite having deliberately courted papal legates for years when they could serve his own political ends, Henry spent the following six months carefully avoiding those sent to negotiate his absolution for Becket's murder because he had in mind a different way of winning Rome's support. On 16 October he landed with a largely mercenary army at Waterford and set up winter quarters at Dublin for the conquest of Ireland. There, the stormy Irish Sea kept him safe from all but the hardiest papal envoy. The mercenaries were paid out of loans from the Jewish merchant Joshua of Gloucester, despite the Church's ruling that, by involving himself in usury, even a king made himself accomplice to the forbidden practice.[2] Typically, Joshua was never repaid by the king, but ordered to recover the loan for himself out of the proceeds of tax farming.

Since Henry thus had no Christmas court in 1171 which Eleanor and Richard were obliged to attend, they rode far south into Aquitaine to hold their own Christmas court in Bayonne. His mother falling ill on the way, Richard enjoyed more freedom of action as duke for a period, although the military power that should have enabled him to enforce his rule was kept under the iron control of his distant father. Among many disputes settled in his name during the *bombança* or luxurious festivities of the visit was the calculation of the tax due when *eubalaena glacialis* whales were captured in the Bay of Biscay. They represented an important source of food along the littoral and the blubber was rendered down and used for lighting purposes, and continued to be so until the species was effectively 'fished out' at the dawn of the twentieth century. It is likely that it was during this sojourn in the south that Richard came to appreciate the seagoing capabilities of the sturdy *balenier* boats specially designed for hunting whales, which would play an important part in transporting his army on the Third Crusade.

It was not until 17 April 1172 that Henry returned to England, having killed enough Irish to consider the island henceforward a part of his realm for Prince John to govern – which turned out to be a very bad idea, since John and his cronies mocked the native nobility for their unfashionable dress and pulled their beards as a lesson to become clean-shaven like their new overlords. On 12 May Henry was back in France, bringing with him the Young King and Princess Marguerite, who was still uncrowned. To the papal legates waiting at Savigny, Henry repeated his protestations of innocence in the assassination of Becket and rode away declaring that he was too busy to talk to them. His own bishops pursued him to Avranches because the burgeoning cult of Becket the martyr was making Henry II dangerously unpopular both in England and on the Continent. At Avranches, across the bay from the holy shrine of Mont St Michel, he finally confessed that he just *might* have been the indirect cause of Becket's death by taking too much to heart the many provocations he had suffered. As proof of how much the assassination had nevertheless grieved him, he offered to go on pilgrimage to Rome, Compostela or even the Holy Land, should there ever be proof that he had ordered his infuriating archbishop to be killed.

On occasion, Henry made grand gestures. Submitting to the discipline of the Church, he knelt outside the cathedral where sinners and excommunicates belonged. There, he stripped off his outer garments to reveal a hair shirt, submitting to a scourging by relays of monks after this was removed. Among the witnesses watching his father being flogged for the murder of his foster-father was Young Henry, little guessing that the king's talent for spectacular gestures had not yet exhausted the potential of the situation.

From Avranches, Henry II dragged the Young King to Montferrand, now Clermont-Ferrand, in the Auvergne, to

confirm the deal with Count Humbert of Maurienne betrothing
6-year-old Prince John to Humbert's eldest daughter Alix, her
dowry to include the strategic Alpine valleys of Novalaise and
Aosta – with 5,000 Angevin pounds as the bride-price, payable
in five instalments. The Angevin pound was the normal currency
of the Plantagenet continental possessions, and was generally
reckoned to be worth one-quarter of a pound sterling. The
Young King, never remotely interested in court business, fretted
in the sidelines, but Prince Richard's star was in the ascendant.
When Henry headed back to Limoges, Humbert came too.
Not only was he determined to find out what exactly were the
possessions and expectations of Prince John, about which Henry
had been characteristically vague, but he also wanted the second
instalment of the bride-price. Informed that John would be
given the castles of Chinon, Loudun and Mirebeau, the count
departed satisfied, in the belief that his daughter would soon
be married to a son of one of the two most powerful men in
Europe. To complicate matters, Young Henry considered those
three castles as his, and wasted no time declaring that his father
had been acting *ultra vires* in giving them away.

Richard's good fortune was that Raymond of Toulouse confirmed at Henry II's court in Limoges that he held the county
of Toulouse as his vassal, and the vassal also of Young Henry and
of Richard, as duke of Aquitaine.[3] He swore to do homage with
100 knights for forty days, equipped and fed at his own expense,
with the provision that any 'overtime' had to be paid for by
Richard. In addition, he was to pay a tribute of 100 silver marks
per annum or give in lieu ten trained war-horses, each having
a value of not less than 10 marks, or just under £7. As Richard
was not present, the ceremony of swearing fealty was postponed
until Whitsun.

Richard, however, was after bigger fish. At Louis VII's court
in Paris he was knighted by the king of France – an important
step towards what happened shortly afterwards. To defuse the
tensions with his sons, Henry arranged a second coronation for

Young Henry, this time with Marguerite installed beside him, at Winchester on 27 August. With the archbishops of London, York and Salisbury still excommunicate and no new archbishop of Canterbury yet appointed, it was the bishop of Évreux who officiated. Neither of the Young King's parents were present, Eleanor being in Poitou with Richard and Henry II in Brittany.

It took more than that to placate Young Henry. In November, he again demanded to be given the power that went with the title of kingship. When this was refused, he took himself and the Young Queen off to Paris, where Louis VII welcomed them and lent a sympathetic ear to his son-in-law's complaints about his father's parsimony and unwillingness to share power. Henry summoned his son back to Normandy, but the Young King made a show of independence by refusing to attend his father's Christmas court at Chinon, using the excuse that he was too busy giving a banquet for knights called William, of whom 110 were lavishly entertained by him while all his differently named friends were turned away that day.

In the draughty castle of Chinon, perched high above the River Vienne, Eleanor, Richard and Geoffrey had to put up with Henry II's consequent bad temper – not helped by news from Rome that Becket, whose tomb in Canterbury Cathedral was credited with working thousands of miracles, was to be canonised on 21 February 1173. On that day Richard and his parents were at Limoges, entertaining the Spanish kings Alfonso II of Aragon and Sancho VI of Navarre, who had come on pilgrimage to the tomb of St Martial.[4]

In Henry's cortège came the disgruntled Young Henry. With Prince Geoffrey also present, it was the first time in a while that all three elder princes had been together. There had never been any love lost between them – in particular, Young Henry was jealous of Richard's apparent freedom of action in Poitou and Aquitaine, compared with the way his father cramped his own style, and Richard resented the crown and title of Young Henry. Yet all three now discovered that they had one overriding thing

in common: a deep resentment of the way Henry II had manipulated them and used them against each other, all their lives. Young
Henry was 18, Richard 15 and Geoffrey 14. In those times when
lives were short, Richard and his elder brother were already considered to be men and Geoffrey, although only on the threshold
of manhood, was precociously astute. Young Henry already had
a following of barons both in France and England who resented
his father's high-handedness. Richard had, in theory at least, the
fealty of all the knightly class of Poitou and Aquitaine, and was
on his home ground. Geoffrey would never have acted alone, but
was prepared to join the two others on certain conditions. Thus a
conspiracy was born.

Had Henry II not been preoccupied with tying the knots of
his grand design for Italy, he might have smelled rebellion in the
air but, during the week-long festivities in Limoges, his main
concern was finalising the betrothal of Prince John and Alix of
Maurienne, which ended with 4-year-old Alix given into his
keeping, her upbringing entrusted to Eleanor. Had the princes
confided their intentions to a few vassals who could act fast, the
rebellion might have succeeded, but the old king's spies were everywhere among his sons' households and it was from Raymond
of Toulouse that he learned of the plot.

He then rode out of the city with Raymond and a small
escort, on the pretext of a day's hunting. Making a lightning tour
of all the castles in the region and ordering the castellans to put
them on a war footing, the old king appointed Abbot William
of Reading to replace Archbishop Bertrand of Bordeaux, who
had died the previous December, and sent him off to keep control of Gascony before himself returning to Limoges, whence
the restless barons had departed to raise their troops for the
rebellion. As quickly as a man pinning a snake by its head, he
dismissed the Young King's household knights[5] and ordered
the sullen prince to accompany him back to Normandy at the
beginning of March, leaving Eleanor in Poitiers with Richard
and Geoffrey.

Young Henry was kept on a very short rein, required even to share his father's bed at night. Yet, at Chinon on the journey north, he managed to creep out of their bedroom early in the morning of 6 March. Escaping from the castle, he headed north, perhaps hoping that his father would assume he had gone south-east, back to Limoges. Through the early morning mists he covered the 60 miles to Le Mans, another 30 miles to Alençon and twenty more to Argentan. Henry was roused in a fury to thunder in pursuit, making a chase scene worthy of Hollywood's best. The terrified prince rode horses into the ground, as did his furious father, gradually gaining on him.

Hearing that Louis VII was at Mortagne, Young Henry changed direction and sought asylum there on 8 March, while his father was still taking stock of the situation back in Alençon.[6] Under feudal law, the Young King, as invested duke of Normandy, had every right to place his dispute with his father, the count of Anjou, before their mutual overlord the king of France, and Henry was hardly going to put his head into the lion's mouth by following his son to Louis' court. When his emissaries arrived there and announced that they represented the king of England, Louis affected surprise on the grounds that his honoured guest was the crowned king of England because the 'old king' had resigned.[7]

Louis also had made a replica of Young Henry's seal, the original of which was still in Rouen. This was used to validate charters rewarding the barons who flocked to his cause: Count Philip of Flanders was given – on paper, at least – Dover Castle and the county of Kent; his brother the count of Boulogne got the county of Mortain; William of Scotland, currently raiding the north of England, got Northumbria; his brother David received the shires of Huntingdon and Cambridge. At that point, the duty of taking counsel that had been urged on Becket saw Young Henry agree to persuade his brothers to declare openly for him, bringing Poitou, Aquitaine and Brittany into the coalition against Henry II.

Arriving at Eleanor's court in Poitiers to enlist them to the cause, Young Henry must have had doubts. Yes, the princes all resented and hated their father, but Richard was already reputed to be so unreliable as to merit Bertran de Born's nickname for him: Richard Aye-and-Nay (in Occitan, *Ricart oc-e-no*). Vassals, friends and allies never knew where they stood with him, for a promise made on Sunday could be broken on Monday. Prince Geoffrey was a wild card, known for being 'as slippery as an eel'. The key was to convince Eleanor. After listening to the Young King's assurances of support from King Louis and his vassals and allies, she concluded that there would never be a better time to strike against the husband and father they had all come to hate, and therefore put her considerable powers of persuasion to work, to reconcile Richard and Geoffrey to Young Henry's plans.

After she opened her treasury to provide funds, the three princes departed together for Paris, to launch the campaign with Louis' support. From simple prudence, Eleanor should have gone with them, but was too proud to throw herself on the mercy of her first husband, whom she had not seen for twenty years. So she stayed in Poitiers to brave it out in the heady atmosphere of her court, where the young gallants were cock-a-hoop at the opportunity to test the military skills they had spent years acquiring.

Damning his sons for ingrates, Henry ordered all the cities and castles on French soil still loyal to him to be on the defensive. The uprising began on the Sunday after Easter, 15 April 1173, when all his continental possessions outside Normandy rose against him – from Maine and Brittany to the south of Gascony. The Earl of Leicester even landed in Suffolk with a force of Flemish mercenaries said to number over 3,000. In Richard's Aquitaine and Poitou, the list of those declaring for the rebellion read like a directory of the nobility.

Epitomising the brutality of 'knightly warfare', the princes' ally Count Philip of Flanders ordered his troops to burn and destroy *everything* and 'leave nothing for the enemy's dinner'.[8] By fire and sword, his forces ravaged Normandy, substantially loyal to Henry, who shrewdly decided that, although the coalition forces ranged against him looked impressive on paper, they had too many chiefs and no overall commander. The three princes lacked experience in managing large numbers of men and Louis VII had never been much of a general.

Henry's remedy was to augment his feudal forces by recruiting a huge army of 20,000 mercenaries from Brabant – the area around Brussels. He gradually won the upper hand during the summer, and opened negotiations at Gisors on 24 September, where he offered to share out his continental possessions, Richard to receive half the revenues from Aquitaine while his father reserved for himself only four castles in the whole duchy. The princes' resolve was weakening, but Louis had learned the hard way not to trust the promises of Henry II. He explained to them that their father was making these offers now because the titles previously bestowed on them with such pomp were in name only, since he had always intended to keep the revenues from their lands for himself.

Following his advice, the three princes rejected Henry II's terms. Diplomacy and negotiation having failed, he returned to the attack stronger than before. In the south, Richard, recently knighted by Louis, was attempting to rally the Gascons, whose natural rebelliousness required an experienced military leader to impose a co-ordinated strategy. They flocked to Richard's colours less from loyalty to him than from hatred of his father.[9] In a number of cities, like the prosperous port of La Rochelle, the prudent burgesses sat out the conflict behind their stout fortifications in the shrewd expectation that 'the old king' would win this war against his upstart sons. The whole of western France was once again a lawless wasteland of burned crops and razed castles, through which armed bands of looters, supporting one side or the other, raped and robbed their way, with nothing the Church could do to stop them. Indeed, its wealth was often the target of their greed.

Henry ordered Eleanor to leave Poitiers and lend her name to his side in the struggle. A letter from Archbishop Rotrou of

Rouen penned by Peter of Blois threatened her with excommunication if she did not obey:

> To the queen of the English, from the archbishop of Rouen and
> his suffragans, greetings in the cause of peace.
> … a woman is at fault if she leaves her husband and does not
> observe the bond (of marriage) … unless you return to your hus-
> band, you will be the cause of widespread disaster. Therefore, O
> illustrious queen, return to your husband and our master … If our
> pleadings do not move you to do this, at least let the sufferings of
> the people, the threats of the Church and the desolation of the
> Kingdom do so. Against all women and out of childish counsel,
> you give offence to the lord King, to whom however powerful
> kings bow the neck … Truly, you are our parishioner, as is your
> husband. Either you will return to your husband, or we shall be
> compelled by canon law to use ecclesiastical censures against you.
> We say this reluctantly, but unless you come to your senses with
> sorrow and tears, we shall do so. Farewell.[10]

The threats simply stiffened Eleanor's resolve, for Henry had
rejected and insulted her for years before the menopause that followed John's birth. But one after another the rebel fortresses fell
to Henry's Brabant mercenaries, enabling him to appropriate the
treasuries within, with which to pay them. The winter of 1173/74
saw the traditional Lenten truce extended for another fifty days
until the feast of Pentecost.[11] At the end of the ninety-day truce,
Henry struck. His mercenaries took Le Mans and marched south
across a landscape of death and destruction to capture Poitiers on
12 May.

With Richard on the run, silence descended on Eleanor's great
audience hall, her troubadours and *jonglars* far away and the flickering fire of southern culture blown out once again. Too late,
Eleanor swallowed her pride and fled, disguised as a man and
with only a small escort, to seek asylum on Louis' territory. A few
miles from safety, she was overtaken and arrested by knights loyal

to Henry II, her whereabouts having been betrayed by her own most trusted courtiers, whose names had been appended to so many of the charters drawn up during the years at Poitiers.[12]

There is no more dread sound than a key turning in the lock, followed by the jailer's footsteps receding outside. She spent the first night probably in the Tour du Moulin at Chinon, a bleak tower in the most inaccessible part of the castle that was reserved for important hostages. Next morning, she looked south through the narrow unglazed windows towards the duchy she would not see again for many years. One can imagine her feelings when brought a captive before her implacable husband, most probably in Rouen. History was full of noble and royal sons who had risen up against their fathers, but all Christendom regarded her as an 'unnatural' wife for raising their sons in treason against her husband. The pope would grant Henry an annulment if asked, for the degree of consanguinity was even closer than that which provided the grounds for her divorce from Louis VII. However, an annulment would require Henry to give back her dowry of Poitou and Aquitaine – and Henry never gave anything back, not even a son's rejected fiancée whom he kept as his own mistress. Nor would he have her killed, unless in one of the berserker rages that betrayed his Viking ancestry, for then Richard would enter fully into his inheritance.

He offered her a choice: she could either abdicate her titles and take the veil at Fontevraud, or be locked up for however long it took to make her change her mind. She was 52 years old and Henry only 39. Refusing to give in to a man almost certain to outlive her, she was facing the prospect of spending the rest of her life under lock and key. But she did refuse. Poitou and Aquitaine were her identity. She had given Henry everything else, but not this. Henry was in a hurry to break her will and thus shorten the war, so the conditions under which she was kept must have been hard. All she had to cling to was the hope that somehow Young Henry and Geoffrey and her beloved Richard would outwit and outfight the father they hated.

But Richard was retreating southwards – all the way to Saintes, the western terminal of the Via Agrippa, the great east–west Roman highway across central France. His preparations for a stand there were brought to nothing by the tactic that had won Henry II so many victories: speed of attack. While Richard thought he was still in Limoges, his father appeared outside the triumphal arch of the Roman general Germanicus, which then served as a town gate of Saintes. He took it by storm and laid siege to the cathedral, where the cloisters were being used as Richard's arsenal and food reserve. Since there was no escape from it, and because he was never one to waste resources, the old king simply sat and waited until the defenders surrendered, swelling his depleted coffers not only by Richard's treasury, but also by no fewer than sixty ransomable knights and 400 men-at-arms. However, his rebellious son was not among them, for Richard had deserted his followers and fled with his household knights to the reputedly impregnable fortress of Taillebourg on the other side of the River Charente. Having travelled too fast to bring any siege engines with him, Henry left him there for the time being and withdrew northwards with his captives after dividing Aquitaine into six regions placed under military governors. Porteclie de Mauzé, the doyen of those barons who had betrayed Eleanor, was rewarded with the profitable office of seneschal of the duchy.

It was against those appointees of his father that Richard led his reduced forces for the next months in a succession of forced marches and skirmishing that produced little result. The Roman military philosopher Vegetius, in his book *Epitoma Rei Militaris*, wrote that courage is more important in war than sheer numbers and speed more important still. Henry was about to demonstrate that once again. A number of Louis' vassals under Philip of Flanders were preparing to cross the Channel, led by Young Henry, and place him on the throne with the support of King William of Scotland. On 8 July the Young King's party were awaiting favourable winds at Gravelines[13] when Henry metaphorically took the wind out of their sails by putting to sea from Barfleur in a gale with a fleet of forty vessels transporting several thousand Flemish mercenaries and his entire family with the exception of the three princes.

Eleanor, who had been kept incommunicado since her capture, found herself aboard the same storm-tossed ship as her daughter Joanna, Prince John and Alix de Maurienne, the Young Queen Marguerite and Richard's betrothed Alais Capet, Constance of Brittany and Emma of Anjou.[14] They constituted Henry's VIP hostages, whom he would entrust to no other jailer.[15] However fraught the position of Marguerite, Constance and the others, Eleanor knew that a far worse fate awaited her once across the Channel.

The Anglo-Norman vassals had watched the progress of the rebellion in France with interest. Aware that by no means all of them supported him, Henry played a trump card, to bring the Church onside. After confining Marguerite, Alais and Constance of Brittany in the castle of Devizes and Eleanor in Old Sarum,[16] he rode on to Canterbury along the Pilgrims' Way for an act of public penance at the shrine of Becket. On Saturday 12 June he dismounted at the Westgate, donned a simple woollen pilgrim's robe and walked barefoot through the dirt streets to the cobbled precincts of the cathedral.

In the crypt, he took off the robe and knelt at the saint's tomb, to suffer three lashes from each of the eighty monks in the community.[17] Meanwhile, Bishop Gilbert Foliot was outside, preaching the king's innocence to the assembled crowd of townspeople and pilgrims. Some of the monks involved in the flagellation had witnessed the murder and must have taken pleasure in personally punishing the kneeling monarch for polluting their cathedral with a blood crime, as a result of which services had been suspended for a whole year until the bishops of Exeter and Chester formally 'reconciled' the building.

After the flagellation, Henry spent the night on his knees in the crypt before departing next morning for London, exhausted by a three-day penitential fast. At the palace of Westminster he had the cuts on his feet and the welts on his back dressed while getting an update on the rebel forces on English soil. The Scots were moving south and Philip of Flanders' force had already landed in East Anglia.[18] However, the Young King's main force was still in France, waiting out the storms. Before the night was out, a messenger burst into the king's chamber with the news that the Scottish king had been captured and was held prisoner in the castle of Richmond in Yorkshire, his army melting away by the hour. Proclaiming that this was a miracle to reward his penance, Henry ordered all the bells of Westminster to be rung in order to waken the citizens of London with the news that God was on his side again.[19] Three weeks after Henry's return, the rebellion was over in England, its leader, the 78-year-old Duke of Norfolk Hugh Bigod having reaffirmed fealty to his king in return for a pardon. After the advance guard of the Flemish force was permitted to return to Flanders, Young Henry abandoned the idea of invasion and headed for Rouen, to support Louis' siege of the Norman capital. Once again, his timing was off. On 8 August Henry landed at Barfleur with his Brabanters and 1,000 Welsh mercenaries, whose arrival to lift the siege was so rapid that Louis at first doubted the evidence of his own eyes.

Retreating to Paris, Louis advised Young Henry that he could not dip further into his nearly exhausted treasury to subsidise the princes' ambitions and that now was the moment for them to extract the best terms from their father, who was worn out with all the travel and stress of the last eighteen months and so near the end of his resources that he had had to pawn even the bejewelled ceremonial sword used at his coronation.[20] Henry agreed to a meeting with the Young King on 29 September as a way of isolating him from Richard and Geoffrey, still campaigning in Poitou and Brittany respectively. The tactic worked. Richard acted true to his nickname *oc-e-no*, and abandoned his supporters to their fate, riding to Montlouis near Tours on 23 or 29 September to throw himself at his father's feet in tears. Henry raised him up and gave him the kiss of peace, after which they rode east together like the best of friends, arriving one day late for the meeting with Louis, where Prince Geoffrey and Young Henry likewise humbled themselves before their father.[21]

As the broker of the peace, Louis insisted that a treaty be drawn up, under which the princes and the barons who had supported them accepted Henry's sovereignty in return for pardons and guaranteed possession of the lands and castles that had been theirs two weeks before the uprising. For the princes, it was a rewrite of Montmirail, under which Richard was awarded half the tax revenue of Poitou and two unfortified and ungarrisoned castles for his personal residences, with the castles of Chinon, Loudun and Mirebeau – the dispute over which had triggered the rebellion – confirmed as given to Prince John, who was also awarded other properties on both sides of the Channel. In addition, Henry undertook to release 1,000 ransomable captives, which was many times more than the coalition had taken. Of the princes' mother there was no mention. Henry needed to make an example to ensure his sons would think twice before defying him again and it suited the princes' self-interest to let her accept all the blame for the rebellion.

In 1964 some amateur historians cleaning the twelfth-century chapel of Ste Radegonde at Chinon discovered a fresco hidden beneath layers of lime wash (see plates 22 and 23). The painting has been dated to immediately after the rebellion and shows a richly dressed and crowned figure identified as red-bearded Henry of Anjou making a gesture that says, *I am in command here*. He is leading Eleanor away to her long captivity in England. The dark-haired girl with her is Joanna, who is known to have shared the journey. She seems to be begging her parents to stop fighting. The two beardless youths riding behind are the princes Geoffrey and Richard, who is grabbing from his mother's hand a white gyrfalcon, which was the emblem of the duchy of Aquitaine. Geoffrey is copying his father's gesture as a sign of obedience.

That says it all. Richard and Geoffrey renewed their homage to their father; Young Henry was excused from doing this on account of his title making him theoretically equal to Henry. As for Eleanor, all that was known was that she was locked up in one of England's grimmest castles known as Old Sarum, on a wind-swept hill outside Winchester, and was likely to stay there for the rest of her life.

## NOTES

1. As John Calvin was later to comment, if all the extant pieces of the alleged True Cross were gathered together, they would fill a very large ship.
2. J. Attali, *Les Juifs, le monde et l'argent* (Paris: Fayard, 2002), p. 197.
3. Richard, A., *Histoire*, Vol 2, p. 164.
4. Ibid, p. 161.
5. Ibid, p. 166.
6. Roger of Howden, *Chronica*, Vol 2, p. 40–6.
7. William of Newburgh, *Historia Rerum Anglicarum*, Vol 1, p. 170.
8. Jordan Fantosme, quoted in Bartlett, *England under the Norman and Angevin Kings*, p. 255.
9. Richard, A., *Histoire*, Vol 2, p. 173.
10. Abridged by the author. For the full Latin text, see *Recueil*, Vol 16, pp. 629–30.
11. *Recueil*, Vol 13, p. 158.
12. Ibid, Vol 12, p. 420.
13. Ibid, Vol 13, p. 158.
14. Roger of Howden, *Chronica*, Vol 2, p. 61.
15. *Recueil*, Vol 13, pp. 158–9.
16. Ibid, p. 443.
17. W. Stubbs, ed., *The Historical Works of Gervase of Canterbury*, Rolls Series No 73 (London: Longmans, 1879–80), Vol 1, p. 148.
18. William of Newburgh, *Historia Rerum Anglicarum*, Vol 1, p. 194–5.
19. Roger of Howden, *Chronica*, Vol 2, p. 63.
20. Richard, A., *Histoire*, Vol 2, p. 179.
21. Ibid, p. 180.

# 6

# Death of a Prince

enry II held his Christmas court of 1174 at Argentan in Normandy, after which he obliged his sons to accompany him on a lengthy pacification of the continental possessions to ensure they were seen by his vassals to be again under his thumb. In Poitou and Aquitaine, the castles of vassals who had remained loyal to him were strengthened and allowed to stand with garrisons sufficient to put down any further unrest; those castles reinforced by the rebels were reduced to the state in which they had been fifteen days before the outbreak of hostilities. Cities like La Rochelle that had not taken part in the uprising were rewarded with new privileges. That done, he departed for England in May with Young Henry, whose loyalty he still mistrusted.

According to Alfred Richard, the nineteenth-century archivist of the *départment* of Vienne and therefore custodian of the charters of the counts of Poitou, Henry II had no such worries about Richard. He judged correctly that this son would be no threat, once given a significant force, paid for from the taxes of Poitou and Aquitaine, to satisfy his vanity and lust for warfare. Starting in midsummer, Richard set out at the head of a small army, augmented by the household knights of several vassals, to punish his former supporters as cruelly as he had attacked the partisans of his father during the rebellion, tearing down their castles and spreading terror in his wake. By no means every vassal backed down on hearing of his approach. Near Agen, the powerful lord Arnaud de Bouville prepared to withstand Richard's siege of his castle at Le Castillon de St-Puy.[1] Richard ordered a battery of siege engines to be transported there and hammered away at the stout fortifications for two months before breaching them and taking prisoner thirty knights and many sergeants-at-arms, whose ransoms covered the expense of the siege. According to custom, once the castle was razed to the ground that should have sufficed, but he went further. To ensure that nothing could be cultivated there and that no one would be able to live there for years to come, he had the ground around it spread with salt, as the Romans were reputed to have done to Carthage at the end of the Third Punic War.

There were, as always in medieval warfare, interludes of gracious living. The cook was an important member of a noble household because, in that time of poor hygiene, one mistake by him could kill his employer. After a particularly memorable feast, in great good humour Richard impulsively knighted his cook, making him 'lord of the fief of the kitchen of the counts of Poitou' as confirmed by a charter bearing many great names as witnesses and Richard's own as undisputed count. Arise, Sir Cook!

Richard's war against his own vassals was prosecuted by an army of *routiers* – mercenaries attracted by his generous rates of pay. The rebellious barons did the same, so that mercenary fought mercenary, with the rural poor paying the heaviest price as always, when their orchards were cut down, vines torn up and crops burned. At the end of Lent 1176 Richard pursued his victorious march into the Limousin, taking Limoges after a short siege. Retiring victorious to Poitiers, he found that Young Henry had at last succeeded in escaping their father's tyranny by pleading a need to go on pilgrimage to Santiago de Compostela. Instead, the two princes joined forces to besiege Châteauneuf, which capitulated after two weeks. Richard now had the bit between his teeth, or rather an unquenchable thirst for blood and power that led him to besiege Angoulême, in which city were many of the nobles who had fled his invasion of the Limousin. Their combined forces should have enabled a stout defence, but after six days they surrendered the city and themselves. Richard despatched Count Vulgrin III of Angoulême, Aymar of Limoges and other important prisoners under escort to Henry II in England. He sent them back to Aquitaine, where they were confined in a fortress literally 'at the king's pleasure'.

Both Richard and Young Henry obeyed their father's summons to his Easter court of 1176 in England, perhaps already knowing what was afoot. In October 1175 the old king had invited the papal legate Huguet to come to Britain, where he was generously rewarded for using his legal skills to draw up a form of divorce from Eleanor, who was still holding out resolutely in her prison. Had the divorce gone through, no legal means could have prevented her regaining her dower lands and contemporary opinion was that this would have been as gross an error on Henry II's part as when Louis VII divorced her. So it is a mystery why the king even contemplated the step. The answer may lie in his desire to marry 'fair Rosamund' – his mistress Rosamund Clifford – and legitimise his infant son by her, so that he could then disinherit all his sons by Eleanor. The plan, if such it was, came to naught with the child's death and Rosamund's retirement to Godstow convent.[2]

One might have thought the successful campaign in Poitou would form some kind of bond between the two princes who shared command, but they parted in some acrimony, each considering himself superior to the other. Young Henry chose to remain in Poitiers, where an increasing number of young nobles who had taken part in the rebellion of 1173–74 flocked to his standard. As before, the old king had his spies in Young Henry's entourage, one of whom was the Young King's vice-chancellor, Adam de Chirchedun. After a letter from him to Henry II was intercepted, Young Henry had him put on trial before a court of his followers. Their verdict was that Adam should be killed for treason but the bishop of Poitiers interceded to point out that the condemned man was a deacon of York and therefore should not be judged in a lay court. Frustrated, Young Henry instead ordered that Adam be stripped and whipped through the streets of Poitiers, then sent north to prison in Argentan, being whipped also through the streets of every town along the way. The intention, of course, was to ensure that he died without actually being executed.

Richard was, to put it mildly, relieved when his older brother departed, heading into Normandy at the command of Henry II, to escort 11-year-old Princess Joanna across France on the first stage of her journey to Sicily, having been betrothed to its ruler William II, king of the Two Sicilies. On the second leg, through the county of Toulouse and onward, it was Richard who escorted her.

Confident of his authority after the successes in the field during 1176, Richard held his own Christmas court in the ducal palace of L'Ombreyra at Bordeaux before taking advantage of the mild winter weather to lead his Brabanter mercenaries south to attack the cities of Dax and Bayonne, taking particular pleasure in punishing those vassals – the term 'robber barons' described them exactly – who habitually robbed pilgrims en route to Compostela. It was with justifiable satisfaction that he afterwards informed his father that he had imposed a *pax ricardi* upon all his possessions. As happened repeatedly, he abandoned his mercenaries to find their own way home, plundering and raping their passage through the Limousin. So insufferable were their depredations that the barons of the county led by Viscount Aymar of Limoges engaged them in a series of battles near Brive, in which, on the Sunday before Easter 1177, they killed over 2,000 of the Brabanters, including their commander.[3]

Having spent two years in England, Henry II now learned of an agreement between the German emperor and the pope which effectively put a stop to his plans to acquire the crown of Lombardy. He therefore crossed the Channel on 18 August 1177 with Prince Geoffrey, fully resolved to curb the freedom Richard and Young Henry had been enjoying. In Rouen, papal legate Cardinal Pierre informed him that Louis VII's cause had been taken up by Pope Alexander III, who required that Richard be married without further delay to Princess Alais Capet, failing which she and her dowry must be returned to her father. But Alais was now sharing the old king's bed, so he prevaricated, saying that he must first meet with Louis to talk it over.

The meeting took place on 21 September, Henry as usual spinning out the negotiations – this time by agreeing to depart on crusade with Louis, as well as confirming that Alais would marry Richard, bringing the Berry as her dowry, and that Marguerite's dowry was indeed the Vexin.[4] If that was the devious side of his character, he subsequently showed his quality as a law-giver in complying with his bishops' requests to make illegal in all the continental possessions the evil practice of forcing vassals and vavasours to pay the enormous ransoms due when their overlords were taken prisoner in *mêlées*, failing which they could be sent to prison as debtors. Under the new law, it was up to the captive to arrange payment of the ransom by mortgaging future revenue until the debt was discharged.[5] This problem did not arise in England, where the *mêlée* was illegal.

The problem of the mercenaries raised its head again in October, when Henry II ordered Richard back to Poitou, where Count Vulgrin of Angoulême was ravaging the country with several armed bands. Richard's seneschal Thibault Chabot had insufficient troops to put them down, so the bishop of Poitiers followed the example of Limoges the previous year and reinforced Thibault's troops from his own funds to take on the combined mercenaries at Barbezieux, near Angoulême. In the resulting battle, all but a handful of mercenaries were killed, the few survivors taking refuge in a nearby castle. That was not enough for Richard, who proceeded to wreak vengeance on Vulgrin's vassal Viscount Aymar, taking Aymar's fortress at Limoges by storm.

With Poitou and Aquitaine enjoying comparative stability, he then raced into the Berry, where there was some unfinished business that Young Henry had failed to sort out. After the death of her father while returning from crusade in 1176 and the deaths of her two brothers, who drowned in a hunting accident, a whole sweep of territory said to be worth more than all of Normandy was inherited by 3-year-old Denise de Déols. Henry II had demanded that she be handed over to him as her overlord, but she had been kidnapped by the lord of La Châtre who, now, seeing Henry II's Normans and Richard's troops converging on his castle where the girl was kept, lost courage and handed her over without a struggle. Conducted to Chinon, Denise was then despatched to England and married to Baudouin de Revers for reasons unknown. Her husband must have been delighted, seeing his personal fortune grow overnight from a small fief on the Isle of Wight to embrace a large piece of central France including the city of Châteauroux[6] and both Henry II and Richard could congratulate themselves on extending Poitevin influence further into central France, nibbling away at the lands loyal to Louis VII.

Immediately south of Déols-Châteauroux lay another feudal untidiness, in which Richard had an interest. This was the county of La Marche, so called because it lay between his lands and territory of Louis' vassal the duke of Burgundy. Count Audebert IV had killed a knight in cold blood, after catching him paying court to the countess, whom he then sent away. When his only son died, it was taken as divine retribution for the murder, for there were no other close relatives, other than those in holy orders. After fruitlessly requesting Henry's confirmation of his title – and nearly being locked up for this temerity – Audebert decided to atone for his sins on crusade and sell the title to his lands to Henry II. He therefore led all his vassals and vavasours to the abbey of Grandmont, where the old king was staying, and had them do homage to him and to Richard, receiving for his pains 5,000 silver marks plus twenty mules and twenty palfreys – these last to equip him for the journey to the Holy Land.[7]

Temporarily satisfied with these extensions of the continental possessions, Henry II decided to hold his Christmas court of 1177 in Angers, from where he had set out to marry Eleanor a quarter-century earlier. To make the point that he had returned to retake possession of his ancestral lands, he summoned more vassals than had attended his own coronation or those of Young Henry. The effect on the three older princes standing beside him as fealty was sworn by vassal after vassal was a salutary reminder that they were not the absolute lords of the territories whose titles they bore, so long as their father lived. Given the character of Young Henry and Richard, their thoughts on this occasion can reasonably be guessed.

In March 1178 Henry II was on the move again, dragging Richard with him to Normandy and taking the bizarre pre-caution before crossing to England on 15 July of placing all his continental possessions under the protection of his feudal over-lord Louis VII, which can be taken to mean that he, who never hesitated to go back on his word, nevertheless trusted Louis not to do the same thing and invade Plantagenet territory while he was gone.

With his father safely across the Channel, Richard rode back to Aquitaine, the pacification of which Henry had ordered him to complete. As usual, the most unrest was in the south, near the Pyrenees, where Count Centulle of Bigorre had attempted to take Dax but had himself been taken prisoner by the militia of the city. There now ensued one of those feudal negotiations that baffle the modern mind. After Richard reached Dax with a task force of knights and men-at-arms from Bayonne to punish Centulle for defying his and the old king's authority, who should arrive but King Alfonso II of Aragon, pleading his close relation-ship with Centulle, begging Richard's forgiveness and promising that Centulle would never again defy his overlords. Richard gave in and released the count of Bigorre, but only after taking posses-sion of his two most important castles.

Interestingly, when rewarding the lords and people of Bayonne for their support, the wording of the charter made plain that it was made not only in his own name, but also that of Henry II. What could be given with one hand could be taken away with the other. Repairing to the ancient Roman capital of Saintes for his Christmas court, Richard considered how to punish Geoffroy de Rancon – the lord of Taillebourg, who had been given him asylum in 1174 to save him from his father's wrath. Gratitude was, as Alfred Richard observed, not a quality Richard possessed. At the end of the festivities he launched an attack, first on Rancon's castle at Pons, which held out for two months and showed no sign of capitulation. After Easter, Richard changed tack and left the siege in place, departing with part of his forces to reduce the castle of Richemond, which he tore down after only three days of siege. Emboldened by this, he attacked, took and destroyed four more castles held by Rancon's vassals before returning to Taillebourg. Alfred Richard recorded the events thus:

> Richard attacked with his usual savagery. As soon as he was on the lands of the lord of Taillebourg, he tore up the vines, burned down isolated houses and laid waste whole villages, reducing the population to poverty and leaving them no alternative but to join one of the bands of *routiers*. Since he well knew the strong points and weaknesses of the castle from the time he had spent there, he installed his siege engines on the most vulnerable side. Geoffroy made a sortie [to destroy them], but was beaten back by Richard's troops. In the violent combat, a horde of attackers and defenders poured through inside the walls before the gate could be closed, giving Geoffroy no choice but to retreat to the donjon. This was on 8 May. Because many of the garrison had been [killed or] taken prisoner and because provisions were short, a long defence was out of the question. So Geoffroy decided to negotiate. To avoid being taken prisoner, he yielded all his castles, especially the one at Pons. Richard had them razed to the ground, foundations and all.[8]

With Taillebourg taken, it was only a matter of time before the same ruthless tactics forced Count Vulgrin to yield the city of

Angoulême and the fortress of Montignac, which Richard destroyed completely. The region of Saintonge now being pacified to his satisfaction, Richard dismissed his mercenaries, among them many Basques and men from Navarre, who halted outside Bordeaux on their way home to loot and burn everything outside the city walls.

Richard was now 22 years old. Travelling to England, he first made pilgrimage to the shrine of Becket at Canterbury, to cleanse his soul of all the blood he had spilled, then journeyed on to meet Henry. The old king welcomed him, confident that the violence and cruelty of Richard's recent campaigns against his vassals must have alienated them to the point where he could safely be given the authority that went with the title of duke. Since Eleanor had never renounced her title as duchess, he allowed her to emerge from captivity to do so publicly, in Richard's favour. Rumour had it that this indicated some kind of reconciliation between them, but she was afterwards again placed under house arrest, although possibly under less rigorous conditions as a reward.

Feeling that he had not much longer to live, Louis VII decided to crown his son Philip Augustus on 15 August 1179, but the ceremony had to be delayed due to the young prince's illness. Fearing that his son might die, Louis made pilgrimage to Becket's tomb after being given a safe conduct by Henry II, who met him at Dover and escorted him in suitable pomp during the four days he spent in England. Philip Augustus' subsequent recovery was yet another miracle attributed to Becket, and he was crowned in Reims Cathedral on 1 November in the presence of Richard, Young Henry and Geoffrey as his vassals for the continental possessions.

The coronation was not before time, for Louis was terminally ill and transferred power to Philip Augustus on 28 August 1180 when his son was still two months short of his fifteenth birthday. Less than three months afterwards, on 18 September, Louis VII died and his only son, Philip II Augustus, to give him his full title, became Henry II's overlord for the continental possessions.

He would prove a shrewd and cunning negotiator, quite unlike his gentle father.

Richard passed the next months in more or less continual warfare, criss-crossing Poitou and Aquitaine. In Alfred Richard's words, he 'ravaged the country terribly'.[9] On occasion, their differences briefly put aside, he was accompanied by Henry II or Young Henry. Whenever lulls occurred, he betook himself with a small number of familiars to Talmont in the Vendée or another forest for equally bloody sport hunting deer and wild boar. Summoned to Henry II's 1182 Christmas court at Caen, he found there his sister Matilda and her husband Henry the Lion of Saxony, exiled from Germany. They had arrived in France with a large entourage which Henry II, with his habitual parsimony, sent back to Germany so that he would not have to pay for their keep. More than a hundred of the Norman vassals and vavasours attended the celebrations. The troubadour Bertran de Born, as was his wont, grew bored with the civilities and began spreading gossip to liven things up. He was also present to enlist Richard's and/or Henry II's support in the long-running disputes with his brother and co-castellan of Autafòrt Castle. While some troubadours were content to compose odes to their ladies and others wrote tender romantic fantasies or moral treatises, Bertran could not resist flirting with Matilda and indiscreetly composed a risqué poem describing her bodily charms. Matilda was 'not amused' by this. He was on safer ground when praising combat and bloodshed as the heights of masculine virtue:

> Tot jorn contendi e m'baralh,
> M'escrim, e m'defen e m'tartalh
> E m'fon hom ma terra e la m'art
> E m'fai de mos arbres essart …

[I'm always in the thick of the fray. / Skirmishing and fighting, that's my way. / They waste my lands, leave my fields burnt brown. / Now they're hacking my trees all down …]

Although the Church protested at the worst excesses, it seems that none in the ranks of the nobility gave a thought for the suffering of the peasants, the fruit of whose labour financed their violent lifestyle. Bertran again:

> E platz mi quan li corredor fan las gens e l'aver fugir.
> E platz mi quan vei après lor gran re d'armatz ensems venir.
> E platz mi em mon coratge quan vei fortz chastels assetjatz
> e los barris rotz et esfondratz …

[I love to see the skirmishers putting the common folk to flight. / A host of armed men riding them down is a grand sight. / It warms my heart to see great castles under siege / and ramparts gaping at the breach …]

The pleasures of riding with Richard *en chevauchée* did not buy the loyalty of Bertran, who had as little of that quality as Richard himself. Meeting Young Henry at the old king's Christmas court of 1182 in Le Mans, Bertran's devious mind contrived a plan in concert with Viscount Aymar of Limoges, one of many vavasours whom Richard's recent campaigns had alienated. After Henry II demanded that both Richard and Geoffrey do homage to the Young King, Geoffrey did so, but Richard argued that he and his older brother were equals, being both conceived in the same parents' bed. He agreed that it was right that the older should inherit their father's kingdom of England whose crown he wore, in theory at least, and Normandy too, but argued that it was equally right that he, Richard, should enjoy absolute authority in his mother's lands of Poitou and Aquitaine. Choosing his moment well, Young Henry, incited by Bertran, informed his father that the lords of Poitou and Aquitaine had asked him to depose Richard and replace him as their overlord.

To ascertain the truth of this, the old king sent Prince Geoffrey into the duchy to summon the chief vassals to his court at Mirebeau, not knowing that Young Henry had instructed Geoffrey at the same time to raise an armed force there against

Richard, which was not difficult, given the recent history of the duchy. Geoffrey sent this force to Limoges, where Aymar was preparing to attack those vassals still loyal to Richard. Young Henry at the same time despatched his wife Marguerite to her half-brother's court in Paris, to beg for his support in this campaign. Unfortunately, Bertran could not resist composing a *sirventès* in honour of this initiative, which included the names of all the chief conspirators, from which the old king realised that the intention of Young Henry and Geoffrey was to kill Richard, so that they could share out his inheritance.

Determined to nip this defiance of his authority in the bud, he took a small band of knights and rode post-haste to Limoges, where the citizens in arms attacked them until an Anglo-Norman knight recognised Henry II's standard and called off the attack. That evening Young Henry came to plead that it was a simple case of mistaken identity, but his father would not listen, having narrowly escaped being wounded when a sword or spear pierced his clothing in the attack. Young Henry retreated into the city, with his father taking shelter in the nearby castle of Aixe-sur-Vienne. News of the attack reached Richard in Poitou, prompting his immediate departure for the Limousin with a small band of horsemen, who rode for two days and nights without rest, arriving at the castle of Gorre, 14 miles south-west of Limoges, on 12 February, to find Viscount Aymar in the act of besieging it. At the sight of them, Aymar slipped away, making good his escape thanks to the horses of Richard's men being exhausted by the long, hard journey. Travelling more slowly in pursuit of him, they ran into a band of mercenaries in Aymar's pay, who suffered the full force of Richard's wrath. Many were killed in combat, others taken prisoner, executed or blinded, or deliberately drowned in the River Vienne on Richard's orders.

Aymar departed to wreak revenge on his neighbours who had refused to join the uprising, leaving Henry II to enter the city and besiege the fortress, inside which the desperate defenders were praying for divine intervention, having no illusions about their fate if the siege proved successful. Richard camped in the suburb of St Valérie, named after the saint whose bridegroom he was. There, the cold and torrential rain made life uncomfortable and prevented the transportation of the siege engines, without which the fortress could not be taken. Instead, he and Henry II had the new bridge over the Vienne demolished, which did not prevent more mercenaries, sent by Philip Augustus at Marguerite's request, from arriving to devastate the surrounding countryside in order to deprive the besiegers of foraging.

The tactic succeeded. After a two-week siege surrounded by scorched earth, Henry II withdrew to find better foraging elsewhere, leaving a garrison in the monastery of St Augustin to protect the townsfolk from any reprisals by Young Henry. Hardly had he departed than he learned that Young Henry was exacting revenge, and returned to drive him back into the fortress. The Young King was now desperate. His allowance from Henry II had not been paid since the beginning of the revolt, so he was forced to borrow from the citizens of Limoges to pay his soldiers, who would otherwise have deserted his cause. This money swiftly being exhausted, he turned to looting churches and monasteries of their treasures, finally reaching the shrine of Rocamadour – today among the six most visited sites in France – not to pray but to steal its treasure.

It seemed to his contemporaries an obvious example of divine retribution that he fell gravely ill there on 25 May and took to his bed in the town of Martel, where he was tracked down by the bishop of Cahors and other churchmen, who found the Young King preparing himself for death, ready to confess and receive communion. Despite all Young Henry's defiance, the old king was distraught at the news. Deterred by his counsellors from going in person to the deathbed scene, he sent instead Bishop Bertrand of Agen and Count Rotrou of La Perche. As proof that they came from Henry II, they brought a precious ring said to have belonged to Henry I, which Young Henry would recognise. The Young King kissed it, begged forgiveness of Christ and all the saints, dictated to the clerics a plea that his father would pardon not only him but also all the barons who had joined his revolt, and died on 11 June at the age of 27. Since his vow to go on crusade was unfulfilled, his faithful companion William the Marshal swore to go in his stead – and did.

The funeral cortège was a sorry sight, most of Young Henry's supporters being terrified to confront the old king. The few knights who did accompany the corpse lacked even the money to buy food until a valuable horse was sold en route. Even so, one man had also to pawn his boots for food. Papal legates, who had tracked the old king down with letters from the pope threatening excommunication if the fighting were not stopped immediately, found their role overtaken by news of Young Henry's death, relayed to Richard in the act of besieging the castle of Aixe, where the old king had taken refuge a few months earlier.

At the abbey of Grandmont, where the knights in the cortège sought to delay putrefaction in the midsummer heat by having the Young King's body disembowelled, the bishop of Limoges refused permission for the entrails to be buried because Young Henry had died excommunicate for the crime of stealing ecclesiastical property. Only after the prior of Grandmont promised that he would ensure the old king made full retribution were the entrails buried and the rest of the corpse packed in salt and spices for despatch to Le Mans for eventual burial at Rouen in fulfilment of Young Henry's deathbed wishes.

With the Young King dead, Aymar surrendered and was pardoned, leaving Bertran de Born to take refuge inside the stout walls of Autafòrt. When Richard arrived with Alfonso of Aragon to besiege the castle with siege engines sent by Henry II from Limoges, Bertran held out just one week before begging for mercy. His punishment was to see the castle awarded to his brother Constantin, whom he had previously swindled out of his half-share in it. Escorted to Henry II to be punished for fomenting the rebellion, Bertran instead moved him to tears by reciting two *planhs* he had composed during the siege of Autafòrt as an insurance policy:

Si tuit li dolh e'lh plor e'l marrimen

e las dolors e'lh danh e'lh chaitivier

qu'òm anc auzis en est segle dolen

fossen emsems, semblaran tuit leugier

contra la mòrt del jove rei engles …

[If the sadness of all the grief and tears / the pain, suffering and misery /
that afflict a man in a hundred years / were added up, they would weigh /
less than the death of the Young English King …]

The ploy worked so well that the old king undid Richard's award of Autafòrt to Constantin and ruled that the two equally bellicose brothers should share the property equally – a recipe for disaster. Satisfied that the power of the barons had been broken, he returned to Normandy, leaving behind the devastated tracts of the Limousin.

## NOTES

1. Alfred Richard refers to this castle as 'Le Puy de Castillon'.
2. *Recueil*, Vol 17, p. 23.
3. Ibid, Vol 13, pp. 166–7, 199.
4. Ibid, Vol 13, p. 171.
5. Ibid, Vol 13, p. 172.
6. Ibid, Vol 13, p. 172.
7. Ibid, Vol 13, p. 173.
8. Richard, A., *Histoire*, Vol 2, p. 198.
9. Ibid, p. 205.

# Ḥeir to the Empire

Their employer dead, Young Henry's mercenaries raped and plundered their way north through the Berry until stopped by a band of vigilante knights and men-at-arms known as the Pacifiques, who had sworn to protect the region against their depredations. Trapped between them and the hostile people of the Limousin, no fewer than 10,500 mercenaries were killed, as were 1,500 'women of ill repute' travelling with them, allegedly bedecked in jewellery looted from churches. Nor were the Young King's mercenaries the only curse on the land. Dismissed by Henry II, a large band of *routiers* under a Brabanter commander named Mercadier spent the autumn plundering their way through the regions of Périgord and Pompadour. With them, sharing the spoils, rode Constantin de Born, whose sole redeeming characteristic was that he refused to loot churches.[1] Étienne de Tournay, an *abbé* from Paris, was travelling through this country on a mission for Henry II shortly afterwards, and reported, 'I saw everywhere towns consumed by fire, ruined dwellings and churches burned down and destroyed, so that places previously populated by men had become the haunt of savage beasts.'[2]

But Richard was untroubled. It was, to the twelfth-century noble's way of thinking, inevitable that these terrible misfortunes should befall the common people. Henry II was far more moved by Young Henry's death than the plight of those dispossessed, bereaved and suffering as a direct result of his depredations. So Richard celebrated his victory hunting in the forest of Talmont and holding open house for those who wished to congratulate him on becoming the heir presumptive to the throne of England, his previous *familia* or household knights augmented by those of all degrees seeking to hitch their wagons to a new star, all unaware that he had a nasty shock in store.

After Henry restored the county of Brittany to Geoffrey, minus a number of castles which he had garrisoned to ensure Geoffrey's good behaviour, Richard was ordered to come to Le Mans in mid-October. There he was acquainted with the old king's wishes: that John be given Poitou and Aquitaine and do homage for them to Richard, who would then be treated as Young Henry had been, as overlord, but a king without a kingdom. This plan had two flaws: unlike his dead brother, Richard had not been crowned as successor to the throne of England; also, his character was nowhere near as amenable as Young Henry's.

He therefore requested a couple of days to take counsel with his vassals, which Henry II could hardly refuse. Riding post-haste from Le Mans, Richard returned to Poitiers and from there informed his father than he had no intention of yielding the slightest part of his inheritance from Eleanor to John or anyone else. Having other problems on his mind, Henry equipped Geoffrey and John with a small army to launch a new war against Richard, while he faced up to Philip Augustus' demand for the return of the dowry allotted to Marguerite on her marriage to Young Henry now that she was a widow – in particular the castle of Gisors. Replying that this was out of the question because he had given Gisors to Eleanor, Henry had his imprisoned queen brought under escort to France to play the part of *châtelaine* – for which she was rewarded in mid-1184 with release from Old Sarum and permission to live in Winchester with her daughter Matilda of Saxony, who gave birth there to a son christened William shortly afterwards.

Philip was not amused and forced out of Henry the grant of an annual widow's pension of 2,750 Angevin pounds for Marguerite, as well as the promise to finally marry off Richard's betrothed Alais to any other of his sons, since he well knew that Richard had no intention of marrying her or anyone else. As always, Henry was playing several games at the same time and now consented to pay homage to Philip Augustus for all the continental possessions, which implied that none of the three surviving princes had any rights in France, except by his consent. That done, Henry held his Christmas court of 1183 at Le Mans.

The year 1184 resounded with the sounds of battle and the lamentations of the bereaved. Roaming at will over the Auvergne and Limousin were bands of mercenaries under Young Raymond, son of the count of Toulouse.[3] Other *routiers* nominally in the service of princes John and Geoffrey, but actually commanded by Mercadier, re-invaded Viscount Aymar's benighted lands while Richard burned and looted his way through Brittany in between pauses for the pleasure of the hunt and devotions in favourite religious communities pursued with fervour and frequently sealed with generous gifts. Although Henry returned to England in June, fighting in the continental possessions continued until November, when he ordered the three princes to appear before him in London. Richard made sufficient show of contrition and promises of obedience at the Christmas court in Windsor to be given permission to return to Poitou, where a number of important castles were garrisoned by his father and therefore unavailable to him.

He departed within the week, before Henry could change his mind. It seems that Richard had at last realised that his previous manner of ruling his vassals was making him nothing but enemies, and that it was time to enlist some supporters. There were already a number of free towns, where feudal laws did not apply. La Rochelle was one, recently enriched by an influx of Jews, who had their own quarter in the city, after Philip Auguste expelled them from the royal domains in 1182. Richard now created others, called *villes neuves* or *villes franches* because their inhabitants were enfranchised, owing no duty except forty days' military service each year, when called upon. One such town was Saint-Rémy on the banks of the River Creuse at the borders of Poitou and Touraine, where the only tax to be paid was a registration fee of 5 *sous* per inhabitant. He was also more generous when travelling, renewing ancient privileges that had fallen into disuse, allowing monasteries and convents to gather firewood in the forests, or pasture pigs on the fallen nuts. Whether his chaplain Milo was influential in this, we do not know, but his name appears on many of the charters.

Henry played a new card, summoning Eleanor from England and ordering Richard at the Easter court of 1185 in Rouen to return all his titles to his mother, failing which Henry would ride with her at the head of a large army to retake possession of Poitou and Aquitaine by force. Richard's inclination was to refuse, but his vassals talked him out of this, which placed him, as was Henry's intention, in the position formerly occupied by Young Henry – a prince without lands, dependent on his father's largesse. To deflect what Bishop Stubbs called Richard's 'restlessness', Henry gave him a large sum of money to hire an army of Brabanter foot- and horse-soldiers with which to punish the county of Toulouse for Young Raymond's support of the recent revolt. Attacked on two fronts when his other neighbour, Count Guillaume of Montpellier, took advantage of the moment, Raymond's family was forced to flee from city to city, his pleas to Philip Augustus falling on deaf ears as his cities were devastated and seventeen castles captured by the coalition.

Richard had no idea what this humiliation of the future count of Toulouse was to cost him on his return from the Third Crusade in 1192. On the contrary, flushed with satisfaction at what seemed the successful conclusion on the invasion, he spent the winter of 1185/86 in Bordeaux, making many gifts and signing his charters as duke of Aquitaine, no matter that he had formally renounced the title.

Prince Geoffrey had unsuccessfully sought the county of Anjou as compensation for being deprived of Brittany. Despairing of ever coming into what he regarded as his birthright, he departed for Paris, to lay his complaints before Philip Augustus, who, as always, listened sympathetically to one of Henry's discontented sons and honoured him with a great show of feasts and tournaments. In one of these, Geoffrey was unhorsed and trampled, not quite to death but so badly that he died from his injuries on 19 August 1186. He was buried in Notre Dame Cathedral. With only two sons left to inherit the vast Plantagenet Empire and John having shown in Ireland that he could not hold two pennies together, let alone the vast spread of territory amassed by his parents on both sides of the Channel, Henry made a sort of peace with Richard, congratulating him for the successful campaign against Toulouse.

Whether Henry showed any grief at the loss of a son he had never much cared for or about is unknown. What did exercise him after the death was Philip's demand that Geoffrey's daughter, called Constance after her mother, be given into his keeping until she could be married – as was normal under feudal custom. Henry had no intention of allowing Brittany to pass into the hands of a husband found for the girl by Philip, but agreed to meet when he came to France after his Christmas court at Bedford. The meeting failing to find any common ground, a truce was agreed upon, to last until midsummer – the purpose of which on both sides was to prepare for an all-out war. In this, Richard came into his own.

Given a generous budget and another army of mercenaries, he was sent to push deep into Philip's territory in central France, supported by another army nominally under John's command and two more armies under Geoffrey the Bastard and the count of Aumale. The outcome was still in doubt when papal legates arrived to stop the widespread devastation such a war would have caused if allowed to continue. With threats of excommunication on all sides, a truce of two years was forced upon the two monarchs and Richard was ordered by his father to go to Paris and do homage to Philip for the county of Poitou. It was as if the transfer of power to Eleanor had never taken place.

Richard was delighted and in no hurry to return. Indeed, 23-year-old Philip spared no expense to entertain his now famous 31-year-old warrior vassal. Preferring to use cunning rather than force of arms, he updated Richard on Henry's offers at their last meeting. With gossip being the favourite pastime of courtiers, it is unlikely that Richard learned anything new, but Philip assured him Henry intended to give the continental possessions to John, with the exception of Normandy, which would go to the eventual inheritor of the throne of England. As to Philip's demands regarding Princess Alais, Henry had admitted that his young mistress had given birth to a son by him.

Court gossip in Paris had it that Richard spent both day and night with his host, eating together, drinking from the same cup and sleeping in the same bed.[4] When this news reached Henry, he ordered Richard to return – with the usual promises offered as bribes. Richard took no notice, but eventually left Philip, riding to Chinon and forcing Étienne de Marçay, the seneschal of Anjou, to remove from Henry's treasury in the castle funds sufficient for Richard to refortify or build several fortresses, including a castle by the new town of St Rémy. Once again, Bertran de Born was stirring up trouble, in this case referring to Richard as 'the duke who will be king'. This bout of independence did not last. Losing his nerve, Richard met Henry at Angers, publicly repented his recent conduct and swore that he was Henry's liege man.[5] His next act was hardly in keeping.

After news reached Europe of the capture of Jerusalem by the Saracens, Richard took the Cross without consulting his father, which infuriated Henry II. At last, Richard could see a great martial enterprise ahead of him, in which, it seemed, his father could do nothing to frustrate him without incurring the wrath of the Church. But first he had to restore order in Poitou, where Count Vulgrin of Angoulême, Geoffroy de Rancon and the de Lusignan family had captured several of his castles. In one combat, Geoffroy de Lusignan had even killed one of Richard's household knights. With Richard at the head of a band of mercenaries, the result was yet again a winter of devastation and death in the south-west of France.[6]

## NOTES

1.  A. Richard, *Histoire*, Vol 2, p. 225.
2.  Ibid.
3.  Installed as count in 1195, he became Raymond VI, although some say two previous Raymonds had been missed out of the line of succession, making him properly Raymond VIII.
4.  A. Richard, *Histoire*, Vol 2, p. 239.
5.  *Recueil*, Vol 17, p. 23.
6.  Ibid, Vol 17, p. 478.

# 8

# The Hell of Hattin

For a man whose entire adolescent and adult life was devoted to warfare, it is ironic that the battle which was to launch Richard into history was one at which he was not even present – at a place in the middle of nowhere, known as Hattin.

In common with most other Western intrusions into the Middle East, historical and modern, the crusades achieved the opposite of their professed aim. It was one thing to capture Jerusalem by force of arms, but governing it and the hinterland long term proved beyond the succession of Latin kings because more and more of the early crusaders left Jerusalem to live in the temperate climate and relative safety of the coastal cities, or even to return to Europe if they had the means. According to Archbishop William of Tyre's thirteenth-century *Historia Rerum in Partibus Transmarinis Gestarum – The History of Things Done Overseas* – the city 'liberated' by the First Crusade became so depopulated that there was scarcely a place where one could safely spend the night.

So many houses were abandoned that the owner of any dwelling unoccupied for a year and a day forfeited title to it, but that was not sufficient to keep enough able-bodied men in Jerusalem to man the walls and guard the gates, even counting the Knights

Templar and Hospitallers.[1] In desperation, King Baldwin I, who reigned 1100–18, invited the eastern-rite Christians living east of the River Jordan to settle in what became known as the Syrian Quarter of Jerusalem. A gradual repopulation from this and other sources created the problem of finding enough food, the importation of which was heavily taxed until Baldwin II rescinded the customs duty in 1120, allowing local Christians and Muslims to sell affordable food to the population. Two generations after the capture of Jerusalem John of Würzburg wrote a description of the Holy Land in the years 1160–70, noting with surprise that the Holy City was then populated by 'Greeks, Bulgarians, Franks, Hungarians, Germans, Scots, Navarrese, Georgians, Armenians, Jacobites, Syrians, Nestorians, Indians, Egyptians, Copts, Capheturici, Maronites and very many others'.[2] This heterogeneous population spoke, in addition to their native languages used in their own quarters of the city, the common tongue of *lingua franca* – a bastard French with many admixtures – for their daily dealings.

Although the immigrants brought the city back to life, there was no sense of the unity essential for a city largely surrounded by hostile peoples because each nationality in the city ruled itself according to its own traditions. Compounding the problem, the ruling knightly caste and nobility wasted much of its energy in incessant internecine struggles. It was this dissension that triggered the Second Crusade. The Latin states – referred to in Europe collectively as *Outremer*, or 'Overseas' – corresponded roughly to modern Israel plus parts of southern and coastal Lebanon and parts of Jordan. It comprised four baronies – the lordship of Krak or Montréal in the south, the county of Jaffa and Ashkelon on the coast, and the principalities of Galilee and Sidon in the north – and a royal domain of Jerusalem and Judea plus the cities of Tyre and Acre.

To the north lay the crusader buffer states of Tripoli, Antioch and Edessa, whose strategic function was to keep at bay the Muslim Seljuk Turks led by their *atabeg* Zengi. At Christmas 1144

Zengi's forces took advantage of the festivities in the Christian city of Edessa, known as Rohais in the West, to breach the walls of the city, massacre 16,000 of its inhabitants and drive the rest off to the slave market at Aleppo.

Count Joscelin of Edessa was living in sybaritic luxury at his estate of Turbessel on the upper reaches of the Euphrates, and had been buying off the Muslim Turks for years. Zengi, a good strategist, had simply waited for the right moment to besiege Edessa, inhabited by peaceful Armenian and Syrian traders, at a time when it was defended only by a small corps of discontented mercenaries who had not been paid for a year. The Syrian bishop Abu al-Farraj declared that the walls of Edessa were mainly manned by 'shoemakers, weavers, silk merchants, tailors and priests'.[3]

The nearest city from which help could have been dispatched to Edessa was Antioch, the coastal city less than 200 miles away whose Count Raymond was a great uncle of Richard. For personal reasons, he refused to get involved, although the fall of Edessa put his county next in line for Turkish attack. After that, the 'domino theory' so often cited in the Cold War postulated that the various cities and fortresses of the Latin Kingdom would fall one by one.

The fall of Edessa provoked crusading fever in Europe. Pope Eugenius III declared it the duty of every Christian man to fight for the continued existence of the crusader kingdom and Eleanor's first husband, the devout Louis VII, answered the call. Many of his vassals were less than enthusiastic until Eugenius made them an offer they could not refuse by announcing that departing on the crusade conferred on each participant a total remission of sins. Since virtually every knight and noble had blood on his conscience, for which he ought to burn in hell, the fever peaked on Easter Day of 1146 at Vézelay in Burgundy.

Avid for adventure, Eleanor donated her considerable riches to the cause and named her price, which was to come along for the greatest journey of a lifetime in defiance of the papal ban on women accompanying the crusaders, who were sworn to celibacy. But the reality of life in the Holy Land appalled most of the newcomers from Europe, who found Italian merchants making their fortunes there and a life of luxury and indulgence being lived in the Latin cities by the inhabitants they nicknamed *les poulains*. Meaning literally 'the foals' protected by their mares, it reflected their inability, after two generations of easy living in Outremer, to fight their own battles without help from Europe.

Without any real strategy agreed, the Second Crusade achieved nothing except huge loss of life on the outward journey and a failed attack on tolerant Damascus, whose ruler Mu'in al-Din Unar was the only Muslim leader to have signed a treaty of alliance with the Latin states.[4] The abortive siege of his city weakened its defences and contributed to its subsequent capture by the Turks, giving them a stepping stone by which Syria could be politically and militarily united with Egypt. The precariousness of the situation was summed up by Bertrand de Blanquefort, Grand Master of the Templars, who foresaw that if any Muslim ruler managed to unite the realms of Syria and Egypt, it would spell the end of the crusader states, for the Holy City was coveted as a holy place not only by Christians and Jews but also by the followers of Mahomet.

Blanquefort's prophecy came true on 18 June 1173 when such a leader entered Aleppo as conqueror. The slightly built and courteous al-Malik an-Nâsr Salâh al-Din Yûsuf became known in the West as Saladin. By the age of 36, after expanding his northern holdings with several other Syrian cities, Saladin's political acumen and military skills succeeded in effecting the political and military union of Syria and Egypt that eluded Egyptian President Nasser with the collapse of his short-lived United Arab Republic in 1961. Saladin's establishment of a solid power base on the shifting sands of Muslim politics merits a book to itself. In comparison with the political and military skills that won his rise to power and the consolidation of that position, the kings and other nobility of the Latin Kingdom were a rabble of shortsighted, squabbling opportunists.

He was of Kurdish origin, born in Tikrit, the town that was to produce Iraqi dictator Saddam Hussein eight centuries later. Founder of the Ayyubid dynasty, named after his father Ayyub, Saladin became ruler of Egypt in 1169 and of Damascene Syria in 1174. In contemporary Christian accounts, he and his followers were called Saracens, a name said to derive from Sarah, the childless first wife of Abraham. It was she who drove Hagar, the younger wife who had borne Abraham's son Ishmael, from their encampment and into the wilderness, which was the legendary cause of Muslims' enmity for the Jews.

On 4 July 1187 the army of Jerusalem under King Guy de Lusignan and his vassals was soundly defeated at the horns of Hattin by a coalition of Muslim emirs – the title equates roughly with 'colonel' in modern usage – under the generalship of Saladin. Paradoxically, had anyone else been the Saracen commander at Hattin, it is possible that Richard I would never have distinguished himself among the early medieval kings of England because it was Saladin's victory there that triggered the Third Crusade.

Although tensions had been building up for some time, the battle between the twin hills known as the Horns of Hattin midway between the refortified Greek city of Sepphoris, then known as Saffuriya, and the city of Tiberias on Lake Galilee was an all-or-nothing gamble by King Guy under the influence of his vassal Prince Renaud de Châtillon, whom the Muslims called 'Brins Arnat'. He was well known to Saladin, having a history of breaking truces and attacking Muslim pilgrims in defiance of Baldwin and his successor King Guy, on one occasion attacking a caravan in which was travelling Saladin's sister. In 1182 he committed the great folly of setting out to attack the holy city of Mecca. The only men of his expedition to reach their goal were prisoners taken there to be beheaded after Châtillon's main body was driven off. After the politically weak and unintelligent King Guy assumed the crown of Jerusalem in 1186, he was unable to control the bellicose Renaud de Châtillon who, in flagrant breach of the 1180 treaty between Damascus and Jerusalem that permitted the free circulation of people and merchandise in the region, attacked a caravan of merchants, killed all those bearing arms and stole all their goods.

Saladin's diplomatic requests that the prisoners be liberated and their goods returned in keeping with the treaty were ignored. He therefore summoned support from all over the dual realm to deal forcibly with 'the Franj', as all the crusaders were called because the majority of those who settled came from France.[5] Similarly, the crusaders referred to Muslim fighters as Turks, no matter their ethnic origins. Saladin's forces included pale-skinned Turks, swarthy Levantines and Egyptians and black Nubians. In June he was able to assemble a mixed force of 12,000 cavalry and about 20,000 foot soldiers midway between Damascus and Tiberias, a Herodian city lying on the western shore of Lake Galilee. This was a sizeable army for the times. Given the difficulties of command and control in battle conditions, Saladin's method was to reward handsomely the various emirs who obeyed firm instructions to position their contingents before each battle exactly where he wanted them.

In retaliation, the bellicose Châtillon persuaded King Guy to assemble the largest Latin army seen for many years under the protection of a relic of the True Cross borne by the bishop of Acre, deputising for the patriarch Heraclius, who was ill in Jerusalem. The combined Christian forces totalled some 1,200 knights from Jerusalem and Tripoli and a handful from Antioch. Their numbers were doubled by locally recruited mercenary light cavalry and foot soldiers known as Turcopoles, who were paid partly with funds sent by Henry II to the Templars in token fulfilment of his oath to make the crusade. Knowing their movements, Saladin set a trap, sending a third of his forces to besiege Tiberias as a feint.[6]

As so often, there was fatal dissension among the crusader commanders before the battle, Count Raymond of Tripoli arguing that the Latin army should remain within the safety of Saffuriya's defences for the time being and Châtillon pumping adrenalin as he incited King Guy to get to grips with Saladin and destroy his forces once and for all, despite the odds against that happening. The problem was that Guy was described by some as half-witted and certainly had neither the intelligence nor the authority to command obedience or be more than a puppet king.

The fortress-city of Tiberias belonged to Countess Eschiva, the wife of Count Raymond. After the city wall had been breached by Saladin's sappers, she and her garrison forces withdrew within the walls of the citadel, which the Muslims set about undermining. When this news was received in Saffuriya on 2 July a council of war was held, Raymond accepting the loss of Tiberias as just one more move in the long drawn-out chess game of the Latin Kingdom – in which important prisoners were always ransomed and women often liberated as an act of courtesy. However, King Guy was unable to control the fighting talk of other nobles who wanted action at all costs – always a recipe for disaster. He was also subjected to what amounted to blackmail by Châtillon's supporters and informed by Gérard de Ridefort, Grand Master of the Templars, that the support of his Order's fanatical knights would be withdrawn if Guy backed down before Saladin.

Discretion was cast to the winds. There were two routes to Tiberias, but the southern one was blocked by Saladin's forces, forcing the Franj onto the northern route, where all the water sources were either dry in midsummer or had been poisoned or blocked up by the Turks. On 3 July, when his scouts reported Guy's forces setting out on the northern route, Saladin knew they had fallen into his trap. Harassed all the way by his mounted archers and with insatiable thirst weakening man and horse, the Latin army moved with increasing slowness through arid and inhospitable country.

As the vanguard came in sight of Tiberias towards nightfall, they could see in the valley below them the enticing waters of Lake Galilee, urgently needed by horse and man alike, but they also saw Saladin's forces drawn up between them and the lake. With the army strung out over several miles, it was too late in the day for them, even had they been in much better fettle, to advance and cut their way through the besieging force to reach the lake shore. They therefore had to spend the night tormented by thirst and in no state to fight the next morning. Under cover of darkness, Saladin positioned a blocking force behind the Latins to cut off their retreat towards Saffuriya, and kept the rest of his army in positions north and south of Hattin.

Came the dawn and King Guy's army rushed towards the lake, only to be caught in a classic pincer movement from north and south as they passed between the twin peaks. With the dry grass and brush fired upwind, their eyes blinded by smoke, the knights and foot soldiers fought desperately but were repeatedly cut down by Muslim attacks until only 150 parched and exhausted knights were still fit to fight around King Guy and Renaud de Châtillon. After they surrendered, Saladin invited King Guy to sit beside him in his pavilion. Suffering torments of thirst, Guy was given cool water to drink, but when Châtillon took the pitcher from Guy to slake his own thirst, Saladin upbraided him for repeatedly breaking his word. Since he had not given the water as a sign of hospitality to Châtillon – who was perfectly aware of Muslim etiquette, having been a prisoner in Aleppo for fifteen years – Saladin had no obligation to spare his life, and personally executed him.

Conflicting accounts claim that many of the Frankish forces fled the field of battle, but only 3,000 or so are actually recorded as having escaped with their lives. Among them was Count Raymond, who had led a desperate charge against Muslim cavalry between the main battle and the shore of Lake Galilee. Saladin's nephew Taqi al-Din commanded his men to open formation so that the undisciplined Frankish horde could pass through, which it did, causing few casualties. Taqi al-Din then re-formed ranks, blocking any return for Raymond and his knights, who then rode off in frustration, heading for safety inside the walls of Tripoli.[7]

For the noble prisoners at Hattin, ransom was their lot. For the rank-and-file, slavery lay ahead. For the Templar and Hospitaller knights taken prisoner, with the exception of their Grand

Master, Saladin decreed immediate beheading because they were regarded as too dangerous to be kept for ransom, whereas Gérard de Ridefort was a valuable hostage, the price of whose eventual release was the key city of Gaza between Jerusalem and Egypt. The fragment of the alleged True Cross was carried off as a spoil of war to Damascus. Countess Eschiva surrendered the citadel of Tiberias on the following day and was, with Saladin's customary gallantry, given an escort to take her children back to their father's protection. As usual after a battle, some of Saladin's forces abandoned the campaign and headed homeward after looting the fallen and taking their allotted number of slaves with them, but sufficient men remained for him to sweep through the Christian states carrying all before him and taking Acre, Nablus, Caesarea, Jaffa, Sidon, Beirut and the crusader fortress of Toron by mid-September.

The crusader states had been reduced to the three northern coastal cities: Tripoli, Antioch and Tyre, the last of which was saved after negotiations for surrender under siege had already begun by the chance arrival of the redoubtable Marquis Conrad of Montferrat, whose fief lay in the north-west of modern Italy. Known to the Muslims as al-Markish, Conrad was a handsome and polished, politically astute and physically brave military commander – the epitome of manly virtues, praised by the Occitan troubadour Peiról d'Auvérhna as *lo marques valens e pros*, or the valiant and worthy marquis. Conrad had fought for the Byzantine emperor Manuel I Comnenus against the Holy Roman Empire and also helped him to suppress a rebellion, for which he was rewarded with the hand of Manuel's sister Theodora. However, so rampant were the murderous intrigues of the Byzantine court that he decided to try his luck in the Holy Land, where his father held the castle of St Elias. What happened to Theodora is uncertain because Conrad set sail for the Holy Land in July 1187 and arrived in Tyre aboard a Genoese merchant ship as a single man after discovering that Acre was in Muslim hands. Once installed in Tyre, he used a considerable fortune brought from Constantinople to strengthen the defences before Saladin returned for a second siege of the city in November.[8]

The city had been an island until Alexander the Great had a mole or causeway constructed between it and the mainland, against which currents built up sediment, turning it into an isthmus. Tyre was therefore easy to defend and difficult to attack by land after Conrad had strengthened the walls on the landward side. He also organised the Italian merchants long resident there on the lines of the newly emergent trading republics in Europe, a movement that he had resisted in his homeland. His refusal to surrender the city was unshaken even when his aged father, who was one of the captives taken at Hattin, was paraded outside the walls. Saladin offered rich rewards if Conrad would capitulate. Instead, Conrad aimed a crossbow at his father, saying he preferred to kill him himself rather than be intimidated. Intrigued by this lack of filial sentiment, Saladin permitted Conrad's father to live and be ransomed the following year.[9]

There was a Saracen fleet offshore blockading the port. On 30 December 1187 Conrad's ships sailed out of the harbour of Tyre and attacked the blockade ships, capturing some galleys and forcing others to beach so that their crews could flee on land. At the same time, Saladin launched a land attack, which was broken up by a sally in force from the city, led by Conrad. At this, Saladin burned his siege engines and some ships to stop them falling into crusader hands and withdrew to consolidate his hold on the southern crusader ports, which cut off the beleaguered city of Jerusalem from all hope of relief arriving from Europe by sea in the foreseeable future. Among the runaways from Hattin who had fled to the safety of Tyre was Balian of Ibelin,[10] the lord of Ramlah, a sub-fief of the kingdom of Jerusalem. When he begged a safe conduct from Saladin to return to Jerusalem and escort his Byzantine wife Maria Comnena and their family to safety, permission was granted on condition that Balian swore not to take up arms again, nor to remain in Jerusalem for more than one day to settle his family affairs there.[11]

Once inside the walls, Balian was released from this oath by the patriarch Heraclius – on the dubious grounds that an oath given to a non-Christian was invalid – so that he could organise some sort of defence with the slender means available. Word of this reached Saladin via a deputation from the city that rejected the sultan's proposals for a negotiated surrender. Despite the broken promise, Saladin nevertheless provided an escort for Balian's family to safety in Tripoli while Balian himself set about organising some sort of defence with a force totalling only fourteen knights, the city having been stripped of the pride of its knighthood by Guy's failed gamble at Hattin. In desperation, Balian knighted sixty squires and other young men and stocked the city, whose normal population was swollen by thousands of refugees from the surrounding countryside, with all the provisions that could be found in the surrounding countryside.

After Jerusalem was surrounded on 20 September it was immediately obvious that Balian's inadequate forces had no hope of sustaining a long siege. Medieval Jerusalem was no fortress constructed on military lines, but a large city that had been defended by several thousand armed insurgents when besieged by Vespasian's son Titus at the end of the Jewish Revolt in 70 CE. Against that, Balian had less than 100 knights, including those newly dubbed and inexperienced, plus some Hospitallers and Templars. To buy time, he conducted negotiations through a dubious spokesman: Yusuf Batit was a Byzantine Orthodox priest understandably resentful of the repression of his church under the Catholic rulers of Jerusalem and hoping for far better treatment from the Saracens. In fact, his congregation acted as a kind of fifth column *intra muros* for Saladin.

Like other wise generals, Saladin preferred accepting the surrender of a besieged city to the rigours and destruction of a prolonged siege, but Balian and his supporters refused to submit. With the Saracen army encamped on relatively level terrain within easy distance of the Damascus gate on the north wall of the city – surrounded by broken ground on the other sides – skirmishes began, each advance of the besiegers met by sorties from the city. In a re-run of the Roman investment of Jerusalem eleven centuries earlier, siege towers were constructed by the Saracens and rolled up to the walls but driven back each time. After six days of skirmishes in which the besiegers suffered higher casualties than the defenders, Saladin moved his main camp to the Mount of Olives above the site of the *gat shemanim* or olive press revered by Christians as the Garden of Gethsemane where Christ was arrested. Although opposite the eastern wall of the city, in which there were two gates, the new camp was protected from sorties by the steep-sided valley of the Kidron stream, across which any sortie by Balian's much reduced forces would have to come.

After three further days of ceaseless assaults on the north wall by siege artillery whose operators were protected by a barrage of arrows and crossbow bolts that kept the defenders off the walls, a sap was fired and the Muslims attempted to force an entrance through the resultant breach. According to William of Tyre, the clergy led a barefoot procession around the walls, emulating that of the priests with the First Crusade in 1099. In desperation, children and adults did penance for their sins but 'God was not listening'. At the end of September, while skirmishing continued, Balian led an embassy to Saladin to plead for the surrender terms he had previously refused. Saladin granted terms in order to avoid a repeat of the senseless massacre by the men of the First Crusade who killed all the inhabitants of the city when they captured it in 1099.

Ransom was initially set at 20 *bezants*[12] for a man, 10 for a woman and 5 for a child, with the destitute majority of the 20,000 people inside the walls to be sold into the cruel fate of slavery. The vaults of the Templars, however, still held some of the treasure sent by Henry II, although this had been seriously depleted by payment of the mercenaries who had failed to win the day at Hattin. Continued negotiations that illustrate Saladin's goodwill and patience led to a renegotiation of the terms, the ransom being reduced to 10 *bezants* for a man, 5 for a woman and 1 *bezant* for a child. Since this was still beyond the combined resources of the Christians, Saladin proposed that 100,000 *bezants* would suffice.

This was eventually reduced still further to 50,000 *bezants* for 7,000 people and eventually 30,000 bezants, two women or ten children counting as one person. On 2 October Balian symbolically surrendered the keys to the crucial fortress known as the Tower of David. He and Heraclius offered themselves as hostages for the freedom of the unransomed, but this was refused, although they were allowed to ransom many poor people with their own money. The ransom for some others was paid by Saladin and his brother Saphadin in an act of charity. A buyer's market then ensued, with householders selling their property to Jews and Syrian Christians, who were allowed to remain unmolested in the city.

The fortunate thousands began the long journey to the coast and safety, as they thought, in Christian Tyre or Tripoli, the first two convoys being escorted by Hospitaller and Templar knights and the last convoy under the leadership of Balian and the patriarch, who was permitted to take with him many religious treasures and relics. The value of these scandalised Saladin's treasurers, who maintained that the ransomed prisoners should be permitted to remove only their personal property, but Saladin ordered them to let the priests go with their treasure, so that his generosity would bear fruit in the future.[13] At the coast, the mass of refugees separated, those believing that safety lay in Egypt heading south in the hope of finding a port where an Italian merchant ship might take them back to Europe. The thousands heading north up the coast to the cities still held by their coreligionists met a sad fate when refused entry to Tripoli as 'useless mouths' who would consume hoarded food in the event of a renewed siege, and then robbed outside the walls of that city of most of the possessions they had managed to carry with them from their homes. Those healthy enough and strong enough continued along the pilgrimage route to Antioch and the relative safety of Byzantium.

Inside Jerusalem Latin-rite priests who had been permitted to stay in the Church of the Holy Sepulchre – as the Jews had been allowed to retain their synagogues – were there surprised to find a few unarmed Christian pilgrims from Europe arriving unmolested among the Muslim and Jewish pilgrims under the tolerance granted to 'people of the Book'. Saladin meanwhile satisfied the hunger of his troops for loot and a share-out of the ransom money before consolidating his victories by capturing several crusader fortresses of the interior.

Saladin freed the exiled king of Jerusalem in the summer of 1188 and returned him to Queen Sybilla at Tripoli, together with ten other noble prisoners who had promised to leave the Holy Land and return to France, never again bearing arms against the Saracens. At the same time, the old Marquis of Montferrat was restored to his son in Tyre. Considering the number of Latin nobles who had broken such vows in the past, it is unlikely that Saladin placed any credit in Guy's promise, and far more likely that he released him and his followers with the intention of exploiting the antagonism between Guy and Conrad to divide the Frankish forces in the Holy Land.

## NOTES

1. E.A. Babcock & A.C. Krey, *A History of Deeds Done beyond the Sea* (New York: Columbia University Press, 1943), Vol 1, pp. 409, 507.
2. John of Würzburg, *A Description of the Holy Land 1160–1170 by John of Würzburg*, ed. A. Stewart (New York: Palestine Pilgrim's Text Society, 1971), Vol 5, pp. 40–1, 69.
3. A. Maalouf, *The Crusades through Arab Eyes*, trans. Jon Rothschild (London: Al Saqi Books, 1984), p. 134.
4. Ibid, pp. 147–50.
5. H. Yule and A.C. Burnell, *Hobson-Jobson – The Anglo-Indian Dictionary* replica of 1886 edition (Ware: Wordsworth, 1996), pp. 352–3 explains, 'They call Franchi [*sic*] all the Christians of these parts from Romania westward.' (Pegliotti, 1340) and *non a Francia sed a Franquia* – 'not from France, but from the land of the Franks'. (Marignolli, 1350).
6. Maalouf, *The Crusades*, pp. 185–91.

7. For a fuller account of the battle, see G. Hindley, *Saladin* (London: Constable, 1976), pp. 125–30.

8. Runciman, *A History of the Crusades*, p. 18.

9. Hindley, *Saladin*, pp. 134–5.

10. *Yibna* in Arabic; *Yavne* in Hebrew. On the coastal plain near Jaffa, the crusader castle was built there in 1141.

11. Maalouf, *The Crusades*, pp. 188–97.

12. The *bezant* was a Byzantine gold coin widely accepted as currency in Mediterranean countries.

13. Maalouf, *The Crusades*, pp. 198–200.

# The Call of Destiny

Thus far in Richard's life there was little to distinguish him from any number of European princes and barons of the time, incessantly squabbling at much cost of life and misery over taxes, treasure and territory supposedly once held by their forebears or due to them through the marriage alliances in which their female relatives had been exchanged, effectively as hostages required to bear children to their new owners – or simply through envy and greed.

Confirmation of the fall of Jerusalem was carried to Europe by Bishop Joscius of Tyre as well as some returning pilgrims and the more fortunate refugees from Jerusalem, but was anticipated by Pope Gregory VIII, who issued the papal bull *audita tremendi*[1] on 29 October 1187 in response to the disaster at Hattin in July. The kingdom of France was now ruled by Louis' very different son Philip Augustus, known as Philip One-Eye on account of an albugo or opaque patch making the other eye sightless. His first response, which matched that of the Plantagenet Empire, was the levying of a Saladin tithe – a tax of 10 per cent of all incomes and moveable property, with the exemption of a knight's weapons, armour and horses, the clergy's vestments and Church treasures. It was to be collected not by the usual officials and tax farmers but by bishops and their subordinates in holy orders and the unlettered priests who lived among the population. In theory, this was to prevent the money raised simply being swallowed up in the general expenses of the state and ensure that it was kept intact to finance a new crusade that would recapture Jerusalem – although at least one collector, a Templar knight named Gilbert of Hoxton, stole the money he had collected.

It was called the Saladin tithe to deflect onto the conqueror of most of the Latin states the opprobrium associated with this additional tax burden, but was nevertheless widely resented in the Plantagenet domains both in France and England. To encourage those who could not or would not pay, a tax exemption was granted to every man who swore an oath to join the new crusade. Many took advantage of this and the attendant advantages: deferment of repayment of any debts until their return from the Holy Land and protection of their property by the Church's power of excommunication during their absence. What the common people made of the pope's ordinance that Wednesdays and Saturdays be meatless days, in addition to which he and his cardinals would fast on Mondays too, defies imagination since they subsisted mainly on soup, rough bread and porridge of one kind or another all the time.

It is not known where exactly Richard was when the news of Hattin reached him, nor that of the fall of Jerusalem, but the papal bull came as a heaven-sent opportunity for him to dun his vassals for the money to fund the greatest military adventure of his lifetime. In a fit of adolescent enthusiasm, even his atheist brother Prince John took the Cross, despite their kinsman Count Philip of Flanders having travelled all the way to the Holy Land ten years previously and returning more than somewhat disillusioned by the situation there. Richard was on campaign somewhere in the county of Toulouse, treating his unransomable captives with his accustomed brutality until his chaplain Milo persuaded him to swell the numbers in his eventual crusading army by letting them live on condition they swore to accompany him on 'the pilgrimage to Jerusalem'.[2]

Having outlived poor Louis Capet, Henry II had no intention of leaving his empire on both sides of the Channel at the mercy of Philip II Augustus while he went on crusade, but making promises had never worried him and even a vow as solemn as this could always be undone by some complaisant churchman. On 22 January 1188, while he was negotiating a truce with Philip at Gisors, Archbishop Joscius of Tyre killed three birds with one stone and pinned red cloth crosses to the cloaks of Philip's retinue, with white ones for Henry's courtiers and green ones for the count of Flanders' entourage. Philip Augustus likewise did not intend to absent himself for at least two years, leaving his lands at the mercy of Henry meanwhile. True, they would be protected by the Church, but Henry was quite likely to defy it, and talk his way out afterwards. Philip was also painfully aware that the tax base available to finance his crusade was very much smaller than Henry's.

With all their vacillation and manoeuvring, the bellicose troubadour Bertran de Born was not alone in deploring 'the journey that the kings have forgotten to make' [*el pasatge qu'an si mes en obli*]. Meanwhile, many knights and barons departed on their own initiative. A mixed fleet of Danish, Flemish and Frisian crusaders arrived by sea in Portugal in June 1189 en route to the Mediterranean. Widening somewhat their original oath 'to free Jerusalem', they assisted King Sancho I – known as Sancho o Povoador, or settler king, because he encouraged immigration from Burgundy and Flanders to settle lands taken from the Moors – to wrest the strategically important area of Alvor from the Almohads of al-Andalus. Later that summer a fleet of English, German, Breton and Flemish ships brought another contingent of independent crusaders who also joined in the struggle to capture the strategically important fortress-city of Silves from the Moors.[3]

The ageing Holy Roman Emperor Frederik Barbarossa was the first European ruler to answer the call of *audita tremendi*, departing at the head of an army variously estimated as comprising 3,000 or more knights and 15,000 foot soldiers, squires and hangers-on in the spring of 1189. Barbarossa was, how-ever, destined never to reach his destination, being drowned on 10 June 1190 in the river Cadnus (now Göksu) in Anatolia. Some sources say he had a heart attack while swimming in its cold water, coloured blue by minerals, on a hot day. Others allege that he fell from his horse while fording the river and drowned under the weight of his armour, but this is a rather Hollywoodian explanation: despite what one sees in all the medieval re-enact-ment films, it was not normal to ride in armour, but rather to have it carried on a palfrey, ready to be donned when danger threatened. Whatever the cause of his death, after the tragedy two-thirds of his army returned home, leaving a much depleted German contingent of around 5,000 men to continue its way via the land route to the Holy Land under the leadership of his son Duke Frederik VI of Swabia. He, in turn, died at the siege of Acre early in 1191. Fatefully for Richard Plantagenet, command of the German-speaking contingent was then assumed by Duke Leopold V of Austria, of whom more later.

Meanwhile, Henry had been bending the spirit of the crusad-ing oath: that those who had taken the Cross be as brothers to one another. In the summer of 1188 he commanded an army of English and Welsh mercenaries in alliance with Richard's force of Gascons and Basques in the old game of tit-for-tat in central France. In November 1188 Philip called a conference at which he proposed a long-term peace on condition that Henry II marry Princess Alais to Richard and declare him the legal succes-sor to the dual realm. When Henry did not agree, Richard knelt in homage before Philip Augustus for Normandy, Anjou and all the other lands on French soil held in fief by Henry.[4]

Henry was now 55 – a fair age for the time and, in his case, exacerbated by a broken leg that had mended crooked and damage to his vertebrae and severe haemorrhoids resulting from so many years' hard riding in peace and war that made it extremely painful to sit on a cushion, let alone mount the hard leather saddle of a *destrier*. Philip rightly pressed home the advantage this gave him as recurring bouts of illness found his principal enemy so enfeebled and lacking in authority as to be unable to compel his vassals' attendance at his Christmas court that year in Saumur. With hostilities suspended until the end of Lent, Henry attempted and failed to wheedle some concessions from Philip through Cardinal John of Agnani.

The end of Lent 1189 therefore saw hostilities resumed, but with Richard and many of Henry's vassals having switched allegiance to Philip's side. When that coalition approached Le Mans, where Henry was holed up with some 700 cavalry, the outlying suburbs were deliberately fired – by which side is unclear – and flames engulfed the whole town. At the last possible moment Henry left the shelter of the walls, his escape with the mounted knights being covered by the rearguard of Welsh foot soldiers. In hot pursuit, Richard neglected to don his armour and over-hauled these sacrificed Welshmen at a ford, where he had the good fortune to confront William the Marshal, whose skill and speed of reaction deflected his lance at the last moment, so that it killed Richard's mount and not the rider. As the fight moved on, William is said to have shouted, 'Let the devil kill you, for I shall not.'

It might be supposed that the control of a powerful, heavy *destrier* bearing an armoured knight was partly a matter of luck, but the record of William the Marshal in countless *mêlées* and under battle conditions proves that it was a question of training and the level of strength, skill and split-second timing one might find today in an Olympic athlete. A vassal of William of Tancarville, William turned the knightly sport of the *mêlée* into a profession. At his first meeting in 1167, for which he had to borrow a horse because he was too poor to own a *destrier*, he won a total of nine horses and all their riders' equipment. Teaming up with another young knight, he became a professional, capturing 103 knights with their horses and equipment in one ten-month season.[5] To such a warrior, even in the heat of battle, every move was a precision action.

On 3 July 1199 Tours fell to Philip and Richard's forces. Next day, Henry's eldest surviving legitimate son suspected his father of bluffing with talk of illness until he saw approaching the castle of Colomiers-Villandry the frail figure of a man dying from septicaemia and who had to be supported in the saddle. Henry acceded to all Philip's demands, agreeing to swear allegiance to him, to repay the costs of the campaign and pardon all those who had abandoned him – with one exception. Miming a kiss of peace for Richard, he hissed into his ear, 'May God let me live to avenge myself on you.'[6]

He was by then so frail that he had to be borne back to Chinon Castle on a litter, cursing his sons. By the next day it was obvious that he had not long to live, and consented to confession and absolution by the archbishop of Canterbury and the bishop of Hereford. The final straw came when a list provided by Philip Augustus of the vassals to be pardoned for changing sides was handed to Chancellor Geoffrey the Bastard. In the great rebellion of 1173–74, while bishop-elect of Lincoln, he had proven himself so competent and faithful in his father's cause that Henry II said, 'My other sons are the bastards. This one alone has shown himself my true and legitimate son.' It was now Geoffrey's duty to read out the list of those who had betrayed him, first of which was Prince John, whom Henry had thought to be the one legitimate son who was loyal.[7] His last hours on 6 July 1189 were spent with only his bastard son to console him.[8]

Because of the hot weather, his wishes to be buried at his favourite abbey of Grandmont in the Limousin were disregarded and the corpse was hurriedly transported before decomposition set in to the nearby abbey of Fontevraud, where Richard stayed beside the bier only for the few minutes it took to assure himself that his father really was dead before heading for the Angevin treasury at Chinon. He found it empty, every last *denier* having been expended on Henry's final campaigns. Either then or at another time when the treasury was so depleted he composed a *sirventès* containing the crystal-clear line: there's not a penny in Chinon.

His remedy was to fetter hand and foot in a dungeon Étienne de Marçay, his father's seneschal of Poitou, who was kept there until he disgorged from the profits made in a quarter-century of tax-farming the small fortune of 30,000 Angevin pounds. Meeting William the Marshal for the first time since the encounter at the ford, Richard accused the Marshal of having tried to kill him. William replied coolly that his lance could just as easily have been aimed at the rider, not the mount. The reward for that frankness and William's loyalty to his father was one promise that did Richard keep, marrying the Marshal to one of the richest heiresses in the Plantagenet Empire, whom he had previously promised to his supporter William of Béthune. Whichever husband was decreed for 20-year-old Countess Isabel of Striguil, it must have come as great relief to her after being held in the Tower of London by Henry as a ward of the Crown for thirteen years, both to prevent her wealth being used against him and to be the bait in a succession of promises that were never fulfilled.

With that, the Marshal was despatched to England, to liberate Queen Eleanor from her fifteen-year imprisonment under Henry. Without awaiting his arrival, that lady of 67, who had been confined as Henry's prisoner for nearly a quarter of her life and was never, before or afterwards, known for letting grass grow under her feet, liberated herself at the first news of her husband's death and immediately announced to all and sundry that she was still the crowned queen of England – which was true. On this authority, she took the reins of state into her capable hands, and required:

> that every free man in the whole realm swear that he would bear
> fealty to the Lord Richard, lord of England, the son of the Lord
> Henry and the lady Eleanor, in life and limb and earthly honour,
> as his liege lord, against all men and women who might live and
> die, and that they would be answerable to him and help him keep
> the peace and justice in all things.[9]

Her personal tribulations of the past fifteen years prompted her prudently to require the archbishop of Canterbury to witness with her the Anglo-Norman barons' oaths of loyalty to Richard.

In a general amnesty, those exiled by Henry were pardoned, Eleanor anticipating Magna Carta by pardoning in Richard's name and releasing several thousand men languishing in gaol under the cruel forest laws 'for the protection of vert and venison', although never judged and sentenced. This was the background of anguish and injustice lurking behind the script of every Robin Hood film.[10] Illustrating just how oppressive the implementation of Henry's laws had become in his last years, all those imprisoned by his justiciars but not sentenced by any duly constituted court of law were also released, providing they could supply sureties that they would later present themselves for trial. Not everyone thought this a good thing. William of Newburgh remarked that: 'The prisons then were heaving with multitudes of guilty men awaiting either trial or punishment, but when (Richard) came to the throne these pests, by his mercy, were released from prison, probably to transgress more confidently in the future.'[11] The appointment of justiciars was very important. When the king was in England, the chief justiciar was head of the judiciary. With the king abroad, as Richard intended to be for an unforeseeably long time on crusade, the chief justiciar acted as his regent.

Across the Channel in France, Richard hastened to put Philip right about the new relationship on which they were embarking. Gone was the former intimacy and talk of brotherhood; nor had he any intention of honouring Henry's undertakings at Villandry. As to the castle of Gisors, in whose shadow they met, he refused to hand that back on the grounds that he would marry Alais after returning from the crusade, on which women were forbidden with the exception of honest washerwomen. Had his word been trustworthy, it would have been a reasonable argument.

At Sées the archbishops of Canterbury and Rouen absolved Richard from the mortal sin of bearing arms against his father while both were bound by their crusader oaths. In the presence of Prince John, he was invested as plenary duke of Normandy on 20 July and the symbolic ducal sword duly belted around his waist. He then bought John's loyalty – or so he thought – by confirming his possessions in France and England, particularly the Norman county of Mortain. While the king of England had no right to appoint bishops, their half-brother Geoffrey the Bastard was politically neutered by Richard ordering the canons of York to elect him archbishop of that diocese, an office that debarred Geoffrey from any eligibility to wear the crown.[12] On 10 August some of the canons obediently elected Geoffrey archbishop. The result was another of the Church *v.* monarch spats: the dean of York, Hubert Walter, and the bishop of Durham protested that they and many of the canons had not been present to vote aye or nay and therefore contested the appointment by writing to the pope. For once, Queen Eleanor sided with the Church hierarchy, as did Ranulf de Glanville, although in her case, the motivation may simply have been a dislike for all Henry II's bastards.[13]

As so often, there was a way out of this maze: Richard now arranged the promotion of Hubert Walter to the see of Salisbury and rewarded Hugh of Le Puiset for withdrawing his objection to the rigged election by settling on his son the post of treasurer of York. No sooner were they out of that maze than Archbishop Geoffrey did a Becket and refused to accept the other recent appointments, for which Richard deprived him of all his lands, both secular and religious, on both sides of the Channel.[14] To frustrate permanently Geoffrey's temporal ambitions, for which he would need to delay consecration, as he had done at Lincoln, Richard first despatched a posse of his household knights to suggest forcibly that it would be a good idea to accede to the king's wishes. When that did not work, he sent a deputation of bishops and other clergy to Geoffrey's manor at Southwell, with orders to consecrate him willy-nilly. The deed was duly done by Geoffrey's own suffragan, Bishop John of Whithorn.[15]

In Normandy too, Richard had problems with the Church, in the person of Cardinal John of Agnani, who had been Henry's go-between with Philip Augustus, and who now wished to attend the coming coronation in England. That might seem harmless enough, but in the current expansion of papal power, it could later have been seen as creating a right for papal legates to attend future coronations or even, as in the Holy Roman Empire, to play a part in the selection of English monarchs. So, the worthy cardinal was firmly told that he was *persona non grata* in England.

After putting his continental possessions in order, on 13 August Richard stepped ashore in Portsmouth and looked out on the country where he had been born, but spent only two brief visits, at Easter 1176 and Christmas 1184. Within forty-eight hours of the landing, he was supervising the weighing of the state treasure, estimated to have a total value of £90,000.[16] From this he took 20,000 marks, or just under £14,000, to pay Philip Augustus' costs in the recent war, settling the debt Henry had agreed to in their final meeting. To this, he added another 4,000 marks to be quit of any claim from Philip.[17] He then rode to Westminster to be reunited with the mother he had betrayed when playing the part of Henry's puppet after the rebellion.

On 29 August he had Prince John married to Isabel of Gloucester, also known as Hawise, riding roughshod over the objections of the archbishop of Canterbury on the grounds of their consanguinity, the bride being a great-granddaughter of Henry I, who was also John's great-grandfather. The couple's estates were, however, immediately placed under interdict, pending a dispensation from Rome. To gain the support of the Church on another tack, Richard rescinded Henry's ordinance that every monastery keep a string of horses ready to service his unpredictable and gruelling progresses throughout the realm. To gain that of the nobility, who resented the way that Henry I and Henry II had diluted their power by creating *novi homines* or new nobility and elevating their favourites through arranged marriages to heiresses of title, Richard declared all such marriages void.

The Welsh took advantage of the change of English monarch to invade the marches. It was Eleanor who had to curb her son's impetuous instinct to ride out and drive them back across the border forthwith, riding instead with him to Westminster for the coronation on 3 September. In the absence of any consort – the unfortunate Princess Alais was still languishing in Winchester – Eleanor played the grand role of dowager queen surrounded by her own retinue of ladies- and maids-in-waiting. Led into the cathedral by William the Marshal bearing the gold sceptre beneath a silk canopy borne by four barons in the presence of nineteen archbishops and bishops, thirteen abbots, eleven earls and seventeen barons, Richard walked between bishop Reynald of Bath and Hugh of Le Puiset, the bishop of Durham who had disputed Geoffrey the Bastard's appointment.

Before the high altar, he prostrated himself and swore the triple oath to keep the Peace of God, to enforce the laws of the realm and to exercise justice and mercy in his judgements. Physically, he was everything that a king should be: tall, bluff, well-built, with a clear gaze from those bright blue eyes. The assembled nobles agreed to accept him as king – they had no choice, but the formality had to be observed. Richard was then disrobed down to his drawers and shirt. The dean of London, Ralph of Diceto, handed to the archbishop of Canterbury the sanctified oil to anoint Richard on hands, chest, shoulders and arms. This done, the chrism – doubly sanctified oil – was used to anoint his head as a token of the sacrament of kingship. Richard was clad in a tunic and long dalmatic robe. He was then girded with the sword of state, two earls affixed golden spurs to his feet and he was crowned by the archbishop and two earls before being invested with the ring, the sceptre and the rod of state. At that point he was at last formally the king of England and, seated on the throne, he listened to the consecrational Mass.

# NOTES

1. The title of a bull was simply formed from its first words, in this case translated as 'having heard the terrible news'.

2. Richard, A., *Histoire*, Vol 2, p. 243.

3. A. de Sousa Pereira, 'Silves no itinerário da terceira cruzada: um testemunho teutónico', *Revista militar*, 62 (2010), pp. 77–88 at www.revistamilitar.pt/artigopdf.php?art_id=538.

4. Benedict of Peterborough, *Gesta Henrici II et Ricardi I Benedicti Abbati, known Commonly under the Name of Benedict of Peterborough*, ed. W. Stubbs (London: Longmans/HMSO, 1867), Vol 2, p. 50.

5. A. Hyland, *The Medieval Warhorse* (Consohocken, PA: Combined Books, 1994), p. 88.

6. Gerald of Wales, *De Principis Instructione Liber in Giraldi Cambrensis Opera*, ed. G.F. Warner (London: Eyre, 1894), p. 296.

7. *La Vie de Guillaume le Maréchal*, ed. P. Mayer (Paris, 1901), p. 327.

8. The events of 1188 and 1189 are covered in greater detail in Boyd, *Eleanor*, pp. 227–35.

9. Benedict of Peterborough, *Gesta Henrici*, Vol 2, p. 75.

10. Roger of Howden, *Chronica*, Vol 3, pp. 4, 6.

11. William of Newburgh, *Historia Rerum Anglicarum*, Vol 1, p. 293.

12. Benedict of Peterborough, *Gesta Henrici*, Vol 2, p. 100.

13. Stubbs, *Gervase of Canterbury*, Vol 1, p. 457.

14. Roger of Howden, *Chronica*, Vol 3, p. 17.

15. Benedict of Peterborough, *Gesta Henrici*, Vol 2, p. 88.

16. Pipe Roll 1 Richard I, p. 5.

17. Roger of Howden, *Chronica*, Vol 3, p. 8.

# 10

# The Enemy Within

alking out of Westminster Abbey to the celebratory banquet in Westminster Hall, this was a king with no knowledge of, or interest in, the country or the people over whom he ruled, and whose native language he could not speak. The language of the court, the nobility and the growing merchant class was, of course, Anglo-French – a bastard tongue whose speakers sometimes felt they had to apologise to those freshly arrived from France for 'not speaking proper French'.

One should never speculate what went on in the mind of a historical personage, but in Richard's case there is no need to. His actions make it plain that the island realm was to him nothing more than a source of wealth to finance his achievement of the great enterprise in which his father had failed, and thus ensure that the name of King Richard I of England would not forever be overshadowed by that of Henry II. Having taken the Cross in November 1187, his overriding priority was to depart on crusade to the Holy Land as soon as the necessary funds could be raised and there make his reputation as the king who recaptured Jerusalem from the Saracen. Among many other factors in his reasoning was a personal tie to Guy de Lusignan, the king of Jerusalem who had so signally failed to out-general Saladin at Hattin. He came from a Poitevin family – troublesome vassals, but vassals nonetheless and therefore arguably under Richard's feudal protection as count of Poitou.

Somewhere in Richard's mind was also a repeat of the glad news from Rome – terrestrial source of all communications from God – that those who died on the crusade, not necessarily in battle against the Saracen, would gain a straight pass to heaven. In the case of a warrior like him, whose adult life oscillated between Christian devotions and callous bloodshed, and who had many deaths on his conscience, both in combat and in cold blood, that must have been a benison worth every sacrifice he would require of his subjects.

The coronation banquet at Westminster literally cost a fortune: out-of-pocket expenses included purchase of 900 cups, 1,770 pitchers and 5,050 plates and dishes. As to what was on those dishes and in those drinking vessels, there was a wide gulf between what the high nobility expected and what the common people ate. From a shared pot the latter spooned straight into their mouths a pottage made from anything that could be boiled up to make a stew or thickened soup: vegetables, herbs and some scraps of meat or fish if available, often from poaching, for which the penalties were savage, if caught. Their carbohydrates came in the form of bread usually made from the cheapest wheaten flour, but often rye flour and even pea flour when all else failed. Their vitamin needs were fulfilled by cabbages, turnips, onions and leeks with other home-grown vegetables, plus fruit either cultivated or foraged for in season. Some of their vegetables would have looked strange to modern eyes: carrots, for example, came in shades of white, yellow and purple and the potato had not yet been introduced to Europe.

Universally available and heavily used, if judged by modern tastes, the habitual seasoning for the tasteless staple diet included native mustard and evaporated sea salt, with sweetening by honey. To quench their thirst, the rural poor drank home-brewed ale made from malted barley. This had to be consumed fast as it 'went off' quickly, especially in hot weather, although some hops were

already being imported from the continent and used in ale produced commercially in the cities, both to improve the flavour
and impart their preservative properties to the brew. In town and
country, cups and plates of the poor were of treen – turned wood
that was more robust than pottery.

In contrast, the nobility and the moneyed urban classes also
had sugar, known to be imported from the Mediterranean countries during Henry II's reign. Imported spices, for those with
the money to buy them, included very expensive pepper – one
single shipload arriving in London weighed two tons – and mace,
cloves, cumin, cardamom, nutmeg, saffron, cinnamon. Along the
coasts, oysters, cockles, mussels and other shellfish were harvested,
both for home consumption and for sale. Salt-water fish were
often available far inland, kept fresh on the journey by being
packed in wet grass. Salted fish was also a common item. Because
of the considerable demand for fish in monasteries where meat
was banned during Lent, on Fridays and other holy days, and
for penitents who were denied meat as punishment, fish were
farmed in specially constructed ponds in the grounds of many
religious foundations and fishponds were to be found in most
manors of reasonable size.

But all that had little directly to do with the coronation feast
Richard was planning, with three or four courses and many
different dishes in each course. The later coronation feast of
Richard III listed three courses, totalling forty-eight dishes in
all, presented to the table in no discernable order. The idea was
to provide an eating binge with plentiful alcohol that everyone
would remember as a sign of the new king's wealth and generosity. German officer Ernst Jünger, who was posted to Paris during
the occupation of the Second World War, noted in his diary that
eating a copious dinner at a luxury restaurant in a city where
most people went hungry, day after day, conferred an immense
feeling of power on the diner.[1] Certainly, all the guests at Richard
I's coronation feast enjoyed that feeling of power, riding away past
the common folk after their dinner.

So what were they eating, that day at Richard's coronation feast in Westminster Hall? A fair idea can be gained from the wedding feast half a century later of Henry III's daughter Margaret and King Alexander III of Scots, when the food available, the manner of cooking and people's eating habits were pretty much the same. Detailed planning of this feast began in early summer, with beasts being purchased in July to be pastured and fattened for slaughter shortly before the festivities on 26 December 1251. At the same time, orders were given for the killing of 300 red and fallow deer, their carcases to be salted immediately. In August, 100 tuns – about 25,000 gallons – of wine were ordered. In October, sheriffs of the northern counties were ordered to supply 7,000 hens and seventy boars and vast quantities of game birds, rabbits and hares. In November another 100 boars and 1,000 more roe, fallow and red deer were ordered, as were vast quantities of rice, sugar and almonds. Forest wardens were ordered to collect huge quantities of charcoal produced in the forests, for most cooking was done over charcoal blown into a red heat with simple wood and leather bellows whose basic design has not changed in a thousand years. Fish ordered in December included 60,000 herring, probably salted, 1,000 unsalted cod, 10,000 haddock and 500 conger eels. Other fresh fish were kept alive until the last moment in the royal stew pond. No less than 68,500 loaves of bread were baked for the guests.[2] At Richard's coronation, ale may have been available at the lowest tables – the monks of Westminster consumed 80,000 gallons annually – but most guests would have been drinking white and red wine imported from La Rochelle, although chronicler William of Malmesbury considered that some English wine produced at this time during the medieval warm period, when vineyards stretched as far north as Norwich, was excellent.

The new king and his most important guests had armchairs, but the majority sat on benches at long trestle tables and were served with one dish placed between each 'mess' of four guests, who then helped themselves from it. Some idea of behaviour can be gleaned from early medieval books on etiquette, which advised guests not to whisper to each other, lest they be accused of slander, not to pick one's nose or spit on the table, but to use the floor – also not to belch into a neighbour's face, lick the plate clean, throw half-eaten food back onto the serving dish, snatch a tasty morsel from a neighbour's hand or wipe one's greasy hands on the table cloth.[3]

Ceremonial was important, with the *plats de résistance* being carried in to the accompaniment of music played on wind instruments. These dishes would include, in addition to the stuffed boar's head celebrated in the famous carol, swans and pheasants cooked and reclad in their skins to resemble live birds. Since the skins were raw, this defied the basic rule of kitchen hygiene, never to allow contact between cooked and uncooked animal products, but it did impress the guests. Each needed his own knife to cut pieces of meat and stab other tasty morsels, plus a spoon for the liquid courses. Forks for use at table were known in Italy, but had not yet reached northern Europe.

In addition to the musicians – Richard had a good ear and enjoyed both singing and listening to music, so only the best would do for him – entertainment during the second course would have included tumblers and mummers. At the end of the meal, the waferers served delicate sweet wafers, candied fruit and other delicacies, and doubled as after-dinner joculators telling ribald jokes for the amusement of the all-male company. Richard had banned women and Jews from the guest list.

The latter had been permitted to settle in England by William the Conqueror because of their usefulness as a source of loans in a time when lending at interest was forbidden to Christians, and also for the taxes that could be wrung from them. Because, as incomers, they fit nowhere else in feudal society, they were under the direct protection of the monarch. A few intrepid representatives of the community therefore attempted to curry favour by bringing gifts for their new overlord to Westminster Hall. However, they were turned away so roughly that it was rumoured to be an expression of the king's ill-will. This, in turn, sparked a pogrom in which men, women and children were killed and homes ransacked. The restoration of order produced exactly three culprits who were hanged – one for theft from a Christian during the riots and two others because they had set fire to Jewish property and accidentally burned down adjacent Christian homes.

To prevent anti-Semitic riots spreading to Normandy and Anjou, messengers were despatched across the Channel expressly forbidding this in the name of Richard, by the grace of God, king of the English, duke of Normandy and Aquitaine, count of Anjou and Poitou. The idea of a country as such was still not clear in most people's minds; a king was therefore described as the ruler of the people in his territory. Philip Augustus was thus *rex francorum* – king of the French – not of the land mass that is modern France, of which the German emperor ruled the eastern third. In the remainder, Richard owned many times more land, albeit nominally as a vassal of Philip, than did Philip himself. Nor did language provide a definition of statehood: in the north-west of Philip's realm, people spoke Celtic Breton; in the north-east, Germanic Flemish; in the southern half of the land mass people spoke Occitan, which was closer to Castilian Spanish than the language of the Franks.

In Richard's England everything was for sale. He is reputed to have said, 'I would sell London if I could find a buyer.'[4] Even if this attribution is apocryphal, it expresses well his state of mind, for on 6 December he did sell two towns – Berwick and Roxburgh, which had been annexed by Henry – back to William of Scotland for £10,000, including a release from vassalage to the English crown.[5]

Henry II's experienced administrators found themselves required to repurchase their offices in competition with anyone else who wished to turn a handsome profit in exercising them, as was the custom of the times. Even that doyen of knighthood William the Marshal jumped on the bandwagon and bought himself the sheriffdom of Gloucestershire for the knock-down price of 50 marks. The wholesale dismissal of experienced administrators left the country in chaos. On 17 September, to squeeze out of him a fine of £15,000 of silver, Richard removed from office and threw into prison 77-year-old Ranulf de Glanville, who had been Henry II's chief justiciar for nine years and effectively his regent during the frequent absences of the old king from England. He was only stopped from ordering Glanville's execution by the intervention of Eleanor, whose chief gaoler Glanville had been *ex officio*, yet who recognised him as corrupt but astute. The old man was ruined anyway and had to take advantage of the fiscal immunity granted to crusaders by swiftly departing for the Holy Land, where he died at the siege of Acre.

To govern the administration of justice, Glanville was replaced by two mutually distrustful justiciars. Bishop Hugh of Durham had governed much of northern England for Henry II and now bought the earldom of Northumberland, which caused Richard to jest that he had magicked a new earl out of an old bishop.[6] William de Mandeville, earl of Essex, was also appointed justiciar under a dispensation of Pope Clement III, which allowed men essential for government to remain at home without sin when the crusaders departed.

Money flowed in from all directions. The bishop of Ely had died intestate, so Richard confiscated his entire estate, including 3,000 marks in coin. Another source of easy money was in the sale to the highest bidders of the many rich heiresses, like Isabel of Striguil, whom Henry II had kept for years as wards so that he could control their assets. Whereas his father had ruthlessly kept in check rebellious barons by destroying any adulterine castles, in the space of these few weeks he was in England Richard undid several decades of Henry II's prudent governance by selling building permits to any baron who could pay the price. It is not possible to know exactly how much money was raised in the turmoil of these weeks, since most of the sums were paid directly to Richard and only appear on the Pipe Roll records if the purchaser needed time to pay. The sub-prime mortgage bubble of the twenty-first century was foreshadowed in the hundreds of manors that passed into the hands of the Church under mortgages that could never be redeemed.

Some opportunists will profit from any situation, however dire. One who did at this juncture was a strange character called William Longchamp, who had been Richard's chancellor in Aquitaine. Knowing nothing of the English, their customs or their language, Longchamp paid £3,000 to become the king's chancellor and bishop of Ely despite the bishop of Bath offering £1,000 more for the office. It would seem then that past supporters of the new king had preferential treatment in the general scramble for power. Being entrusted as chancellor with the seal necessary to validate every document of state, Longchamp raised the fee for affixing this in order more swiftly to recover his outlay in buying the chancellorship. Given three castles and the Tower of London to look after, he spent an immense sum of well over £1,000 during one year on restoring and refortifying it.[7] To his see centred on the recently built cathedral at Ely his generosity was confined to the gift of some relics, including what were supposedly a few teeth from the head of St Peter.

For most of the fourteen weeks Richard spent in England, he was chasing money all over the prosperous southern half of the realm, travelling as far north as Warwick and Northampton, holding a Great Council of bishops and barons at Geddington, and covering the country as far west as Marlborough and Salisbury to squeeze from office-holders and property owners money owing to the Exchequer of Receipt – the term comes from the checked cloth spread over the table on which tax payments were counted. On 19 November 1199 he was at Bury St Edmunds, celebrating the feast of the martyred East Anglian king who had given his name to the town. Apart from selling offices and property in a nationwide auction, the new 'king of the English' showed little interest in the administration of his realm. It was Eleanor who responded to the arrival of the persistent Cardinal Agnani at Dover on 20 November, ostensibly to arbitrate in a monastic dispute at Canterbury but in defiance of Richard's known wishes. She ordered Agnani to remain where he was in Dover until the king should decide what to do with him.[8]

On 27 November the court arrived in Canterbury, processing grandly through the Westgate and into a city that had been much enriched by the cult of St Thomas Becket, whose shrine was visited by tens of thousands of pilgrims each year. After two days of negotiations with Archbishop Baldwin and the monks of the community, Richard gave both sides what they wanted. Only then did he summon the cardinal from Dover, and made the point that he could solve the problems of his kingdom without interference from Rome. Agnani was a wily man who drew up a deposition stating that the monks had been obliged to give way to Baldwin under threats from Richard, so that the accord was invalid. Prince John saw in this a chance of having the interdict on his lands, due to his marriage to Isabel of Gloucester, lifted. Agnani, sniffing the winds of change, and perhaps flattered that the king's brother showed him more respect than did the king, complied.

One important person was immune both to crusading fever and the reorganisation of society caused by Richard's tax gathering, but not to the need for wealth. Queen Eleanor, who was to act as regent with the support of the two justiciars during Richard's absence, required an income appropriate to her new station – and perhaps some compensation for all those years spent as Henry II's prisoner. Not only had she retaken control of her dower possessions, but she also persuaded Richard to bestow on her the lands and income allotted by Henry I and Stephen of Blois to their queens, to cover the necessary expenditure of their households.[9] At her discretion, she could also levy the traditional 'queen geld' at the rate of 10 per cent on all fines payable to the king.

With her long political experience, she must have known that Philip Augustus, Henry's long-term enemy who had been Richard's bosom friend of yesteryear, would return from the

crusade – if he survived – intent on revenge for the humiliation and wrongs both political and personal inflicted on him by
Henry. Knowing her sons as she did, she was also able to guess
that Philip and Richard's joint leadership of the crusade would
not bind them as brothers, but lead to a permanent rift between
them. History was to prove any such fears justified: the acrimony
between the two rulers during the crusade resulted, a few years
after her death, in Richard's successor John losing Normandy to
Philip Augustus in the long process of erosion of the empire that
Eleanor and Henry had made, ending in the English defeat at the
Battle of Castillon in July 1473 and the surrender of Bordeaux to
the French in October that year.

So much for the enemy without. As to the enemy within,
capable of every betrayal himself, Richard at first insisted that
Prince John must accompany him to Outremer so that he could
not mount a coup either in England or in the continental possessions during his brother's absence, but Eleanor fought this
on the grounds that it was unthinkable to risk both sons dying
in the Holy Land and thus putting up for grabs the whole
Plantagenet Empire. So John was heavily bribed to behave in his
brother's absence. His hunger for power and riches might have
been sated by Richard granting him the castles of Ludgershall,
Marlborough, the Peak, Lancaster and Bolsover, the honours
of Peverell and Wallingford, the town of Nottingham and the
whole of Derbyshire, plus lesser properties and honours.[10] To
these he later added the counties of Devon, Cornwall, Somerset
and Dorset, together constituting a greater single block of territory in England than had been granted to anyone else since
the Conquest. Instead, these possessions made John dangerously
powerful and impoverished the Exchequer considerably, since he
did not have to account to the Crown for the taxes he levied in
his possessions.[11]

These gifts illustrate Richard's inability to deal with John's
treacherous and deceitful nature. Time and again he forgave
the brother who had turned his coat so publicly by deserting

the father against whom he had no argument, for Henry II had
repeatedly shown his youngest son every favour and even implied
that he would succeed to the throne of England. As events were
to tell, Richard would have done better to lock up his younger
brother for the duration – for which there were precedents. His
father had done exactly this with Eleanor after the rebellion of
1173–74 to prevent her causing him any further damage, and
his great-grandfather Henry I had locked up his elder brother
Robert Curthose for twenty-eight years after grabbing power
following the death of William Rufus.

## NOTES

1. Quoted in D. Boyd, *Voices from the Dark Years* (Thrupp: Sutton, 2007),
   pp. 157–8.
2. P.W. Hammond, *Food and Feast in Medieval England* (Thrupp: Sutton,
   1998), p. 127.
3. Ibid, p. 119.
4. William of Newburgh, *Historia Rerum Anglicarum*, Vol 1, p. 346.
5. Benedict of Peterborough, *Gesta Henrici*, Vol 2, p. 98.
6. Ibid, Vol 2, p. 87.
7. Roger of Howden, *Chronica*, Vol 3, p. 28.
8. Ralf of Diceto, *Radulfi de Diceto Opera Historica* ed. W. Stubbs, Rolls
   Series No 68 (London: Longmans, 1876), Vol 2, p. 72; also Benedict of
   Peterborough, *Gesta Henrici*, Vol 2, p. 97.
9. Roger of Howden, *Chronica*, Vol 3, p. 27.
10. Benedict of Peterborough, *Gesta Henrici*, Vol 2, pp. 73, 75, 78.
11. Roger of Howden, *Chronica*, Vol 3, xxxiii.

# Part 3:

# The Crusader King

# So Many Ways of Dying

In the Holy Land, the dissension that was the curse of the crusader states continued. In the spring of 1188 William II of Sicily sent his *ammiratus ammiratorum,* or Grand Admiral Margaritus, with a fleet of sixty ships and 200 knights to control the sea lanes to and from the Holy Land and to protect the coastal cities against Saladin's depredations. The Sicilians sided with Guy de Lusignan. On 6 April 1189 Archbishop Ubaldo Lanfranchi of Pisa – a great maritime power – arrived with a fleet of fifty-two ships. Being no friends of the Holy Roman Empire, in whose territory lay Conrad's home territory of Montferrat, this contingent also sided with King Guy. This gave Guy the confidence to demand that Conrad cease his pretension to the throne of Jerusalem. The reply was again a resounding *Non!*

Guy again marched south, with the Sicilian and Pisan fleets sailing a parallel course just off the coast, to besiege Muslim-occupied Acre after setting up camp a mile from the walls on 28 August 1189, near the water supply of the River Belus, which flowed into the sea just south of Acre. The city itself, on the site of modern Akko, a mere 15 miles south of what is now the Israel–Lebanon border, was garrisoned by 6,000 Muslims. On 15 October 1189 Saladin partially surrounded the crusader force, thereafter obliged to fight on two fronts. The dispute dragged on and cost so many lives because Acre was both an important commercial centre of the Levant and a key port for the resupply of the crusader states.[1]

Constructed on a peninsula jutting southward into the Gulf of Caiaphas (modern Haifa), Acre was protected to the south and west by the sea and a stout sea wall. The north-eastern and eastern walls barring access from the landward side were double and provided at strategic intervals with towers from which enfilading fire could be directed at enemy forces approaching the outer walls. One was called the Accursed Tower, in memory of all the men who had died there. There were two land-gates and two sea-gates opening on to the harbour and an outer anchorage. The walls, repaired and strengthened by Saladin after capturing the city, plus the natural advantages of the site, made Acre a very tough nut to crack.[2] Protected by a decaying mole of Roman construction was a fortified harbour sheltered against all but offshore winds. The harbour entrance was blocked by a heavy chain between the Tower of Flies and another tower, which was lowered to allow friendly ships to enter and winched back up afterwards. The Tower of Flies, so called because it was the site of executions, where corpses attracted swarms of flies, also served as a lighthouse and a customs checkpoint under normal conditions.[3]

Early in September the Danish and Frisian crusaders arrived, but their performance in combat on land was unimpressive. They were therefore used to augment the naval blockade of Acre, by which Guy hoped to force a surrender when the supplies of food and arms in the city were exhausted. When news came of the death of William II of Sicily in November, the Sicilian contingent was called home by his successor, Tancred of Lecce.

Wrested from Byzantine rule in 902, the island had been a Muslim emirate until the Norman conquest in 1091. Its resulting population was a mixture of Christian, Muslim and Greek Orthodox. Although Joanna's husband was known as 'William the

Good', because he had been the first Western monarch to send aid to the beleaguered Latin Kingdom, he also spoke and wrote Arabic – and took his sexual pleasures in his harem of beautiful Christian and Muslim girls. Many of his counsellors had been Muslims and it was feared that they might take advantage of his death to mount an uprising under the banner of religion. In addition, the Sicilian possessions on the mainland were threatened from the north by forces of the Holy Roman Empire.

After the departure of the Sicilian contingent, troops in the siege camp were also augmented by a scattering of French and Flemish bishops and barons with their vassals. Additional reinforcements came from Tyre after Markgraf Louis III of Thuringia, a cousin of Conrad's mother, arrived by sea and used his diplomatic skills to persuade Conrad to send troops to the siege of Acre – which he did, on condition that they were not placed under Guy's command.[4] In November the independent fleet of Londoners at last arrived, cock-a-hoop over their success against the Moors in Portugal.[5]

This piecemeal reinforcement and retirement from the fight by European contingents was a feature of the long 'holy war' that lasted two centuries, beginning with the First Crusade in 1095 and ending with the fall of the Latin states after the abortive Ninth Crusade in 1273. It mirrored Saladin's difficulties in holding his army together for any length of time, composed as it was of knights and foot soldiers drawn from Syria, Mesopotamia, Egypt and Turkestan. They did not owe him any personal loyalty, but stayed fighting only as long as their own emirs could keep them in the field.

Conditions inside the walls of Acre, whose exact positions at the time of the siege cannot now be determined as the area has all been built over, were as grim as in any other besieged city. Food was in such short supply that the normally discarded offal such as entrails, heads and feet were all consumed. Christian prisoners in the city were executed, expelled and hanged from the walls, to reduce the number of useless mouths. Only a small

number of healthy young male captives were kept alive to oper-
ate the siege engines driving off each crusader attack. Outside
the walls, three massive wheeled towers were constructed by
the besiegers, said to be 60 cubits or almost 100ft high and
rolled close to the walls by muscle power. A huge battering ram
with an iron head was also made. To foil the work of sappers and
besiegers scaling ladders and in the towers, the defenders hurled
great beams down on them, as well as boulders, pots of boiling
water and Greek fire. At first, the Greek fire failed to burn the
siege towers covered in dampened cowhide, but an improved
formula was devised by a Damascene in the city, which did
ignite the siege towers, forcing the men inside to run for their
lives, pursued by showers of arrows. The man from Damascus
refused payment, saying that he had done his work 'for the love
of God'.[6]

By the time Saladin attacked the siege camp outside Acre on
4 October 1189, Guy was nominally in command of 400 knights
and 7,000 foot soldiers. The numbers in the other contingents
are not known. In the ensuing battle, Christian losses were heavy,
especially among the dedicated Templar knights, whose losses
included their Grand Master Gerard de Ridefort, after an estimated 5,000 men of the Saracen garrison sallied out of the city
and took in the rear the Christian forces engaged with Saladin's
army. In the confused fighting Conrad was at one time surrounded by the enemy until rescued by Guy. Fighting was so
intense and prolonged that Saladin's chancellor reported to his
master that he had counted 4,100 Frankish dead on the Christian
right wing alone.[7] However, Saladin lacked sufficient forces to
consolidate this victory, resulting in a stalemate that lasted fifteen
months, during which Conrad sailed north to Tyre and returned
with dismantled siege engines that were immediately assembled
and used to batter the city walls until destroyed during a sortie on
5 May 1190.

He later travelled north to escort the remnants of the German
army arriving by land under Emperor Frederik Barbarossa's son

Frederik of Swabia. The rump of Barbarossa's army, whittled away by battles en route in Syria and an epidemic in Antioch, arrived at Acre on 3 October.[8] About this time Archbishop Baldwin of Canterbury landed at Tyre and rode down to Acre at the head of Richard's advance party. By the time it reached Acre, conditions in the blockaded city and the siege camp outside had become so unhealthy that Queen Sybilla's two daughters had died. When their grieving mother also succumbed to the contamination of water from human and equine corpses, Guy's claim to the throne of Jerusalem was extinguished, the title passing to Sybilla's half-sister Isabella, but Guy refused to stand aside for her. Rank was no protection from illness: nobles and men-at-arms alike suffered scurvy, with painful lumps on limbs and faces and teeth falling out of bleeding gums. Life was little better for the men of Saladin's relieving army; he himself suffered an outbreak of boils from waist to knee, which made sitting in the saddle agony for him.[9]

Nor were casualties and deaths from disease limited to humans. Numerous diseases such as glanders, infectious anaemia and equine venereal disease – the last usually fatal for stallions – were transmitted along the closely packed horse lines by droplet and fly bites, killing thousands of horses and making many others unfit for combat. In much the same way as modern warfare causes large numbers of armoured and transport vehicles to be written off, the crusaders lost thousands of horses to disease in addition to those wounded or killed in combat. The march to Jerusalem of the First Crusade was estimated to have cost the lives of 4,500 horses.[10]

Supplying the garrison with food and arms was a perpetual headache for Saladin, due to the harbour being blockaded by crusader ships. Among the ruses resorted to, according to the Muslim historian Baha al-Din, was loading one very large vessel in Beirut in June 1190 with all kinds of food and manning it with sailors dressed in Western style, who had also shaved off their beards, to look like Christians. Crosses were sewn into the sails and live pigs

– forbidden to Muslims – were kept on deck. When stopped and challenged by the blockade, men on board replied in the *lingua franca* and pretended their ship was a French vessel heading for the beach by the siege camp, then making a successful dash for the safety of the harbour before they could be stopped. There, as Baha al-Din comments, 'They were greeted with cries of joy, for hunger was stalking the city.'[11]

Count Henry II of Champagne, known to the Muslims as *al-kond Herri*, arrived in July 1190, bringing news that Philip Augustus and Richard – both of whom were his uncles[12] – were at long last preparing to depart on crusade. By now the assembled barons had had enough of Guy as leader. To confer legitimacy on a universally acceptable replacement, a council of nobles decided to marry Conrad to 21-year-old Isabella. She was already married to the youthful Humphrey IV of Toron, formerly a captive of Saladin, who had released him without ransom, ostensibly because he spoke a fluent and elegant Arabic and was a naturally charming person. Humphrey's marriage was annulled, his wishes in the matter being disregarded since he was considered 'effeminate' and not sufficiently aggressive for a crusader lord. The decision was endorsed by Isabella's mother Maria Comnena, who was married to Balian of Ibelin, one of the *seigneurs* responsible for the disaster of Hattin. The senior prelates in the Holy Land being sick, it fell to papal legate Archbishop Lanfranchi and Bishop Philip of Beauvais to annul the marriage on 19 November 1190 and marry Isabella to Conrad on 24 November.

There is no record of her feelings at being wrested from a young and affectionate husband to be bedded by a hardened middle-aged warrior, who was intent on rapidly getting her pregnant so that he could look forward to being regent to an infant heir on the throne of Jerusalem. This was all done despite Conrad being known to be married, albeit under the Orthodox rite, to Princess Theodora, who was still alive. Furthermore, since Isabella's half-sister had previously been married to her new bridegroom's elder brother William Longsword the match was incestuous under canon law. It was indeed a tangled web to be woven in the middle of a total war! Conrad, having recently been wounded, the newly-weds departed from Acre to the relative safety of Tyre, so that he could convalesce. His potency clearly had not been affected by the wound, because Isabella gave birth to a daughter by him the following year.

Talk of wounds during the crusades perhaps gives a false idea today when most severe injuries in combat come from explosives. In medieval hand-to-hand combat, both knights and men-at-arms suffered injury from slashing blades, stab wounds and broken bones. The worst were those inflicted by cudgels and maces, especially of the ball-and-chain variety – the preferred weapon of Bishop Odo of Bayeux, half-brother of William the Conqueror. It has been said that his choice of weapon indicated great holiness, in that he simply stunned his adversaries, but this betrays a misunderstanding of the weapon and times: Odo's probably spiked weapon crushed skulls and shattered ribs and limbs horribly, but enabled him to claim as a churchman that he was not shedding blood.

It was common for men to have lost fingers, ears and noses, to have permanently damaged legs and arms or to have scarred faces. Indeed, the nasal piece had been added to the basic helmet after thousands of men lost their noses in combat. Because the essence of hand-to-hand fighting was brute strength allied with trained reflexes, in the intervals between combat outside Acre men of all ranks would be seen hacking away at the *pell*, a stout post driven into the ground that had been used since Roman times to practise delivering a blow with all one's strength and recovering control of the sword immediately afterwards to foil an opponent's counter-strike. And no one could ever relax. The Norman *trouvère* and chronicler Ambroise, who travelled with the Third Crusade and was first to use the epithet 'Lionheart', reported an incident in which a knight squatting to relieve himself in the siege camp was surprised by a Turk on horseback.

Warned by his comrades' cries just in time, the knight grabbed a stone from the ground and killed the Turk with it, capturing his horse into the bargain.[13]

In addition to skirmishes, there were some major battles. On 11 October 1190 several thousand men of the garrison made a sortie from Acre, but were repulsed with heavy losses. On 31 October a flotilla of fifty Muslim galleys broke through the crusader blockade, with heavy losses on both sides. Their shallow draught enabled them to sail right into the silting-up port, bringing men, food and weapons to the besieged city, enabling the garrison to make another sortie on 11 November. An even larger fleet from Egypt reached the safety of Acre's harbour on 26 December. In the siege camp, conditions were at their worst, with knights slaughtering their own horses for food and the common troops reduced to eating grass and weeds, just to put something in their stomachs. Shortage of food was made worse by the Pisan merchants, who controlled supplies, inflating prices to levels impossible for the ordinary crusader to pay: a handful of peas for a silver penny or a sack of corn for 100 or 200 gold coins.[14] The common soldiers were so hungry that the bishop of Salisbury had some flogged for resorting to cannibalism, unable to afford the inflated prices where even the common fig sold at seven for 1 *bezant*.

There was in Europe a general prohibition on eating horse-meat because horses were considered noble animals and even poor people tried to avoid eating the flesh of animals that died. These and other prohibitions went by the board in the siege camp, where horses that had died of starvation were butchered to provide the only meat available, however tough, for many starving men.[15] The arrival of supply ships laden with wine, oil and corn brought prices tumbling down, so that the same measure of corn which had been for sale at 200 *bezants* could now be bought for six.[16] Taking advantage of the Christians' poor physical condition and general demoralisation, on 13 February 1191 Saladin's men managed to break through the siege lines and reach the city gates, which were kept open just long enough to allow a fresh garrison to replace the exhausted original force.

With the improved weather, a contingent of Rhinelanders commanded by Duke Leopold V of Austria arrived by ship from Venice. He then assumed command of the survivors of Barbarossa's army, Frederik of Swabia having died the previous month. Leopold must have wondered into what hell he had brought his men, but can have had no idea how famous an insult was to make him, as captor of the king of England.

Conrad was nothing if not a trier. In February he attempted a seaborne invasion, but his attack on the Tower of Flies failed when a ship went aground on a reef. In March a fully laden corn ship arrived and off-loaded its cargo for the crusader camp. After others followed, bellies could again be filled, at a price. News that the kings of England and France were on their way with their armies caused Saladin to write to the Muslim rulers of North Africa and Spain for assistance, but he received little except polite replies.

## NOTES

1. R. Gertwagen, 'The Crusader Port of Acre: Layout and Problems of Maintenance', in *Autour de la Première Croissade*, ed. M. Balard (Paris: Publications de la Sorbonne, 1996), p. 553.
2. Runciman, *A History of the Crusades*, pp. 23–4.
3. Gertwagen, 'Port of Acre', pp. 555, 559–60.
4. Runciman, *A History of the Crusades*, p. 25.
5. See Runciman, *A History of the Crusades*, p. 26 for a comparison of dates given in the various Christian and Muslim histories.
6. Quoted in J. Bradbury, *The Medieval Siege* (Woodbridge: Boydell, 1998), p. 123.
7. Hyland, *The Medieval Warhorse*, p. 163.
8. Benedict of Peterborough, *Gesta Henrici*, Vol 2, p. 143.
9. Bradbury, *Medieval Siege*, p. 124, quoting Baha al-Din.
10. Hyland, *The Medieval Warhorse*, pp. 48, 168.
11. Quoted in Maalouf, *The Crusades*, p. 208.

12. Count Henry's mother was a daughter of Queen Eleanor by her first husband Louis VII.
13. Quoted in Bradbury, *Medieval Siege*, p. 124.
14. Runciman, *A History of the Crusades*, p. 33.
15. Roger of Howden, *Chronica, pars posterior*, p. 69.
16. Benedict of Peterborough, *Gesta Henrici*, Vol 2, p. 145.

# Of Cogs and Cargo

Richard's decision to make the greater part of the journey to Outremer by sea was possibly influenced by
Eleanor, who had not only suffered much privation on
the overland route to the Second Crusade with her first husband Louis VII, travelling via the Holy Roman Empire, Hungary
and Byzantium, but also seen half the French army wiped out by
Turkish hit-and-run tactics in the mountains of Anatolia before
ever reaching the Holy Land. It is possible, too, that unconfirmed
rumours had reached Richard's ears of a secret pact made with
Saladin by the Byzantine emperor Isaac II Angelos to delay the
crusading army of Holy Roman Emperor Frederik Barbarossa on
the fatal overland route through his territory in 1189.

Although British schoolchildren used to be taught that the
Royal Navy could trace its history back to King Alfred (849–99),
this is not true. Most of Alfred's military activity was on land,
although he used ships to intercept Viking raiders at sea. In 875
he put to sea against seven invading vessels, captured one and
drove the others off. In 855 his ships intercepted and captured sixteen Danish ships off the coast of Essex, but were then defeated
by a larger force of Danes.[1]

Alfred's was not the first royal fleet in the British Isles, then divided into several kingdoms. In fact, defensive fleets of these islands dated back to the Roman establishment of the Saxon Shore forts, ports and fleets in the third century. We know from the tenth-century *Senchus Fer n-Alban* – or History of the Men of Scotland – that taxation in the seventh-century Irish/Scottish kingdom of Dalriada included a ship-levy which theoretically provided a fleet of 177 small ships, each manned by fourteen men. However, the only deployment reported seems to be in the year 719, not defending Dalriada against foreign invaders, but in a civil war![2] Alfred's son Edward and his warrior daughter Athelflaed continued to fight the Danes, using ships apparently modelled on the Viking longship and built with taxes levied by the *ship-soke*. They could, on occasion, raise 100 vessels to defend Wessex although, according to *The Anglo-Saxon Chronicle*, by 1001 Ethelred the Unwise was desperately ordering the construction of more and more ships but could not assemble enough to keep the invaders at bay. There was thus no continuing policy of an established navy; rather, each king tried with inadequate tax resources to cope with the complex of current problems confronting him.

The Norman Conquest saw a comprehensive feudal taxation system imposed on the English but this provided no permanent fleet, although a royal transportation system did exist between south coast ports and Normandy so that the king's household and messengers on official business could travel across the Channel conveniently. Richard's father Henry II is reckoned to have crossed the Channel nearly thirty times in his reign – usually in his *esnecca*[3] or 'snake-ship' because it was swift and thin compared with contemporary merchant vessels – but had no fleet to outflank the Welsh when first invading their country, and failing to conquer them. In 1165 he had to hire a Viking squadron from Dublin to harass the coast of Gwynedd. So, inheriting no Anglo-Norman fleet that could transport his army for the crusade when he came to the throne, Richard was faced with a problem. In order to avoid paying the extortionate rates demanded by the shipowners of Pisa and Genoa, who possessed the two great Christian fleets in the Mediterranean, he decided to raise a fleet by purchasing vessels in English ports and his continental possessions. As maritime historian Professor John Pryor has observed:

> Most historians have written about medieval campaigns as though they took place in a geographic, meteorological and oceanographic vacuum. In most books, military forces move from one place to another without the slightest difficulty ... naval forces are given even less consideration. They leave the West and arrive in the Holy Land as though their commanders had merely engaged the engines on their cruise ships and set course by the shortest possible route for the Holy Land ... For the First Crusade the only crusader fleet to attempt to make the passage to the East in one passage was a Genoese flotilla of twelve galleys and a transport ship. The fleets of Pisa and Venice ... wintered over in the Ionian islands and on Rhodes respectively. And even the Genoese took four months to make the voyage.[4]

The intention here is to examine more closely the problems and dangers of Richard's decision to assemble a large fleet for the expedition and send it twice as far as the Genoese on the First Crusade. The twelfth century had seen a number of fleets travel successfully between Europe's Mediterranean coastline and Outremer and some smaller fleets had also reached the Holy Land from Germany and the Baltic, but Richard's plan was a major undertaking, with which he charged Robert of Turnham, or Thornham. Henry of Cornhill, the trustworthy sheriff of London, Kent and Surrey, was comptroller of the expedition's budget and recorded that most of the English vessels acquired in harbours from Hull to Portsmouth and assembled in Dartmouth were square-rigged cogs modelled on the flat-bottomed riverine *Koggen* developed in Frisia.

By the time of the Third Crusade, the cog had a heavy bottom of edge-joined strakes using pegged mortise-and-tenon joints above which the clinker-built sides were of sawn boards nailed to the frames. It had a high freeboard braced by stout through-beams spanning the midships in the area still called 'the beam', enabling increased width and therefore more cargo- or passenger-carrying capacity. With a length of around 60ft and a beam of 13ft or so, the cog was an all-purpose transport. Some were equipped with steer-boards, which were wide oars manipulated by the boatswain at the right side rear of the ship – hence the term 'starboard' – but some may also have had the more efficient central rudder hinged on the sternpost. The heavy bottom construction gave the stability for fore- and after-castles and also top-castles to be added, giving an advantage over lower-freeboard galleys in ship-to-ship combat. The cogs cost between £50 and £66 each, paid two-thirds in cash and the rest by remission of taxes due by their owners or the ports where they lay. At least forty-four ships were purchased in this way[5] – thirty-three of them from the Cinque Ports alone.

The vessels had to be purchased, rather than leased, since it was considered impossible for square-rigged vessels to return through the straits of Gibraltar, due to the strong prevailing westerly winds. Although lateen-rigged Mediterranean craft could progress against the wind and sometimes moored in the ports of Gascony and further north on the French Atlantic coast, the mixed force of 167 English, Norman, Flemish and German vessels that had sailed south in 1147 to help wrest Lisbon from the Almohad Moors in the Iberian *Reconquista* represented the furthest a northern fleet might travel and return to base.[6] Richard's fleet therefore had to be written off and scrapped in the Mediterranean at the end of its crusade service.

Depending on the vessel's size, crew numbers varied from twenty-five to sixty plus the steersman/boatswain aboard the flagship, which was Henry II's *esnecca*, and could be rowed as a galley or proceed under sail with a favourable wind. Whether

there were other *esneccas* in the fleet is unknown. The 1,100 crew-
men were not volunteer crusaders, but paid a year in advance at
the rate of 2 pence per day, with the boatswain/skippers receiving
only twice that amount.[7] Frequently overlooked is the enormous
logistical operation required to provision these ships. Large quantities of hardtack known as 'biskits of muslin'[8] were prepared from
a gritty stoneground mixture of barley and rye grains with bean
flour made into a dough without leavening or shortening, rather
like modern water biscuits or *matzos*. Baked four times instead
of the usual twice for domestic biscuits, they were thought hard
enough to defy the teeth of ship-borne rats, if not also the wee-
vils, and the absence of fat stopped them going rotten.[9]

The biscuits had to be softened in some liquid before they
could be eaten. Tasting this unpalatable food for the first time,
any landlubbers who had been enticed aboard by the wages paid
up front could have had little idea that the time would come
when just one such hardtack would be manna for a starving man
in the Holy Land. Salted meat and fish, hard cheeses and dried
beans and peas made up the balance of the crews' diets while
at sea, although a number of live animals and fowls were carried for slaughter and butchery on the voyage; maritime historian
Benjamin Z. Kedar records 14,000 cured pig carcases among the
victuals loaded.[10] Writing some 300 years later, when little of
shipboard life had changed, Felix Fabri wrote:

> Everything that is on board becomes putrid and foul and mouldy;
> the water begins to stink, the wine becomes undrinkable; meat,
> even when dried and smoked, becomes full of maggots and all of
> a sudden there spring into life innumerable flies, gnats, fleas, lice,
> worms, mice and rats … I have seen few men die on board during
> storms, but many have I seen sicken and die [from these causes].[11]

A considerable quantity of freight had to be stowed in the open
holds and lashed securely down. This included the heavy heart-
of-oak baulks of dismantled siege engines and thousands of bows

and arrows – the English longbows would suffer from the dryness of the Holy Land climate and become brittle – as well as the more robust crossbows with their quarrels, plus swords and side-arms, body armour and helmets and 60,000 horseshoes with the nails to fix them, all hand-forged in the Forest of Dean. These were not easily obtainable in Outremer for European *destriers* and palfreys, larger and heavier than the nimble local breeds, which were bred for speed and their ability to survive on less water, and were also broken and trained differently. To the Muslim eye, European or *afrendji* horses were too fat, meaning too slow, and lacking in endurance, especially in hot, dry conditions. Therefore complete sets of farriers' tools and armourers' workshops had also to be transported, to re-shoe horses and effect the necessary repairs to arms and armour.

Some horses were doubtless carried aboard, for use during landfalls made on the voyage, but the main body of palfreys and *destriers* required by the army is more likely to have travelled the first leg of the long journey by the overland route to southern France before being embarked for the Mediterranean stages. It might seem that medieval logistics were simple compared with the long-distance transportation of a modern mechanised army, with its requirements for spare parts, fuel and mechanics, but the complications of shipping horses were legion. Being unable to vomit, they make poor sailors and, since they had to be closely confined in stalls and supported by slings to avoid them injuring themselves due to the ship's motion – these vessels rolled abominably in even a light sea – would be sick and useless for several days after a long voyage. Their diet was also a problem. Many horses waste hay and will not eat trampled fodder. Most horses drink about 18 litres of water a day under normal conditions. With twenty confined in humid conditions below deck in one ship the weekly requirement was at least 2,500 litres, or 2.5 tonnes, of water. A shipboard diet of hay and oats or dried barley increased water requirement, to avoid impaction of the gut, and too much grain during the voyage would have caused many horses to suffer the muscle disorder azoturia on disembarkation.[12] Known colloquially as 'Monday morning sickness', this can be painful and crippling for horses kept in stalls, instead of loose boxes, over a weekend, let alone for horses confined on ships for several weeks.

There was also a considerable amount of personal equipment to be prepared and we have to thank the chronicler Gerald of Wales for an insight into this. Required to accompany Archbishop Baldwin of Canterbury on a recruiting tour of Wales in 1188, he recorded how the archbishop insisted on his entourage dismounting and walking up and down Welsh mountains to toughen them up for the crusade. Baldwin also had special tents made and erected on his newly purchased estate at Lambeth to test their suitability and give his servants practice in erecting them and striking camp.[13] Baldwin was known as a pessimist, so it is possible that more optimistic religious and lay leaders put less effort into the preparations.

Any vassal who had doubted that Richard the warrior could turn into Richard the monarch could have said I-told-you-so on seeing the keen attention he devoted to all the preparations for the coming campaign and his heedlessness of the consequences of his actions in leaving an unstable realm behind him when he crossed the Channel on 11 December 1189. All but five sheriffs in the land were new to the post and inexperienced; dissident barons were building castles that Henry would have razed to the ground immediately; Archbishop Baldwin of Canterbury and Hubert Walter, newly appointed bishop of Salisbury by Richard, travelled to Outremer ahead of the main crusading party, which left William Longchamp with no ecclesiastical superior to keep him in order. Prince John was flexing his political muscles as the ruler of a virtually autonomous principality. Also, the Welsh were mounting incursions in the marches, in no small part because Rhys ap Gruffyd, the most important ruler of southern Wales, had come to Oxford under Prince John's protection to meet Richard, who had sent word that he was too busy to meet him. The Welsh prince had taken this as a personal snub. It was unlike John to get involved in diplomacy, but his reason was simple: a Welsh invasion would immediately threaten the lands he had acquired by marrying Isabel of Gloucester.

The absence from England of Hubert Walter, a nephew of Ranulf de Glanville who had been trained in the governance of England by his uncle, was to be a sad lack for the country. Described by the monks of Canterbury as 'tall of stature, subtle of wit although not of speech', his rise to political eminence had been slow but steady. In 1185 he was a baron of the Exchequer; in the same year Henry II used him as one of several envoys negotiating with the chapter of Canterbury Cathedral over the election of a new primate; in 1186 he was made a dean of York and nominated for the post of bishop, although not approved by Henry; in April of the fateful year 1189 he was a justice of the *curia regis* at Westminster and later Henry's assistant chancellor in Maine. There, or previously, he must have impressed Richard because his appointment to the see of Salisbury was one of Richard's first acts after coming to England.

The death of William de Mandeville in December prompted Richard to add to Longchamp's other responsibilities the duties of a justiciar. To avoid conflicts with Hugh of Durham, that prelate was told in February 1190 to confine his activities to England north of the River Humber, leaving Longchamp as justiciar for the southern half of the country. In addition, Pope Clement III was said to have received 1,500 marks to confer the post of papal legate on Longchamp. This concentrated far too much power in one pair of hands – or rather, three pairs of hands, because Bishop William brought to England two of his brothers to share in his good fortune. Mandeville's widow Hadwisa was given by Richard to his favourite William de Fors. She was described by Richard of Devizes as 'a woman almost a man, lacking nothing virile except the virile parts'. True to her character, she refused the match until Richard seized her estates in Yorkshire and started selling off her livestock, at which point she submitted to the king's will, if not necessarily that of her new husband.[14]

1 The first seal of Richard

2 The second seal of Richard, showing on his shield the three lions passant, which are still on the British royal coat of arms today

3 The knight as a Christ-like figure at Melle church, shown protecting either a child or a poor person, the comparative size denoting importance, or lack of it. The sculptor here shows clearly how tightly the high pommel and cantle held the rider in position

4 The chivalric fantasy: a knight rescuing a damsel from the dragon of lust. (Angoulême Cathedral)

5 Chronicler Matthew Paris came closer to the reality of knightly violence with this sanitised sketch of William the Marshal unhorsing Baldwin de Guisnes in a *mêlée*

6 The truth of knightly conduct: this eroded carving at Parthenay church shows a knight riding roughshod over a peasant. From the symbolic gyrfalcon on his wrist, this is a duke of Aquitaine – possibly Richard indulging in his favourite activity

7 When not at war, knights relaxed by killing animals instead of people

8 Going on crusade won the pope's assurance that all their earthly sins would thereby be cancelled out. With so much blood-crime on their consciences, knights feared the weighing of their soul after death by an angel and a demon

9 In the twelfth century, everyone could estimate a horse's value and, therefore, the wealth or importance of its owner. A knight would have been judged by his mount, much as people today may be judged by the cost and make of the car they drive

10 Reflecting the importance of the horse, the church at St-Front-sur-Gironde is decorated with twenty-six horse heads (the detail of which is shown in the image above), rather than the usual images of saints and angels

12 Eleanor of Aquitaine as she looked at the time of her death

11 Richard's powerful mother, Eleanor of Aquitaine, aged 22 at Chartres Cathedral

13 No clear contemporary image of Richard exists, but he was said to closely resemble his own father Henry II and his grandfather Count Geoffrey the Fair of Anjou, as seen in this polychrome enamel portrait

14 Detail of a side chapel in La Sauve Majure Abbey

15 Riding from Bordeaux to punish his Gascon vassals with fire and sword,
Richard gave alms to the monks at Cayac Abbey (above) so they would pray for
his soul. He claimed that his favourite abbey of La Sauve Majeure (detail, top)
was 'dearer to me than my own eye-balls'

16 Richard adored singing and music and would dress up for grand occasions

17 The great audience hall in Poitiers, built by Eleanor and Henry II, where Richard held court

18 The Angevin treasure castle at Chinon, as seen from the river

19 The view from the battlements over the Loire Valley. In the foreground is the Tour du Moulin, where Eleanor was imprisoned by Henry II after the rebellion of 1174

20 (above) 21 (below) At the end of the rebellion, Richard took refuge in Saintes Cathedral, using the cloisters (below) as an armoury and magazine. Abandoning his knights and men for Henry II to take hostage, he fled to the mighty fortress of Taillebourg (above). Later, he besieged and destroyed the castle where he had been given asylum

22 In the chapel of Ste-Radegonde at Chinon amateur archaeologists uncovered this fresco, painted shortly after the rebellion of 1174. It depicts Henry II leading Queen Eleanor away to fifteen years' imprisonment in England. The young woman between them is Princess Joanna

23 On the left of the fresco, Eleanor is depicted yielding to Richard a white gyrfalcon, the emblem of the duchy of Aquitaine. Richard is so eager to take it that he is nearly leaning out of the saddle

24 Climbing the scaling ladder into the breach in the walls of Acre, Albéric Clément said: 'If it please God I shall enter the city.' God was not pleased, and he was hacked to death at the top of the ladder

25 After the city surrendered, Richard ordered the slaughter of the 2,700 men, women and children living there

26 In the Manesse Codex, created around 1315, Richard's captor Heinrich VI is portrayed as a strong and wise ruler. Setting the ransom for the release of Richard was complicated by Prince John conspiring with Philip of France to bribe Heinrich not to free the Lionheart

27 In the *Liber ad Honorem Augusti* by Petrus de Ebolo, written around 1196, Richard is shown kissing the Emperor's feet, while begging his pardon. This did not go down well with his Anglo-Norman vassals

28 The *donjon* of Châlus Castle, from which the fatal crossbow bolt was fired

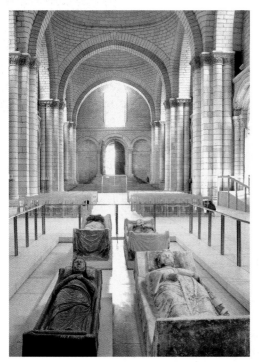

29 The nave of the abbey church at Fontevraud, showing the effigies of Richard (foreground, right) and Isabel of Angoulême (foreground, left), with Henry II and Eleanor in the background

30 Among Queen Berengaria's good works was the founding of the convent of L'Épau, near Le Mans

31 Queen Berengaria was described as virtuous and docile, rather than beautiful or intelligent

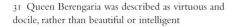

32 At the foot of Queen Berengaria's effigy there is a carving of a lamb being mounted by a lion, in reference to the wifely duty she can rarely have performed for Richard

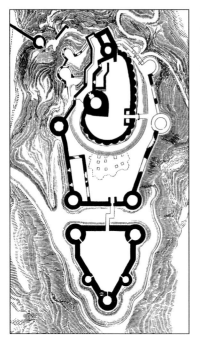

33 A nineteenth-century ground plan of the most costly fortress in the world, drawn by architect Viollet le Duc. Richard's 'impregnable' Château Gaillard incorporated all the latest improvements in castle design

34 Viollet le Duc also produced this reconstruction of the siege of the castle, destroyed by the French king just five years after Richard's death

Crossing to Calais from Dover on 11 December, Richard saw in the harbour a part at least of the fleet of 100-plus vessels he was assembling to transport his army from Marseilles to the Holy Land.[15] At his Christmas court held in the castle of Bures in Lower Normandy the new king of England was so gung-ho and patently delighted to have shaken the dust of that country off his boots that his continental vassals speculated that he would hand England to John and content himself with the continental possessions on his return from crusade. Although he never went that far, it is true that he paid only one more brief visit to his island kingdom – and that was again to squeeze every last penny from his subjects north of the Channel.

Richard's attention was concentrated on continuing preparations, including the acquisition of more ships in his ports on the Gulf of Gascony, mainly the stout clinker-built *baleniers* used for whale fishing in the Bay of Biscay. Meanwhile, his English fleet was being assembled at Dartmouth, ready to sail southward down the Atlantic coast and through the straits of Gibraltar into the Mediterranean. Roger of Howden's account of the voyage is unclear, but it seems that the English ships left Dartmouth with the tide on 25 March. In 1147 a crusading fleet of 167 vessels had left Dartmouth and arrived in Oporto after twenty-four days' sailing, including one or more stopovers in Spanish Biscayan ports.[16] However, on 6 May Richard's ships ran into a storm in the Bay of Biscay that separated the vessels and was so frightening that three Londoners in one ship claimed to have seen a vision of St Thomas Becket telling them not to fear because he and two other saints were looking after them. Having rounded Cape Finisterre, they certainly made landfall at Lisbon, and maybe Oporto, to obtain fresh supplies and, more importantly, clean water for men and horses.

While the English flotilla was moored in the estuary of the Tagus awaiting the arrival of the squadron from Richard's continental possessions commanded by Guillaume d'Oléron, there occurred a shameful episode that foreshadowed the sacking of

Constantinople by the Fourth Crusade. Welcomed at first by
King Sancho, grateful for the armed assistance of the London
crusaders at Silves in the previous year, some of the crews volun-
teered to assist Sancho's army to repel another attack under the
king of Morocco. After his death and the subsequent withdrawal
of the Moors, the crusaders ran amok back in Lisbon, burning
down houses, fighting among themselves and with the townsfolk,
stealing property and raping women. Sancho put a stop to this by
closing the gates of Lisbon and throwing into prison 700 riot-
ers trapped within the walls.[17] The episode was whitewashed in
many contemporary and later accounts by the pretence that the
fleet was delayed by these men heroically capturing Silves from
the Moors.

Released by agreement with Robert of Turnham and Henry
of Cornhill, the men were forced to swear that in future they
would abide by the rules of conduct laid down by King Richard.
On 24 July William de Fors arrived with thirty more big ships,
divided into five squadrons commanded by Archbishop Gérard
of Auch, Bishop Bernard of Bayonne, Richard de Camville,
Guillaume d'Oléron and Robert de Sablé, who was in overall
command. After mooring in the estuary of the Tagus, they were
given two days to re-provision before sailing away on 26 July, to
the evident relief of the Portuguese, and passed the point of no
return at the straits of Gibraltar on 1 August. The land on both
sides of the strait was occupied by the Moors, but with insufficient naval power to prevent so large a Christian fleet passing
through. In any case there was, as Saladin discovered, little sense
of solidarity among Muslims of the Maghreb with those fighting the crusaders in Outremer. However, southern Spain was all
Moorish territory, so, after Gibraltar, they were unable to land
and re-provision until reaching Christian territory at the mouth
of the Ebro in north-east Spain. From there, the plan was to rendezvous with King Richard and the bulk of his army, travelling
by land, at Marseilles on the southern coast of France.

## NOTES

1. N.A.M. Rodger, *The Safeguard of the Sea* (London: Penguin/National Maritime Museum, 2004), pp. 6–7.
2. Rodger, *The Safeguard of the Sea*, p. 5.
3. Also spelled *snecca*, *enecca* and *énèque*.
4. B.Z. Kedar, 'Reflections on Maps, Crusading and Logistics', in *Logistics of Warfare in the Age of the Crusades*, ed. J.H. Pryor (Farnham: Aldershot Publishing, 2006), p. 288.
5. Rodger, *The Safeguard of the Sea*, p. 45, quoting Pipe Roll 2 Richard I, pp. 7–8, 53, 104, 112–13.
6. Rodger, *The Safeguard of the Sea*, p. 45.
7. Ibid, p. 47 and endnote.
8. Possibly from 'Muslim' or 'Mosul' as in the case of cloth muslin.
9. See www.royalnavalmuseum.org
10. Kedar, 'Reflections on Maps', p. 263.
11. R. Gertwagen, 'Harbours and Facilities along the Eastern Mediterranean Sea Lanes to Outremer', in *Logistics of Warfare*, p. 103, quoting from *The Book of the Wanderings of Brother Felix Fabri*, trans. A. Stewart (London: PPTSL, 1893–96).
12. Hyland, *The Medieval Warhorse*, pp. 144–6.
13. C. Tyerman, *Who's Who in Early Medieval England* (London: Shepeard-Walwyn, 1996), pp. 240–1.
14. *The Chronicle of Richard of Devizes of the Time of King Richard the First*, ed. and trans. J.T. Appleby, Nelson's Medieval Texts (London: Nelson, 1963, p. 10.
15. Roger of Howden, *Chronica, pars posterior*, Vol 3, p. 46.
16. Kedar, 'Reflections on Maps', p. 263.
17. Benedict of Peterborough, *Gesta Henrici*, Vol 2, pp. 119–20.

# 13

# Seasickness and Siege

With 70 per cent of the money raised in England already spent on the fleet and other preparations, Richard made a compact of mistrust with Philip Augustus on 18 January 1190, under which they swore to depart together and return together, meanwhile behaving as brother crusaders, their territorial disputes put on hold for the duration of the crusade. Expanding the peace treaty of Villandry, they also imposed a truce on all their vassals remaining in France for as long as the crusade lasted.

Richard's travels throughout his continental possessions, exacting more taxes and punishing vassals who failed to pay up, were interrupted by the arrival of Queen Eleanor, crossing the Channel and bringing with her Prince John, Geoffrey the Bastard and a posse of prelates that included both William Longchamp and Hugh of Durham. Also in the party was Princess Alais, a hostage of the Plantagenets for twenty-one of her thirty years. Eleanor was by this stage desperate that Richard should marry and father a legitimate child, so that if he died on crusade, John would not succeed to the throne. And if Richard's heir were an infant, who better than his astute and experienced grandmother to act as regent until it came of age? Marrying Alais, who had been betrothed to Richard for more than two decades, would have solved this problem. She had borne at least one child to Henry and was therefore known to be fertile. Since the marriage would also cement a new alliance between the Capetian royal family and the Plantagenets, it would have been a political masterstroke. Refusing the match at this moment was one of the worst moves in Richard's erratic reign.

To correct another ill-considered decision, he forced Prince John and Geoffrey the Bastard to swear that they would not return to England in the following three years – the likely duration of the crusade – without his express permission. Eleanor was rightly alarmed: with John itching to lord it over his possessions on English soil, it was extremely probable that, if forced by this oath to remain idle in France, he would collude in some way with Philip's vassals, with incalculable results. She therefore persuaded Richard to release John from the oath, so that he could occupy himself with governing his English territory. Geoffrey the Bastard was obliged to remain in France – an archbishop of York forbidden to set foot in the country of his diocese! A factor in this decision was the considerable income of the see that was to go to the Exchequer during his absence.[1]

England was a ferment of crusading fever; knights who did not take the Cross were presented with a distaff, symbolising the women's work of spinning. Some of the stay-at-homes were even derisively labelled 'Holy Mary's knights'.[2] A few courageous individuals argued publicly that it was wrong to rejoice in the slaughter of thousands of Saracens, who were human beings, although unbelievers. The chronicler Radulphus Niger, a future dean of Lincoln Cathedral, went so far to declare that the obsession with terrestrial Jerusalem was a chimera that distracted men's minds from the true goal of a spiritual Jerusalem or 'heaven on earth'. But he was swimming against the tide. For many people, the idea of killing Saracen unbelievers in the Holy Land became confused with killing non-Christians closer at hand, as it had in the two previous crusades. England's Jewish community was seen as an obvious target with the spurious justification that its property could afterwards be sold to raise funds for the crusade.

A series of pogroms climaxed in a mass suicide at York on 16 March 1190 – the feast of *shabbat ha-gadol* or the Great Sabbath at the end of *Pesach* or Passover. The former leader of the community, named Baruch – Latinised to Benedict – had already been killed during the pogrom in London at the time of Richard's coronation. In the renewed violence his palatial home was set on fire, his family murdered and their possessions looted. This prompted the 150 surviving Jews in the city to take refuge in a wooden fortress standing on a motte and known as Clifford's Tower.[3] Fearing that the constable of the tower would betray them, the Jews refused to let him in, arguing that the tower was the property of the king, under whose direct protection they were. When the sheriff John Marshal was told that they had illicitly taken possession of the tower, the militia was ordered out. This in turn attracted a mob intent on 'tasting Jewish blood', in which a prime mover was one Richard Malebisse, a noble deeply indebted to Jewish creditors at a very high rate of interest in the region of 250 per cent per annum, comparable to the interest rates of the instant cash companies of today. So high was the risk of default on loans from Jews that interest rates like this were the norm.

A friar celebrated mass in front of the motte each day. After he was killed by a stone thrown from the tower, the terrified Jews suffered several days of anguish while small siege engines were dragged into position below the motte. After a fire broke out in the wooden building from causes unknown, in the smoke and confusion, a French rabbi from Joigny advised the men to kill their wives, rather than have them raped before death. This they did, after which the rabbi killed sixty of the men in a scene reminiscent of the Roman siege at Masada. Many bodies were thrown from the tower onto the mob outside.[4] The remaining Jews, trusting to promises of safe conduct if they converted to Christianity, emerged to be massacred by the mob, whose ringleaders never had any intention of sparing them. Malebisse then led a group of other debtors to the cathedral to destroy the copies of their loan agreements stored there, before making good his escape, reputedly to Scotland.

At Bury St Edmunds fifty-seven Jews were murdered on Palm Sunday, and many others died in similar pogroms at Kings Lynn, Stamford, Colchester, Thetford and Ospringe in Kent. Probably the richest man in the kingdom, Aaron of Lincoln had founded a nationwide banking organisation, financing major works like the construction of cathedrals and monasteries. On his death in 1186, so great had been his fortune that a *scaccarium judeorum*, or Jews' Exchequer, was established under the Exchequer of Westminster to administer the estates of deceased Jews. Although cloaked by the argument that the Jews 'had killed Christ', most pogroms were incited by Christians who owed them money and had good reason to kill their creditors, loot their property and destroy evidence of the debts. In a few places, wise administrators forestalled this. At the first sign of trouble in Lincoln, the sheriff Gérard de Camville allowed the community to take refuge in the castle with all their valuables while he and his officers restored order in the town.

Furious that so much taxable wealth had been destroyed or stolen elsewhere, Richard ordered that, in future, copies of Jewish loan documents be held by the Crown, so that, when the lenders were killed, debts due to them automatically became enforceable as property of the king, removing the prime motive for murder by their debtors, although, as a Christian, he could not demand interest on the outstanding loans.[5] Hubert Walter later arranged the other details.

In the immediate future, Richard ordered William Longchamp back to England with his brother Osbert to arrest and punish the instigators of the pogroms and the office-holders who had failed to prevent them. Sixty pairs of iron fetters were purchased at a cost of 15 shillings for those arrested in Lincoln and the diocese was placed under interdict. Before Longchamp was finished, among his prisoners was Bishop Hugh of Durham, arrested ostensibly for his responsibility for what had happened at York on 16 March. Trusting to letters from Richard confirming him in

office, he had returned to England, only to be shown later letters
from the king justifying his Aye-and-Nay nickname by giving
Longchamp jurisdiction. These were used to deprive him of his
offices, most of his wealth and his liberty.[6]

By now far too much power was concentrated in the
Longchamp family, the third brother, Henry, having purchased
the sheriffdom of Herefordshire. But Richard's attention was
firmly fixed on Aquitaine, where several vassals were defying
his authority. He agreed with Philip Augustus' kinsman Count
Robert II of Dreux that the joint departure on crusade be postponed until July – which would mean a year's delay in reaching
the Holy Land – and then rode south with Henry of Saxony,
son of his sister Matilda and Henry the Lion, to give the youth a
blooding. And a blooding it was, with at least one castellan named
William de Chisi hanged from his own battlements as a lesson to
other Gascon dissidents.[7]

Still apparently trying to get Richard into bed with an appropriate spouse, Eleanor spent the spring and summer of 1190 in or
near Chinon, to judge by the number of charters issued in that
area stamped with her seal. He, meanwhile, was organising the
crusading fleet in five squadrons commanded by two bishops and
two laymen, only one of whom had experience of naval command. Also at Chinon in June, he published rules for shipboard
conduct and laid down the punishments for various misdemean-
ours. From their harshness it is evident that he had no illusions
about the men hired to crew the ships: for murder at sea, the penalty was to be bound to the corpse and thrown overboard with it;
for murder on land, the penalty was to be buried alive with the
victim; for non-lethal bloodshed, the perpetrator was to lose a
hand; for an attack without bloodshed, he was to be keel-hauled
three times; a fine was to be levied for foul language; and for theft
the penalty was to be tarred and feathered and abandoned ashore
at the next landfall.[8]

With both Richard and Eleanor in France, there was no one
in England to hold Chancellor Longchamp in check. With no

friends in England to favour, he taxed everyone so savagely that William of Newburgh said he had two right hands with which to grab money. The chronicler Gerald of Wales described him as:

> short, crippled in both haunches, with a big head and hair on his forehead coming down almost to his eyes like an ape. His chin was receding and his lips were spread apart in an affected, false and almost constant grin. His neck was short, his back was humped and his belly stuck in front and his buttocks at the back.[9]

So large was the entourage with which he travelled, amounting sometimes to 1,000 riders, that accommodating it for one night could cost a monastery its revenue for the following three years.[10] Longchamp was also a pederast, which made defaulting parents extremely reluctant to hand over their sons to him as hostages for payment of tax.[11]

On 1 July 1190, with Alais, a VIP prisoner in the fortress-city of Rouen, the kings of France and England rendezvoused at Vézelay in Burgundy, together with their armies. It must have been an impressive sight: thousands of barons and knights, each of whom required at least four horses; one or more *destriers* kept exclusively for combat; a palfrey to ride; another for his squire leading the *destrier*; and another to transport his armour and other belongings kept close to hand. In addition were the draught animals of the long wagon train of ox-carts bearing tents, cooking utensils and provisions.

To make the point that they were all pilgrims, albeit with murderous intent, the two kings were each presented with a symbolic staff and scrip, but Richard had put on so much weight that when he casually leaned on his staff, it snapped in two, which was taken as an evil omen. Although the two monarchs had sworn to be as brothers to each other and to share equally any loot taken on the expedition, stresses in the *entente* were already apparent. Richard controlled almost all the Saladin tithe collected in his possessions, but Philip had been able to collect the tithe only in his far smaller domains in the Île de France, his vassals elsewhere tending to keep the tithe for their own crusading needs, which had enabled many of them to depart before their king, eager to carve out some glory in the Holy Land before Philip could claim the credit. There was no particular reason why they should not, since small parties of knights, and even individual knights, regularly travelled to Palestine in the years between the major crusades. William the Marshal, as one example, had spent nearly three years there in fulfilment of his deathbed promise to the Young King.

An armed mass of the size of the combined armies was rare. Its sheer size imposed severe strains on the countryside through which it passed like a plague of locusts, moving slowly at the pace of the wagon train. With no sanitation, the army left behind a trail of human and animal excrement several miles wide on the 200-mile journey from Vézelay to Lyons, where the Rhône was crossed. That problem was left behind them, but the impossibility of finding feed for so many horses and oxen along the way forced a decision to diverge after crossing the river. Philip's contingent crossed first because it was fewer in number, but such was the press of the English following them that the bridge collapsed – a not uncommon event of the time. Many were drowned and the crossing of the rearguard was delayed while ferries were improvised.

Here the two armies separated, with the French heading for Nice and eastwards along the coast to Genoa to hire shipping that Richard had thought too expensive. He led his contingent south to Marseilles, where the combined Plantagenet fleet should have been awaiting him, had they not been delayed first by the events at Lisbon and by contrary winds at the straits of Gibraltar.[12] Impatient as ever, on 7 or 16 August (accounts vary)[13] Richard hired some Pisan merchant vessels to take his immediate entourage to Genoa while his rank-and-file swiftly ran out of money during the unexpected delay and caused problems in Marseilles.[14] Meeting Philip in Genoa, he was asked for the loan of five galleys when the English fleet arrived, but haggled the number down to three, which Philip took as a personal insult as well as a blow to his royal purse.

The English fleet arrived eventually at Marseilles on 22 August 1190 to embark the main force of Richard's army while he was making a Grand Tour of western Italy, riding from one port to another, where the hired Pisan ships were waiting to transport his party to the next stopping place. It was a curious and time-consuming diversion, attributed to his fear of the sea and susceptibility to sea-sickness: on 20 August he was in Pisa; then came a meeting with Bishop Octavian of Ostia at the mouth of the Tiber and on to Naples, which he reached on 28 August and stayed for eleven days.[15] The Plantagenet fleet was meanwhile coasting down to Messina on the eastern coast of Sicily, arriving there on 14 September, two days before Philip Augustus sailed in and was given Tancred's palace in the city as accommodation for his household.

Archbishop Baldwin, Bishop Hubert Walter and Ranulf de Glanville set off from Marseilles as soon as the Plantagenet fleet arrived there with an advance party to sail direct to the Holy Land and reached the siege camp outside Acre eight months earlier than Richard and the main force. With the harbour fiercely defended by the Saracens, autumn storms obliged the incoming ships to sail north to Tyre and take shelter there. On finally entering the siege camp, spread over half a mile east–west by three-quarters of a mile north–south, that had been set up by Guy de Lusignan on and around the low hill known as Tel al-Fukhar a mile to the east of the city of Acre – and therefore out of range of catapulted missiles from the ramparts – the new arrivals found there a horror even worse than the conditions of medieval sieges in Europe.[16]

The Christian besiegers had dug deep ditches to protect their camp from surprise sorties by the garrison in the city and, on the landward side, from Saladin's forces who were besieging the Christian invaders. With blocking forces much closer to the city covering the area from the camp to the sea both north and south of Acre, at times de Lusignan's forces controlled far more territory than this; at other times they were driven back inside the defensive perimeter of the ditches, where a festering mass of sewage and decaying animal and human corpses attracted millions of flies. Since nothing was known of contagion, these were tolerated – as they would be for centuries to come – as a simple nuisance by men unaware that these pests contaminating their food represented far more of a threat to health and life than the missiles aimed at them from the city walls or Saladin's attacks on the camp.

Unfortunately for archaeology, the site of the camp lies beneath the modern city of Akko, but it is known from the *Estoire de la Guerre Sainte*, written by Ambroise from notes he made during the crusade, that the Saracen siege lines extended in a loose crescent a couple of miles to the east of the crusader camp, and moved backwards and forwards as the fortunes of war favoured first one side and then the other in the intermittent skirmishes, a few of which could have qualified as minor battles. Even Saladin's personal pavilion had to be moved several times. South of the camp, the Muslim siege lines extended nearly to the beach but to the north a corridor was kept clear by the crusaders, to permit convoys to enter and leave, evacuating casualties to Tyre and returning with supplies and reinforcements.[17]

On arrival there, finding the Patriarch of Jerusalem ill, Archbishop Baldwin took his responsibilities as the senior churchman seriously until the atrocious conditions claimed him as yet another victim. He died in November, leaving a specific bequest to finance twenty knights and fifty sergeants-at-arms, the balance of his treasury to go to the over-stretched fund to provide for the increasing number of impoverished and sick crusaders. Hubert Walter rose to the occasion, negotiating with the leaders of the other contingents, providing for the sick and wounded, leading diplomatic missions to the Saracens and on occasion leading forays against them.[18] He was to serve Richard and John, when he came to the throne, with loyalty and a perhaps excessive zeal.

The one city Richard had no desire to see on his tour of Italy was the dilapidated field of ruins that had formerly been the

Eternal City, because Pope Clement III was no friend of his and Italy was riven by tensions between the Holy Roman Empire occupying the north of the peninsula and the Norman kingdom of Sicily embracing a large part of the southern Italian mainland. Its mixed-race inhabitants spoke Latin, Greek and Arabic and were of western Catholic, Greek Christian and Muslim faiths. Under King William II, known as 'William the Good' and whose consort was Richard's now 25-year-old sister Joanna, it had enjoyed two decades of quiet prosperous co-existence, symbolised by a coinage with Greek Christian images on one side and Muslim symbols on the reverse. The Norman kingdom had also been a considerable support for the crusader states, but when William II died on 11 November 1189 Grand Admiral Margaritus led the fleet back to Sicily on orders from William's successor, formerly Count Tancred of Lecce, who was faced with insurrection by his Muslim subjects and incursions into his territory on the Italian mainland by German forces under the newly elected Holy Roman Emperor Henry VI Hohenstaufen.

The last leg of Richard's long ride down the length of Italy was apparently accomplished with only one companion.[19] One has to wonder why a king would put himself at risk in that way, which nearly proved fatal at the small Calabrian town of Mileto, just off the modern A3 *autostrada*. The story is that he heard the cry of a hawk coming from inside a peasant's hovel and assumed that common folk, as in his own possessions, had no right to own such a bird. Trying to steal it from them, he was badly beaten by the peasants before making his escape, which put him in a foul mood, no matter that his troubles were of his own making.

Mooring in the port of Messina on 23 September and riding into the city in grand pomp, Richard was insulted that his 'crusading brother' had been accommodated in the royal palace, which he thought should have been reserved for him instead of a smaller palace outside the walls that Tancred made available. With the French and Plantagenet fleets bringing thousands of hungry men clamouring for fresh food, the profiteering inhabitants of Messina had put up the price of bread and all other provisions, leading to disputes and injuries on both sides. Knowing of the events during the stop over in Lisbon, the Greek-speaking inhabitants of Messina, whom the crusaders nicknamed *Griffons*, had no desire to see their city taken over by all these armed men pumped-up with adrenalin and spoiling for action after the confinement on board ship, but on 3 October a quarrel outside the walls over the price of food took on the dimensions of a riot, causing the city gates to be closed against the foreigners and Richard's ships to be refused moorings in the harbour.

The following day Philip tried to defuse the situation by arranging a meeting at Richard's borrowed palace with Admiral Margaritus and a number of local notables. Whatever progress might have been achieved was undone when Richard heard himself being insulted, through the open windows, by a crowd of Messinans outside. Dismissing the negotiators in a fury, he decided to do what he always did when thwarted or insulted: use violence.

The gates closed, the undisciplined civilians inside Messina loosed off volley after volley of arrows at the Plantagenet army outside the walls. Richard ignored this, waiting until their armoury was exhausted before launching his attack with a shower of crossbow bolts to clear the battlements of defenders. After only five hours' fighting, his banners were raised on the battlements, symbolising that the city was his to loot as he wished. His men invaded the city, robbing everyone they met and pillaging houses, except in the quarter where Philip was lodging. All the important residents of Messina fled, among them Admiral Margaritus, who could have lent considerable support to the crusade, had Richard not driven him out of house and home and burned all his ships in the harbour. It was an ill-considered move that may have been critical, since Margaritus had been a pirate and a privateer before becoming William II's admiral, and not only knew the eastern Mediterranean better than anyone else, but had also conducted a campaign against the tyrant of Cyprus, Isaac Comnenus.

Using timber carried to make siege engines in the Holy Land, a wooden castle was erected close to the city walls and named Mategriffon or Kill the Greeks Castle. There seems to have been some disagreement as to whether it was the business of sworn crusaders to launch a small war against fellow Christians because, to ensure that all his vassals, knights and men-at-arms played their parts, Richard announced punishments for a less than enthusiastic participation. These included amputation of a foot for a rank-and-file soldier and deprivation of his privileged status for any knight found guilty of holding back.

Philip, whose men did not take part in the fighting, insisted on his banner being raised alongside Richard's on the battlements and claimed half the loot under the agreement made between the two kings. Some hard haggling ensued before Richard conceded him a share in the proceeds. For the rest of the stay on Sicily, Messina was the crusaders' winter quarters, a well-used gallows between it and Mategriffon warning the natives to behave themselves.

The stay at Messina was intended not only to avoid the winter storms which could easily have wrecked many ships. Roger of Howden recorded that most, if not all, of Richard's fleet was hauled ashore at some point in order for timbers eaten by that curse of marine archaeology, the teredo wood-boring mollusc, to be removed and replaced with Sicilian timber.[20]

## NOTES

1. Benedict of Peterborough, *Gesta Henrici*, Vol 3, lxvii.
2. Howlett, R., *Newburgh*, Vol I, pp. 304–6.
3. Rebuilt in stone in the thirteenth century.
4. William of Newburgh, *Historia Rerum Anglicarum*, Vol 1, pp. 304–6.
5. Benedict of Peterborough, *Gesta Henrici*, Vol 2, p. 107.
6. R.B. Dobson, *The Jews of Medieval York and the Massacre of March 1190*, Borthwick papers No 45 (York: University of York, 1974).
7. Roger of Howden, *Chronica*, Vol 3, pp. xlv–xlvi; Benedict of Peterborough, *Gesta Henrici*, Vol 2, p. 109.
8. Benedict of Peterborough, *Gesta Henrici*, Vol 2, p. 110.

9. Ibid, Vol 2, pp. 110–11.

10. Gerald of Wales, *De Vita Galfredi*, ed. J.S. Brewer, Rolls Series No 21 (London: Longmans, 1861–91), Vol 4, p. 420, abridged by the author.

11. Benedict of Peterborough, *Gesta Henrici*, Vol 2, p. 143.

12. Runciman, *A History of the Crusades*, p. 6.

13. Benedict of Peterborough, *Gesta Henrici*, Vol 2, p. 114.

14. Ibid, Vol 2, p. 112.

15. Ibid, Vol 2, p. 115.

16. This is the best estimate of the siege camp's position and size, all traces of which have vanished due to subsequent intensive cultivation of the plain of Acre (personal communication with Professor Pryor).

17. According to Carta catalogue (Paris: UNESCO 1971–72), p. 102.

18. Tyerman, *Who's Who*, pp. 241, 262.

19. Runciman, *A History of the Crusades*, p. 37.

20. Roger of Howden, *Chronica*, Vol 3, pp. 71–2; also Pryor, ed., *Logistics of Warfare*, p. 266.

# 14

# A Bride for Richard

ichard also at some point decided that many of the ships that had sailed from the North were not suitable for use in Mediterranean naval warfare, any more than the lightly built Mediterranean galleys would have been usable for much of the year in the weather conditions of the Channel and North Sea. He therefore hired an unknown number of galleys locally. These were either monoremes with single banks of twenty-five oars a side or biremes, with a total of 100 oars in two banks, one below deck and one above deck, pivoted either on a pin in the wale that later became the gunwale or poked through an oarport in a sort of outrigger that gave extra leverage. The rowers were not galley slaves, but paid labour. If life pulling an oar in the upper bank was hard, the conditions for men rowing in the lower bank below deck were appalling: cramped, dark, ill-ventilated and stinking.

To take advantage of favourable winds, there were two masts carrying lateen sails, which gave many advantages over the square-rigged cogs, but required trained men to manoeuvre the rigid yard around the mast rapidly when going about on a new tack or if the wind changed direction. By this stage in the evolution of Mediterranean shipping, the standard ship's complement was 108 men, plus officers, marines, a carpenter and the steersman (or men) to manhandle the two rudders fixed on either quarter at the stern. At just over 100ft long, these ships had after-castles and fighting castles just aft of the foremast. There was also a raised deck at the prow, below which it was the Byzantine custom to house the force pump that ejected a powerful jet of naphtha-based Greek fire for short distances as galleys closed for combat – a forerunner of the modern flamethrower.[1]

For the horses to be transported to the Holy Land, specially designed oared ships known to westerners as *chalendres* or *taridae* (from the Byzantine Greek *chelandion* and Arabic *tarida*) could carry forty or so horses each, with let-down ramps several metres long at the stern quarters for embarking and disembarking the animals, if necessary with their riders already mounted for rapid deployment into the shallows and up the beach after the shallow-draught galleys were driven ashore backwards in the medieval equivalent of an amphibious invasion. These ramps had to be soundly caulked with moss, tar and pitch before putting to sea, as they were hinged well below the water line.[2] This was a great improvement on the former northern European custom of loading and unloading horses over the side of the ship one at a time in a sling suspended from temporary sheerlegs, as shown in the Bayeux Tapestry. Modifying a ship like this was not, however, without its dangers: in 1096 a horse-transport carrying horses and mules for Stephen of Blois and Robert of Normandy on the First Crusade broke up at sea, drowning all the crew, passengers and animals onboard.[3]

The thousands of knights, men-at-arms and hangers-on having attracted merchants and moneylenders who saw a market for their goods and services, the long sojourn on Sicily made a considerable hole in the savings of many crusaders, since everything from food to clothes had to be purchased. Typical of the transactions is an extant document acknowledging a loan of 60 silver marks from a Genoese merchant to two squires in the retinue of Jean de Chastenay, a vassal of Hugues III of Burgundy, against a list of jewels he deposited as security.

When Sicily's King William II had died in November 1189 the council of nobles had elected his bastard nephew Tancred of Lecce to succeed him in order to prevent the German emperor from claiming the throne by virtue of his marriage to William's aunt Constance. Not only had Queen Joanna's dowry not been restored to her on William's death, but she was also being held hostage by Tancred in his capital of Palermo, at the opposite end of the island from Messina. Richard demanded both her release and the delivery of valuables, provisions and two fully manned galleys that William II had promised to Henry as his contribution to the crusade. Hoping thus to hasten the departure of the two crusading armies on his island kingdom, Tancred liberated Joanna and had her escorted into her brother's safekeeping on 28 September with 20,000 ounces of gold in lieu of her dowry and a further 20,000 ounces to compensate for the legacy William II had left to Henry II for the crusade.

Again, some of this wealth was shared with Philip, as agreed before the departure from France. Recently widowed himself, Philip welcomed Joanna to his palace, seeing in her a suitable replacement for his dead queen, for she was as beautiful and regal as her mother, and had been queen of Sicily for thirteen years. Richard again failed to seize the chance to unite the houses of Plantagenet and Capet. Instead of using Joanna's marital availability in this way, he sent her across to the mainland, appropriating for her accommodation the priory of Bagnara.[4]

Advised by his Muslim counsellors to play the two crusader kings off against each other so that they could not gang up against him, Tancred favoured Philip with gifts but sent none to Richard. Instead, he took him on a tour of the island's holy sites, during which he disclosed letters allegedly received from Philip that described the king of England as an unworthy cheat against whom the French and Sicilians should unite. Richard was only too ready to suspect Philip of their authorship and had Robert de Sablé negotiate a treaty in his name that recognised Tancred's title as king of Sicily, pledging to defend him against any conflicting claim from the German emperor. In an exchange of gifts, Tancred restored the last 40,000 gold *bezants* of Joanna's dowry. Then Richard declared his 3-year-old nephew Arthur of Brittany his heir to the throne of England and all his continental possessions, and betrothed him to Tancred's elder daughter in the ultimate gesture of feudal alliance.[5]

When the news reached Eleanor, she must have been distraught. Richard's adoption of a toddler was a declaration that he had no intention of marrying and begetting a legitimate heir. Not only that, but her carefully contrived political web to keep Prince John from grabbing power in the king's absence was undone at a stroke, for once John learned that his quite reasonable chance of succeeding to the throne if Richard died on crusade had been wiped out like this, he had no incentive to behave himself. The final straw was that allowing a child of Arthur's age, living in France and owing feudal obedience to Philip Augustus, to succeed to the title to the continental possessions was as good as handing them to Philip on a plate.

The complications Richard was piling up for himself on Sicily were also alarming. When he showed Philip the incriminating letters bearing what appeared to be the Capetian seal, he was brusquely informed that they must be forgeries made by Tancred's scheming Muslim counsellors to create tensions between two Christian monarchs. It was, Philip declared, yet another insult to the House of Capet that Richard had given them credence. His list of the insults endured at the hands of Henry and Richard included the unresolved matter of Alais: either Richard should marry her immediately or she should be returned to Philip with her dowry. To this, Richard retorted that it was unnatural for any man to wed his father's former mistress, who had borne him a child.[6] That final repudiation, after two decades of trickery and deceit by Henry, was all Philip needed to declare undying enmity between himself and the Plantagenets.[7]

On 8 October the two kings met to agree frostily the future conduct of the crusade. Prices were laid down for foodstuffs, with profiteering to be punished – in extreme cases on the grim scaffold beside Mategriffon. It was also laid down that half of every knight's money was to be devoted to the welfare of his men; debts contracted on the crusade must be honoured; and gambling was forbidden, except for knights and clerics – who were to be punished for excessive gaming, which the churchmen present said would include excommunication for transgressors.

Other bones of contention between the two kings were less easy to resolve. One of the many nobles related by blood or feudal duty to both sides in their dispute was Count Philip I of Flanders, shortly to die at the siege of Acre. At some point during November he avoided a schism that would fatally have split the crusade by brokering a settlement under which Richard was released from any obligation to marry Alais in return for a promise to return her and her dowry to Philip Augustus at the end of the crusade, plus a compensation of 10,000 marks[8] – which meant that she would be an asset for Philip Augustus to marry off to whomever he chose.

Whether or not the two Philips knew the true reason for Richard accepting the deal is not recorded: he had to clear the decks for an adventure he would rather have done without. Casting about for a match that would, so to speak, kill two birds with one stone, his mother had travelled across the Pyrenees to the court of King Sancho VI of Navarre to obtain the hand of his 25-year-old daughter Princess Berengaria, whom she considered a suitable bride for a king with Richard's notorious lack of interest in marriage. It is true that he had once, while visiting Sancho's court, written a poem for Berengaria, but that was just gallantry and indicated no emotional relationship. Although Richard admitted paternity of a serving wench's child begotten long since, there was no trace of the litter of bastards traditionally left in the wake of a heterosexual duke of Aquitaine.

Historians disagree over how prevalent was the *jus primae noctis* or *droit de seigneur* – the law of the first night. It was in any event not a law, but a custom; troubadour poetry has many instances of a travelling knight coming across a lone shepherdess and raping her as by right, in contrast with the anguished yearning for a lady of his own class. Spreading his semen far and wide in this way was regarded as an enrichment of the common people's bloodstock and there are many people in Aquitaine whose surnames are masculine first names, such as Pierre, which would originally have been 'de Pierre' because an ancestor had been a bastard offspring of a noble of that name.

After Eleanor dangled in front of Sancho the Wise the idea of becoming father-in-law to the king of England, he consented to the match and Berengaria was hustled away on a 1,300-mile journey to meet her unwilling bridegroom. Richard's mother had been an extraordinary beauty in her youth and was still an impressive lady of great presence, but the bride she had chosen for her son was described as prudent, gentle, virtuous and docile – in short, a submissive wife with whom Richard might be able to perform his marital duty to provide an heir. Eleanor could feel satisfied with her mission: the second reason to marry Richard into the family of the king of Navarre was that it afforded an excellent way of safeguarding the common frontier of Aquitaine and Navarre. The deal she had made with Sancho did not include the marriage portion to which Berengaria should have been entitled as queen of England because Eleanor intended keeping that for herself. In compensation, she offered Berengaria the county of Gascony, the Ile d'Oléron and several towns on both sides of the Channel. The old queen and the queen-to-be hastened towards Sicily, so that Richard could be married – and the union hopefully consummated to get her with child – before he proceeded to the Holy Land.

With Joanna safely out of the way on the mainland, Richard spent much of Tancred's money in a series of magnificent Christmas banquets designed to flaunt his wealth and show Philip Augustus up as the poor relative. The 'entertainment' was usually a *mêlée*, or mock free-for-all battle in which tempers could run dangerously high. In one of these Philip Augustus' cavalry commander Guillaume des Barres, who had broken his parole when taken prisoner by Richard after the Battle of Châteauroux in August 1188, was unwise enough to wound the vanity of his erstwhile captor by unhorsing him. Some of Philip's vassals had grown bored with the long stay on Sicily and departed with their own retinues in the hope of reaching the Holy Land before the spring gales, taking with them some of Richard's vassals too. Tales soon filtered back of shipwrecks, disease and deaths in combat in the Holy Land.

Meanwhile Eleanor was chaperoning Berengaria, using a series of safe conducts to travel across Toulousain territory and down the length of Italy through the rigours of a hard winter. Coming after her journey into Navarre, all this travelling made considerable demands on a woman of 68, but she was taking no chances that Richard would wriggle out of the arrangement with Sancho the Wise if Berengaria arrived alone on Sicily. It would have been all too easy for him to invoke his crusader's oath of chastity or the papal prohibition on women accompanying the crusade in order to continue celibate to the Holy Land.

Keeping up to date on the journey south was hardly as easy as picking up e-mails on one's laptop in the overnight motel, but Eleanor did have a continuing feed of news from both the continental possessions and England: from time to time her cortège crossed paths with *nuncii* carrying letters from Sicily to the crusaders' homelands and back. One significant meeting on her journey south came at Lodi, between Milan and Piacenza. Whether by accident or design, her visit coincided with that of Henry VI Hohenstaufen, eldest son of Barbarossa, who was on his way to Rome to receive the papal blessing on his succession to the throne of the Holy Roman Empire. He was deeply displeased with Richard's endorsement of Tancred's claims to Sicily and southern Italy but the meeting passed with the usual courtesies, Eleanor being invited to witness a charter before leaving his court.

With repairs proceeding apace, Richard's combined fleet had some 200 vessels lying idle at Messina, yet he did not send one to facilitate the journey of his mother and bride, letting them travel by land. This may well have been so that Philip was not presented with yet another insult in meeting Eleanor's replacement for his half-sister, still locked up in Rouen, when Berengaria arrived on Sicily. On 30 March 1191, one day after Philip's diminished fleet set sail, the old queen arrived at Messina with Richard's bride-to-be. However, this was in the forty-day period of Lent, during which not even the archbishop of Canterbury could celebrate a marriage. There was also the crusader's vow of celibacy to get around, if the marriage was to be consummated.

It was for Eleanor a brief reunion with her favourite son and Joanna, a daughter whom she hardly knew, having sent her to Sicily as a 12-year-old bride for William II fourteen years earlier. Affairs of state caused Eleanor to set aside any tiredness from the long journey and commence the return journey four days after arriving on Sicily.[9] She had learned that Prince John was using the time to acquire political leverage, taking advantage of the universal loathing for William Longchamp to bring over to his camp many of the nobility of England who outwardly professed loyalty to Richard but were all too aware that he showed no interest in his Anglo-Norman vassals, except to tax them. Statistically, there was one chance in four of a knight returning alive from crusade and the odds were even higher against Richard's return, since he prided himself on always being in the forefront of any combat. So, to the dissident nobility of England it seemed very likely that John would wear the crown of England before long.

Armed with letters from Richard appointing Archbishop Walter of Rouen, who had been born in Cornwall, to replace Longchamp, Eleanor headed north after leaving Berengaria at Bagnara with Joanna acting as her chaperone until they could be safely embarked for the next stage of their journey to the east. The two royal pawns were said to be as happy in each other's company as 'two doves in a cage'[10] – a gruesome simile for the lives of noblewomen even of the highest rank. Because of the papal prohibition on women accompanying the crusade, they did not travel with Richard's main fleet, but departed on 7 April in a fast Byzantine armed vessel of the type loosely referred to as *dromon*, having fifty oars a side, each rowed by one man, and a lateen sail. A word of caution is needed here. To landsmen, many ships look the same. As Professor John Pryor says, today people talk and write of yachts, but what exactly is a yacht? He makes the point that although the chroniclers of the Third Crusade called various Mediterranean vessels *dromons*, the true *dromon* had been replaced in the Mediterranean by swifter galleys before this time.

The royal vessel had both fore- and after-castles designed for defence against boarding by pirates on the high seas, and would have provided ample accommodation for the two royal ladies with their entourages and baggage, the decks being sheltered by awnings during fair weather. It sailed in convoy with two galleys, whose job was to see off any importunate pirates seeking to take hostage these important passengers. The arrangements should have ensured a safe and reasonably comfortable voyage to the Holy Land, but sea travel was never certain. Even the formidable Queen Eleanor had disappeared in these waters for six undocumented weeks on her return voyage from the Second Crusade after an encounter with Byzantine pirate galleys whose captains were intent on holding her to ransom.

On 10 April the rest of Richard's fleet upped anchor or cast off mooring ropes and set sail, to the great relief of Tancred and most of his subjects who had at least avoided the fate that was about to befall their neighbours on Cyprus. Various contemporary estimates of the size of the fleet exist. Richard of Devizes gave the number as '156 *naves* under sail (some of which were *taridae* or *huissiers*, each carrying twenty horses), twenty-four *buscae* (or northern round ships) and thirty-nine galleys'. Roger of Wendover gave the numbers as 'thirteen three-masted *buscae*, 100 *naves* under sail and fifty galleys'.[11] Whatever the exact numbers, the fleet at this point was a mixture of ships that had sailed from England or Richard's continental ports and hired

Mediterranean vessels, together carrying some 8,000 men and
the knights' horses. Richard of Devizes recorded that this mass of
shipping was divided into eight squadrons, so formed that a bugle
call from one squadron could be heard by the next squadron and
a man's shout could be heard from one ship to the next in the
same squadron; the king's *esnecca* and the more manoeuvrable galleys brought up the rear, rounding up stragglers and towing them
where necessary during calms.[12] As maritime historian Dr Ruthy
Gertwagen comments, such station-keeping could only work
with this number of vessels of dissimilar speeds during good visibility and calm sea conditions.

In case the idea of a sea voyage in those days seems like a
chance to relax, on the Seventh Crusade half a century later, Jean
de Joinville spoke for many when he wrote:

> You may appreciate the temerity of the man who dares, with
> other people's property in his possession, or in a state of mortal
> sin, to place himself in such a precarious position. For how can a
> voyager tell, when he goes to sleep at night, whether he may be
> lying at the bottom of the sea next morning?[13]

At night, Richard ordered lanterns to be hoisted to the mastheads
to aid station-keeping, but this was of no effect on the night of
13 April when a terrifying north-easterly storm, locally called *la
tormenta*, sundered the fleet and forced those vessels that managed
to keep station with Richard's flagship to take shelter in the lee of
the island of Crete, probably at the Gulf of Chandax, where the
crews went ashore to replenish water barrels from streams that
flowed down to the beach.[14]

By this time, Mediterranean navigation was not totally devoid
of scientific aids. Foremost of these was the compass, described
by Richard's milk-brother Alexander Neckham as a magnet-
ised needle on a pivot in his book *De Utensilibus* and listed as an
essential piece of on-board equipment in his *De Naturis Rerum*,
published in the 1180s, together with its *modus operandi*:

When in cloudy weather they can no longer profit by the light of the sun, or when the world is wrapped up in the darkness of the shades of night … [the sailors] touch the magnet with a needle. This then whirls round in a circle until, when its motion ceases, its point looks directly to the north.[15]

Richard, with his fascination for all technology with military application, would certainly have known of this and required at least some of the ships to be equipped with compasses.

On 22 April they reached the island of Rhodes, which had been recaptured from the Muslims during the First Crusade,[16] but a third of the journey still lay ahead. On that day Philip was already being welcomed to the siege of Acre by his cousin Conrad of Montferrat after an uninterrupted voyage of twenty-two days from Messina, which indicates that he had enjoyed moderate favourable winds all the way. As Dr Gertwagen remarks:

Galleys of all kinds were poor sailers because they were designed to be rowed and could use their sails only with moderate breezes astern. Nor was the upwind performance of *naves* much better than that of galleys. Because of their rounded hull configuration and lack of deep keel, they made much leeway and with winds abeam it was difficult to hold a … course.[17]

In fact, it was probably impossible to do so. The great advantage of galleys, of course, lay in calms when they could not only keep going on the right heading, but also tow becalmed vessels powered only by sail.

Richard's crossing was very different from Philip's. From Crete onwards, the seas were rough. Having suffered greatly from seasickness, he prolonged the stopover on Rhodes for ten days to take on provisions and especially fresh water, which was important for the horses, to exercise them a little and also to allow straggling ships to catch up. Fed on dry grain, with only stale water to drink while on board and their digestive systems upset

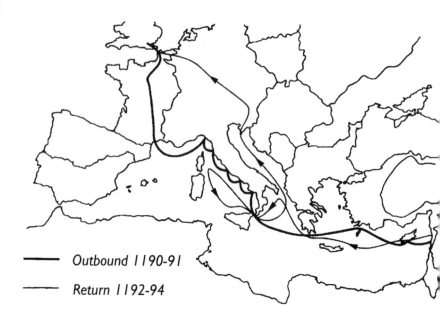

Outbound 1190-91

Return 1192-94

Richard's routes on the Third Crusade

by the motion of the ships, horses emerged from their stalls with problems that required several days of convalescence on land before the voyage could continue. Even more recuperative time would be needed on arrival in the Holy Land before the *destriers* would be fit for combat.[18]

The third landfall may not have been intended, since the island of Cyprus lies less than 200 miles from Acre. In taking the Cross a crusader swore not to be deflected from the journey to Jerusalem for any reason. Yet the relief of Acre was unilaterally put on hold by Richard after another storm drove Joanna's small convoy onto the coast of Cyprus. The *dromon* carrying her and Berengaria reached Limassol on the southern coast of the island, but the two escorting galleys were wrecked on shoals before reaching this haven and their cargoes impounded. The survivors of the wrecks were imprisoned on the orders of the tyrant Isaac

Comnenus, who had seized power in 1184 and declared himself emperor of Cyprus. He instituted a reign of terror on the island after securing a niche within the balance of power in the eastern Mediterranean by signing treaties with William II on Sicily to the west and Saladin to the east.

Isaac refused permission for the *dromon* with its two royal passengers to moor in the calmer waters of Limassol harbour, hoping to oblige them to accept his offer that they should step ashore.[19] Refusing to be taken hostage so easily, Joanna replied to Isaac's invitation with a polite apology, saying that she first needed her brother's permission. In spite, Isaac refused supplies and even fresh water to her ship, but the number of armed men on board discouraged any further action.

On 6 May, five days after Joanna's arrival, Richard's fleet staggered into Limassol after another tempestuous crossing from Rhodes in which several vessels had been sunk and Richard's *esnecca* narrowly missed the same fate. Foul-tempered from prolonged seasickness, he swore vengeance for the insults to his sister and Berengaria, and gave orders to trans-ship a landing force from the larger vessels into shallow-draught galleys and small boats to make for the shore, which had been fortified by Isaac and was defended by his troops. With Richard commanding a force of archers in the first landing craft, a hail of arrows fell on the defenders, giving the advantage to the invasion force. A great slaughter ensued, forcing the surviving defenders to flee inland and save their lives by taking paths through the mountains unknown to the crusaders.[20]

Never one to let an enemy escape easily, Richard ordered horses to be disembarked and took advantage of the unpopularity of Isaac among the non-Greek merchant families of the port to hire guides, with which he pursued the Cypriot army, surprising its camp before dawn with such violence and bloodshed that Isaac fled in his nightclothes, leaving behind his treasury, tent, horses and even the royal seal. Next day, many of the Cypriot nobility came to the crusader camp and swore to support the

king of England in his war against Isaac, giving hostages as witness of their good faith. Seeing himself thus abandoned, Isaac
asked for and obtained a safe conduct to meet Richard, where he
agreed to terms: a payment of 20,000 gold marks; the prisoners
to be freed; and himself to join the crusade with 100 knights, 400
Turcopole mercenaries and 500 infantry. In addition, he ordained
that supplies bought by the crews and passengers of the fleet
would be duty free at fair prices. He also did homage to Richard,
acknowledging him as overlord of Cyprus. Yet another example
of the fate of women in those times was his gift of his daughter,
for Richard to marry to whomever he chose.

It was a very satisfactory outcome for two days of combat –
until Isaac took advantage of the camp being asleep and slipped
away to what he thought was the safety of Famagusta on the eastern coast, despatching his wife and daughter to the fortress-port
of Kyrenia (modern Girne in north Cyprus) and ordered the
crusaders to leave his territory. On the same day a ship berthed in
Limassol bringing Guy de Lusignan and a coterie of supporters
including Humphrey of Toron to lobby Richard's support in the
political struggle with Conrad. Richard's impulsive endorsement
of Guy – who was generally considered dim-witted and lacking
in princely authority – as the rightful king of Jerusalem was a
knee-jerk reflex on hearing that Philip Augustus had given his
support to Conrad.

Richard broke promises all the time, but decided to punish
Isaac's effrontery by conquering Cyprus after the new arrivals
pointed out to him the strategic significance of the island. If it
became a haven for crusading ships, so much the better; but if
Isaac were allowed to make a firm alliance with Saladin, it could
be used as a base for Saracen ships to intercept and capture
Christian convoys bearing men, money and supplies to and from
the Holy Land – which would spell the end of the Latin states.

Richard therefore divided his army into three regiments: one
was to pursue Isaac overland and the balance boarded the galleys,
whose number was swollen by five of Isaac's galleys that had been

taken as prize. These were divided into two flotillas, one under himself and the other under Robert of Turnham, to circum-navigate the island in both directions, in his words so that 'this perjurer may not slip through my hands'.[21] In a time of no charts, the circumnavigation of an island beset by rocks and shoals was a hazardous undertaking that must have required pressing into service local seafarers as pilots and the use of the tallowed lead to ascertain the depth of water beneath the ships and the composi-tion of the bottom when nearing shore. The mini-campaign was successful: every one of Isaac's galleys and other ships encountered was taken as prize, and, seeing the crusader flotillas approaching, the castellans of Isaac's littoral castles abandoned them and took refuge in the mountains.[22]

Already feeling confident that he was the de facto ruler of Cyprus, Richard took a day off. On Sunday 12 May, Lent being ended, the 33-year-old king of England married Berengaria in the garrison church of St George at Limassol and then watched the bishop of Évreux crown her as queen of England. There was no shortage of bishops to perform the ceremony. No detail of Berengaria's appearance was recorded by the celibate chroniclers, although the bridegroom is known to have been wearing a gor-geous rose-coloured *cotte* of samite, embroidered with glittering silver crescents, a scarlet bonnet worked with figures of birds and animals in gold thread, a cape decorated with shining half-moons in gold and silver thread and slippers of cloth of gold. His spurs and the hilt of his sword were of gold, and the mounts of his scab-bard were silver. What his bride made of this display, which defied the austerity decreed for crusaders – or, indeed, of his penance in Sicily, where he had been flagellated publicly in his underwear before being given absolution for sodomy in order to take the sacrament at the wedding mass – is not recorded. Whether he ever shared her bed is unknown. There was in any case no issue.

Ignoring pleas from Philip Augustus to hasten to Acre with all possible speed and not waste time fighting Christians, albeit of the Orthodox rite,[23] Richard pursued Isaac to Famagusta, his

army travelling partly on land and partly by sea. Isaac retreated to
Kantara in the north of the island, placing his faith in the reputed
impregnability of the fortress-port of Kyrenia and the castles of
Kantara, St Hilarion and Buffavento, which, although ruined, are
still impressive works of fortification today. The inland city of
Nicosia was among those that surrendered without bloodshed.
At some point Richard fell ill, probably from malaria, which had
troubled him for years, leaving it to Guy de Lusignan to command the force that captured Kyrenia. Isaac's queen and their
daughter had taken refuge in the castle of Kantara, but when she
saw the army approaching, the daughter came out to throw the
castle, her mother and herself on Richard's mercy.

Realising that all was lost, Isaac had fled to the furthest point
on the island, at Cape St Andrew on the extremity of the Karpas
Peninsula, where he finally surrendered on 21 May, pleading with
his captors not to treat him like a common criminal by putting
him in irons. As one king to another, Richard agreed, but had
chains made of gold and silver before delivering his prisoner thus
fettered as a hostage to the Knights of St John, who kept the self-
appointed emperor of Cyprus confined at their castle of Margat
in the principality of Antioch for three long years. Before sailing
away, Richard entrusted the island to Robert of Turnham and
Richard of Camville as regents in his absence.

Isaac's daughter, who was referred to simply as *la demoiselle de
Chypre*, joined Joanna and Berengaria for the rest of the voyage,
arriving at the siege of Acre on 1 June and returning to Europe
with them.[24] It was, for her, the start of an adventurous life
that reads like the plot of a novel. After being bought from the
Plantagenets as part of Richard's ransom agreement negotiated in
1193, she was released – as was her father – into the care of Duke
Leopold V of Austria, who was a distant relative of her branch
of the Comnenus family. In 1199 she was recorded as living in
Provence, where she met Count Raymond VI of Toulouse, who
was then married to Joanna, the former queen of Sicily. Joanna
was pregnant by Raymond for the second time but, shortly after

what one supposes was a happy reunion with her erstwhile travelling companion, Countess Joanna was dumped by Raymond,
who set up home with the Cypriot princess.

That did not last: in 1202 she married a bastard son of the Count
of Flanders named Thierry, with whom she set sail, ostensibly
on the Fourth Crusade. While the main body of the European
crusaders forgot their sworn oaths and turned aside to sack the
Christian city of Constantinople, thus destroying Europe's bul-
wark against the Muslim Turks, the two adventurers headed
for Cyprus with the ambition of reclaiming Isaac Comnenus'
realm in the name of his daughter. In the interim Richard had,
although briefly styling himself 'king of Cyprus', sold the island
to the Knights Templar for 100,000 *bezants*, 40,000 down and
the balance on a mortgage. Unfortunately, the Templars' rule of
the island proved as unpopular as Isaac Comnenus' had been, the
heavy taxation of the islanders causing a series of uprisings. These
culminated in Nicosia on 5 April 1192, when the Templars were
forced to take refuge in the citadel, emerging to beat off their
attackers in a savage combat in which they narrowly missed being
wiped out. Wisely, they returned the island to Richard, who sold
it again – to Guy de Lusignan, the exiled king of Jerusalem, under
whose descendants it knew comparative peace and prosperity for
many years. The impromptu invasion by Isaac Comnenus' daughter and her lover failed dismally. They were last reported seeking
asylum in Armenia.

## NOTES

1. For the balance of Professor Pryor's paper on these ships, see www.
   cogandgalleyships.com/blog/497372-ships-of-the-crusade-era-part-11/
2. William of Tyre, *Chronicon*, ed. R.B.C. Huygens (Turnhout: Brepols,
   1986), p. 927.
3. Fulcher of Chartres, *A History of the Expedition to Jerusalem, 1095–1127*,
   ed. and trans. F.R. Ryan (Knoxville, TN: University of Tennessee,
   1969), Vol 2, p. 239.
4. Benedict of Peterborough, *Gesta Henrici*, Vol 2, p. 126.

5. Ibid, p. 133.

6. Gerald of Wales, *De Principis Instructione*, p. 282.

7. Roger of Howden, *Chronica*, Vol 3, p. 99.

8. A mark was at that time worth two-thirds of a pound sterling, or 66 pence.

9. E.R. Labande, 'Les filles d'Aliénor d'Aquitaine – Etude Comparative', *Cahiers de Civilisation Mediévale*, XXIX (1986), p. 109.

10. Pierre of Longtoft, *The Chronicle of Pierre de Longtoft*, ed. T. Wright, Rolls Series 47 (London: Longmans, 1886–88), Vol 2, p. 49.

11. Personal communication from Professor Pryor, who points out that there are four contemporary, but mutually contradictory, accounts of the voyage from Messina. Even in the same account, a given ship may be referred to as an *esnecca* and a *nef*, plural *nes* or otherwise, just for the sake of rhyme.

12. Gertwagen, 'Harbours and Facilities', p. 97.

13. Joinville and Villehardouin, *Chronicles of the Crusades*, ed. M.R.B. Shaw (London: Penguin Classics, 1963), p. 196.

14. Gertwagen, 'Harbours and Facilities', p. 98, quoting Cristoforo Buondelmonte, and p. 104.

15. Alexander Neckham, *Alexandri Neckham De Naturis Rerum Libri Duo with the Poem of the Same Author, De Laudibus Sapientiae*, ed. T. Wright, Rolls Series 34 (London: Longmans, 1863), facsimile edition (Whitefish, MT: Kessinger, 2010), p. 183.

16. Benedict of Peterborough, *Gesta Henrici*, Vol 2, p. 162.

17. Gertwagen, 'Harbours and Facilities', pp. 97–8.

18. Hyland, *The Medieval Warhorse*, p. 146.

19. Benedict of Peterborough, *Gesta Henrici*, Vol 2, p. 163.

20. Ibid, Vol 2, p. 164.

21. Personal communication from Professor Pryor.

22. Benedict of Peterborough, *Gesta Henrici*, Vol 2, p. 165–6.

23. J. Bradbury, *Philip Augustus* (London: Longmans, 1998), p. 89.

24. Roger of Howden, *Chronica*, Vol 3, p. 111.

# 15

# If it be God's Will ...

On 5 May 1191 the Plantagenet fleet sailed away from Famagusta after Richard had restored the former laws of the island under the less tyrannical rule of Byzantium before Isaac Comnenus' *coup d'état*. He arrived at Tyre in a flotilla of twenty-five of the fastest ships, with the slower transports following and several of them lost en route. On the orders of Conrad, the garrison of the city denied entrance to the new arrivals, obliging them to camp outside the walls, which cannot have put Richard in a good mood.

Setting sail down the coast for Acre, the lookouts aboard his flagship *Trenchemer* espied a very large ship flying the French flag. Since Philip had no such vessel in his fleet, the faster galleys approached to board her – at which the crew took up arms, revealing themselves as Saracen reinforcements for the garrison at Acre who initiated combat using arrows and Greek fire. After a short and bloody fight the Saracen ship was rammed or otherwise damaged so severely that it sank, to Richard's great satisfaction. There were allegedly 1,500 men aboard, all of whom drowned with the exception of the few taken hostage.[1] The crusader flotilla arrived at the siege of Acre two days later, on 8 June 1191 – a week after Joanna, Berengaria and Isaac's daughter, who had been escorted there by another flotilla.[2]

With the German contingent having largely aborted the crusade after their emperor Frederik Barbarossa drowned in Turkey
and the Sicilians having departed after the death of William II,
plus all the other departures, the brunt of the recent fighting had
fallen on Philip's men. So, despite the disputes between the two
kings on Sicily, Philip had good reason initially to be glad to see
the Plantagenet reinforcements. The great rejoicing in the crusader camp produced a corresponding gloom in the garrison,
watching from the city walls as all these well-armed, relatively
healthy and well-equipped European knights and foot soldiers
disembarked on the open beach to the south of the city, instead
of the 1,500 reinforcements they had been expecting to sail into
the harbour.[3]

Philip had succeeded in damaging the city walls with his largest catapult called Malvoisin, or Bad Neighbour. But it and the
siege engines of the Templars and Hospitallers had not created any
breach large enough for an attack to break through into the city.
In the camp many men were ill from the midsummer heat, which
made a mail *cotte* uncomfortable even when covered by a surcoat
and turned a helmet into an oven around the head. Among the
victims of the lack of hygiene and bad food was Philip Augustus
himself, suffering from what they called *arnaldia*. Later known as *la
suette* in France, this was possibly a viral contagious fever with copious and debilitating sweating and skin rashes, and which caused the
nails and hair to fall out, lips to peel painfully and whole strips of
skin to fall away from the body. During several medieval and later
epidemics in England it was called 'the sweating syknes' and last
appeared in northern France in 1906.

Scenting a new source of profit in all the hungry bellies
Richard brought with him, both the Pisan and Genoese merchants wished to swear allegiance to him. Knowing the bonds
between Philip and the Genoese, he sent them away empty-
handed, allowing the Pisans to do homage, which placed them
under his protection. His siege engines, shipped dismantled from
Europe and swiftly erected near the walls, proved more effective

in breaching those walls than had Philip's, which were burned down by Greek fire at the Accursed Tower whilst left unmanned.[4] A worse blow to Philip's pride was Richard's poaching of his locally recruited mercenaries by offering them 4 gold *bezants* a month, as against the 3 *bezants* Philip had been paying them.

Morale was already at a low ebb: on occasions groups of besiegers cheered a telling sortie against crusaders from another country or who spoke another language.[5] One of the sorties from the city reached as far as the 'red light area' of the crusader camp. But hostilities were not continuous: in the way of medieval warfare, the kings and nobles took time off for sport. On one occasion when Philip Augustus' white falcon flew into the city, he sent a messenger offering a reward of 1,000 *bezants* for its return, but the bird was apparently considered more valuable as meat by whoever caught it. As just one proof that business was still business, the debt contracted by Jean de Chastenay on Sicily was repaid by his son Gautier the month that he died, and the pawned valuables were returned to him by the lender.[6]

During quieter periods, courtesy visits were exchanged between the knights of both sides. In the Saracen camp Richard was known as *malik al-Inkitar* – meaning 'the king of England', *Inkitar* being an Arabic transliteration of 'Angleterre', which the Muslims had heard used by speakers of *lingua franca* in the East. Despatching a Moroccan prisoner under a flag of truce, Richard asked for an interview with Saladin, to get the measure of his adversary. He perhaps also wanted to impress him with his red hair and tall stature, compared with Saladin's swarthy skin, short stature and slight build. The historian Baha al-Din, who was a member of Saladin's court at the time, commented that Richard's intention was to reconnoitre the weaknesses of the Saracen positions. Instead, Saladin sent his brother al-'Adil, known to the crusaders as Saphadin, to a meeting with the message: 'Kings meet only after an accord, for it is unthinkable for them to wage war once they know each other and have broken bread together.'[7]

It was soon Richard's turn to succumb to *la suette*, so that for a while both kings were ill. Richard also suffered a return of the malaria that had troubled him for years. Both diseases were then common in Europe, let alone in the unsanitary hell of a midsummer siege camp in the Middle East. It is also extremely probable that all the crusaders had brought with them one or more species of parasitic intestinal worms. Recent state-of-the-art analysis of the soil excavated from two crusader-period latrines at Acre has also revealed evidence of rampant amoebic dysentery.[8] Cholera might break out at any moment and rats feeding on the refuse and corpses brought the risk of plague. To the illnesses caused by lack of sanitation and contamination of drinking water must be added severe, and sometimes fatal, fevers from ticks and sand flies biting men who slept on the ground, whether under cover or not. And wounds, however slight, were liable to go septic, leading to gangrene and death.

Night and day, the crusaders catapulted into the city missiles of stone and iron and fire, as well as living and dead prisoners and putrid carcasses of animals designed to spread disease among the defenders, who in turn operated counter-batteries of catapults, often returning the same missiles, and raining down on the besiegers a hail of arrows, stones and fire. At night the thudding of catapults and rams, the yells of exultation and screams of the wounded made sleep impossible for those who were not exhausted. The elegant pavilions of the nobles gave some respite from the clouds of flies breeding in the open latrines, and the sand flies and mosquitoes that bit every inch of exposed flesh, but many men slept in the open, even on the ground, despite the risk of scrub typhus. Nor was rank any protection; those who died included many of the nobles.

Whether through sickness or to spite Philip Augustus, Richard refused to take part in the attack on the city after Saladin's nephew Taqi tried to break through to its relief on 3 July, when the wall was breached. The unsupported French attack was driven back by the defenders' use of Greek fire. Philip then had a relapse of *la suette*, but nevertheless insisted on being carried on an armoured litter to within crossbow range of the walls, so that he could take pot shots at defenders incautious enough to show themselves, as Richard was also later to do.

More to the point, the catapults and siege towers brought from England were causing so much damage to the walls that desperate people were throwing themselves off the battlements. Eight days after the failed French attack, Richard's men made a breach and attacked, but were likewise driven off. By 4 July, when some spokesmen of Richard were in Saladin's camp requesting fresh fruit, sherbets and snow to cool his drinks, the city of Acre had been cut off, except for the intermittent blockade-runners and one relief by land, for nearly two years. Its inhabitants were literally starving, infants and old people dying of thirst. When messages reached Saladin that the garrison could no longer hold and had made an offer of surrender, he wept bitter tears and sent heralds through his camp to summon his emirs for one final attack on the crusader army. The initiative came to nothing because they refused to take part, considering such an attack as a useless waste of life.[9]

Relations between the Plantagenet and French armies deteriorated still further. Philip adopted Conrad as a *curialis* – a member of his court – and possibly on his advice, dunned Richard for half of Cyprus in accordance with the pact they had sworn in France and renewed at Messina. After the death of Count Philip of Flanders, Richard retorted that, since the agreement covered all the gains of both kings during the crusade, he would expect in return half of Flanders and half of all the possessions of all Philip's other vassals who had died on the expedition. To put an end to this pointless haggling where neither would give way, the masters of the Templars and Hospitallers were appointed to rule on the claims – and there the matter rested, in the hands of the lawyers, so to speak.[10]

In that age of superstition and ignorance, rumours were rife. One, which may have been true, was of a Christian spy living inside the city who wrote news of events there, the state of morale, food supplies and weapons, and gave warning of planned sorties. His letters were wrapped around arrows and fired over the walls to land in the siege camp, each bearing the authentication formula *In nomine patris et filii et spiritu santi* [sic] – in the name of the Father, the Son and the Holy Spirit. Since his identity was never established before or after the siege ended, no one could say whether this was just a rumour or the work of a spy caught and executed by the garrison or killed by chance when the crusaders eventually entered the city.[11] About the only thing on which Richard and Philip could now agree was that, when the English army was making a major attack on the walls, the French would guard the landward ditch against any incursion by Saladin's investing army, and vice versa.

Superstition and ignorance also preyed heavily when a total solar eclipse on 23 June lasting three hours made the whole sky so dark that the stars were seen shining brightly. This was taken as an evil omen and caused great terror in the Christian camp, except by the teams of sappers labouring in the cramped tunnels beneath the walls of Acre, who were unaware of the event. Their technique was to excavate a tunnel to a spot exactly beneath the foundations of the walls and there hack out a large cavern whose roof was supported by beams and props. When this was considered sufficiently large, the props were liberally smeared with pitch. Pig carcases, barrels of oil and other inflammable material were hauled into the cavern and set alight. When the props burned through, the roof fell in, bringing down the wall above it. At least, that was the theory. The Saracens naturally suspected what was going on and dug counter-mines to break into the crusader tunnels and kill the sappers in them. In one case, when the counter-mine broke through, the crusader sappers were surprised to hear themselves addressed in *lingua franca*, for the 'enemy' were Christian prisoners labouring underground in fetters. Furious to find that these slaves had been helped to escape along the mine back to the crusader camp, the garrison then blocked both tunnels.[12] After another team of sappers succeeded in undermining a significant section of wall near the Accursed Tower, Philip's marshal Albéric Clément led many French knights into the assault, proclaiming, '*Aut hodie moriar, aut in Achon, Deo volente, ingrediar.*' This day I shall perish, or, God willing, I shall enter Acre.[13]

Apparently, God was not willing. After Clément had climbed onto the damaged walls, his scaling ladder broke under the weight of the men following him, leaving him stranded alone, hacked to death by Saracens in full view of those below. Judged guilty of cowardice on this occasion for failing to go to the aid of the knights trapped between the walls, Conrad of Montferrat retired to Tyre in some opprobrium.

Because it was a generally observed custom for the people of a city that surrendered to be granted their lives, though not much else, whereas death was the penalty for fighting to the bitter end, the defenders again sued for terms on 4 July, offering Richard and Philip the city and all the weapons and treasure therein if they would grant the defenders the right to leave *cum vita et membris* – with life and limb intact. To this the kings replied with their terms: the return of all the lands recaptured by the Saracens since the time of Philip's father, Louis VII, during the Second Crusade, plus the return of the True Cross and the liberation of all Christian captives.[14]

Saladin's instructions to the garrison to hold out were at one point carried by a courier who swam under the blockading Christian ships at night. The following night his master launched an attack on the guards of the landward ditch in the hope that a mass sortie from the city could be made during this diversion. Roused from sleep, the crusaders rushed to the ditch, but the plan for the sortie was foiled by extra guards placed on it close to the walls, allegedly after a warning had been received from the mysterious archer-spy. The on-again off-again negotiations were complicated by the fact that there were three parties to the talks: the French and English kings in council with the other leaders of the national contingents; the garrison spokesmen; and Saladin's envoys. The two last had different agendas.

On 5 July and the following night Richard's siege engines succeeded in making a huge breach in the walls, through which a new attack was launched, with the result that on 6 July a new request for parley was received from the city. This time three commanders came out and were allowed to go to Saladin for orders, telling him that the walls and towers were now falling down and a third of their men had been killed so that the city could no longer be defended.

This produced an astonishing offer. Saladin proposed that the kings of England and France ally themselves with him for one year in a campaign beyond the Euphrates, and cede three named fortresses. In return, he would return to them the city of Jerusalem, the True Cross and all the disputed lands and places. Should the kings not be prepared to go with him, then he would accept instead one year's service of 2,000 knights and 5,000 men-at-arms,[15] the knights to be paid 46 *bezants* a month and the men 15 *bezants* a month – which was generous. There was even an assurance policy in the proposed deal: each Christian knight killed would be replaced by one of his knights and each man-at-arms killed would be replaced by one of his soldiers; all those taken prisoner would be ransomed. The negotiation came to nothing.

On Sunday 7 July all was as before: while the Plantagenet army tended the landward ditch, the French launched a violent attack on a narrow breach at the Accursed Tower, which came to nothing and cost the lives of forty-one of Philip's knights. On 8 July, possibly as a diversion, Saladin put the nearby city of Caiaphus to the sack, laying waste the land around it. That night, to the other horrors of the siege suffered by the people inside Acre was added a violent earthquake that shook the city to its foundations, causing many casualties and terrifying everyone. With no or few buildings in the crusader camp, no casualties were recorded there; on the contrary, many swore that they had seen a vision of the Virgin Mary that night, by which they had been promised a swift end to the siege.

On 11 July Saladin demolished several nearby fortresses to make a wasteland for miles around Acre. Richard's siege engines' ceaseless battering of the walls having made a large breach, he sent in his army supported by Pisan allies, which led to a truce, the city begging terms again. On 12 July the surrender overtures led to an assembly in the Templars' tent of both kings and all the bishops and barons in the combined crusader forces, with whom the Saracens finally agreed terms. They were to surrender the city of Acre with all the gold, silver, weapons and food in it and also all the galleys and other ships in the harbour, plus 300 Christian prisoners. Saladin also agreed to return the True Cross and liberate 1,500 Christian knights and 100 noble captives.[16] As specific ransom for the garrison of 3,500 men and some 300 of their dependants a sum of 200,000 gold *bezants* was to be paid within forty days, although at least one chronicler believed the ransom money was to be paid in three monthly instalments. If the ransom were paid within the stipulated time, they would go free; if not, their lives would be at the mercy of the besiegers.[17]

The kings then sent detachments into the city with orders to lock up 100 of the Saracen commanders under special guard, while the other captives were driven into an empty place. Conditions in the city must have been appalling after two years' destruction of walls, towers and dwellings and thousands of people having been killed there. Within hours the kings received reports that some of the captives had managed to escape under cover of night, so the remainder were locked up more securely in cellars, while the few who accepted Christian baptism were allowed to go free – until reports were received that many of these had gone out to Saladin's camp and there renounced their baptism. From that time on, baptism was denied the captives.

Conrad of Montferrat had been recalled from Tyre at the request of Saladin to negotiate the surrender terms. The garrison disarmed, he entered the city with his banner and those of Philip and Richard, who claimed the royal palace as his quarters, Philip being allocated the former house of the Templars. The banners of other Christian leaders were also displayed on the battlements, as a sign not only of victory but also to mark their claims to the spoils of war while the artificers were still dismantling the petraries and other siege engines, which were then loaded onto the ships of the fleet for the next stage in the campaign.

It was also a time for civilities. Richard, feeling magnanimous in victory to the enemy he considered a worthy opponent, sent fine harriers and falcons of his own as presents to Saladin, who responded with costly gifts in return, but on the same day the two European monarchs found themselves in a Byzantine maze of treachery, when representatives of the lord against whom Saladin had sought their aid arrived with seductive promises, should the kings bring their armies to help him defeat Saladin. Aware of what was going on, Saladin made a better offer. Neither was accepted. This was on 16 July while the bishops were busy reconsecrating the churches of Acre, some of which had been used as mosques.

When Richard discovered that Leopold of Austria – whom he considered a mere honorary duke, although commanding the German contingent – had managed to find quarters as good as those of the king of England, he fell into a rage worthy of his father and had Leopold's banner torn down from the battlements, hurled into the sewage-filled moat and trampled into the filth, as a sign that the Germans were not entitled to share in the spoils. Many of them had been there for up to two years and rightly considered that they deserved a fair share of the spoils. It was not only an ill-considered insult, but one that was to cost Richard's subjects dearly. Many of the German knights actually sold everything except their personal weapons before abandoning the crusade for good and riding away to the north with Leopold, whose hatred of Richard embraced another insult to his family: Isaac Comnenus, still held in Margat Castle, was his mother's first cousin.[18]

It is likely that the members of the surrendered garrison were used as forced labour because the city must have been cleansed of some of the filth and rubble accumulated during the two-year siege by 21 July, when Richard moved into the royal palace with Joanna, Berengaria and Isaac Comnenus' daughter. Outside the palace, all was not peace. Apart from the incessant in-fighting between the various contingents, the surviving Pisan and Genoese merchants and nobility who had been based there before the Muslims drove them out now demanded the return of property and premises they claimed as formerly theirs. This hardly pleased the exhausted, wounded and sick crusaders who had taken possession of those buildings after living so long in the appalling conditions of the siege camp. Conrad approached Philip on their behalf and it was left to him to negotiate the restitution of property, which strained even further his relations with the Plantagenet contingent and its king.[19]

Philip had been ill for three months longer than Richard, and was worn out physically and mentally. He begged Richard to release him, not from his crusader's vow – only the pope could do that – but from the undertaking agreed in France that neither king should return to Europe before the other. On 22 July a number of Philip's barons, including the duke of Burgundy, came to Richard and begged him with tears in their eyes to advise them whether it was lawful to return to France with Philip or not. Strangely, because he was himself adept at the same sort of display when it suited him, he was moved by their entreaties. According to the chronicler, he said to these hardened warriors, '*Nolite flere!*' Don't cry![20]

On 28 July the squabbling continued, not only over the division of the spoils of the siege, but also over the future of the Latin Kingdom. Richard sneeringly agreed that Philip could leave, but would get no share in the eagerly awaited ransom money, on the grounds that it was for the continuation of the war, not for Philip's royal purse. The continuing bone of contention between the two kings was the question of who was now the rightful king of Jerusalem. Richard upheld Guy and Philip stood firm on Conrad. A Byzantine compromise was reached, under which Guy could keep the title 'king of Jerusalem' and have the ports of Jaffa and Caesarea, while Conrad could keep Beirut, Sidon and Tyre and inherit Jerusalem on Guy's death – assuming that Jerusalem could be retaken from the Saracens. At that time and in that place there was a joke about a man called Ali who became rich overnight by telling the sultan he could teach his favourite camel to talk in only three years. His friends said he was mad because no one can teach a camel to talk and that the sultan would chop off his head when the time was up and he had not taught the beast to say a single word. Unworried, Ali replied, 'In three years, the camel may be dead, the sultan may be dead or I may be dead.' There was something of that logic in the compromise over the throne of Jerusalem, given that, even during periods of truce, men and women of all ranks and ages in the Holy Land died suddenly from disease even more frequently than back home in Europe.

Philip again demanded a half-share of Cyprus, in keeping with their agreement to share the spoils of the crusade equally, but Richard again refused. The personal antipathy between the kings had reached the point of no return. When Philip's illness peaked with trench mouth causing his teeth to fall out of rotting gums, rumours circulated in the French camp that Richard had somehow poisoned him. To add to his troubles, Philip heard a malicious rumour started by Richard to the effect that his infant son and heir Prince Louis, known to have been ill, had died in Paris.[21]

Sorting out the inheritance of Count Philip of Flanders, Theobald of Blois, Henry of Troyes, Stephen of Sancerre and the counts of Vendôme, Clermont and Perche, and many others of his magnates, was now a matter of priority for Philip Augustus. Duke Hugues III of Burgundy was shortly to be added to the list, so that it was afterwards said that the French king 'had left the major barons of his father's generation buried in the Syrian sands'.[22] Such a depletion of the old aristocracy, loyal to the House of Capet, inevitably meant instability in France, which its king could not ignore.

Another reason for Philip's urgent desire to leave lay in rumours that Richard's repeated contacts with the Saracens had included a deal for four of the Shi'ite extremists known as the Hashashin or Assassins to shadow his movements and murder him at some propitious moment. If the specific arguments between the two kings are relatively undocumented, Richard's arrogant ability to insult most of the other leaders after Philip's departure is a matter of record. In view of what later happened to Conrad of Montferrat, Philip's fears of assassination were quite reasonable. Richard invoked the crusader's oath not to return home before liberating Jerusalem in order to belittle Philip for breaking it, but that rings hollow today, since Richard himself later abandoned the crusade, leaving Jerusalem in Saracen hands.

His problem was now that if Philip returned to France before him, the continental Plantagenet territories would be vulnerable to his incursions, no matter how strongly the Church protected a crusader's property in his absence. He therefore made Philip swear a new oath, witnessed by the duke of Burgundy and the count of Champagne, that the House of Capet and its vassals would not invade Plantagenet territory until forty days after Richard's return!

Departing from Acre on 31 July, Philip left half his share of the spoils of the city to Conrad and gave to the ill-fated Hugues of Burgundy the command of his troops who elected to remain in the Holy Land, with some treasure and 5,000 marks for their upkeep. To Raymond of Antioch he sent 100 knights and 500 foot soldiers. Conrad departed with him, refusing to serve in an army now commanded solely by Richard and perhaps also because his own contacts with Saracens had given him reason to fear that a contract had been put out on his life. Three days after leaving Acre, Philip and his entourage set sail from Tyre for Europe in a fleet of fourteen Genoese galleys, using the anti-clockwise currents of the Mediterranean to port-hop from Tyre to Tripoli, Tripoli to Antioch, Antioch to Rhodes and Crete through the pirate-infested Aegean islands to Corfu, and across the Adriatic to Otranto or Brindisi on the south-eastern tip of Italy. There, safe conducts were obtained from Tancred of Lecce

and the Holy Roman Emperor Henry VI for them, as returning crusaders, to ride the length of Italy in peace. Stopping in
Rome with the traces of his illness evident on his face and body,
Philip was released from his crusader's vow to liberate Jerusalem
by Pope Celestine III,[23] who also listened sympathetically to his
complaints about Richard's conduct.

Yet Philip's request to be allowed a dispensation from the
Peace in order to seize the moment to right the wrongs of the
Alais/Vexin/Flanders complex met with no such success, pos-
sibly because Eleanor on her stopover in Rome had briefed the
pope on the Plantagenet reaction to any such move.[24] Instead,
Philip was warned that he would be excommunicated, should
he 'commit any evil' to the lands and property of the king of
England during the latter's absence on crusade.[25] From there
northwards, the homeward journey was the same as for Queen
Eleanor and Louis VII on their return from the Second Crusade.
At Milan, Philip met the German Emperor Henry Hohenstaufen,
who was settling scores with Tancred of Sicily and more than
ready to listen to all the Franks' tales discrediting the Sicilians.
He was also related to both the insulted duke of Austria and the
imprisoned king of Cyprus and his daughter, who was still held
prisoner in Joanna's household. However, the claim that he swore
there and then to take personal revenge on Richard should he
pass through any part of the Empire on his way home[26] sounds
like a later invention, for there was then no reason why Richard
should set foot in Hohenstaufen's domains.

## NOTES

1. Benedict of Peterborough, *Gesta Henrici*, Vol 2, p. 168.
2. Runciman, *A History of the Crusades*, p. 47.
3. Maalouf, pp. 208–9.
4. Roger of Howden, *Chronica*, Vol 3, cxxxi.
5. Bradbury, *Philip Augustus*, p. 89.
6. See http//fr.wikipedia.org/wiki/Jean_de_Chastenay

7. Maalouf, *The Crusades*, p. 290.

8. P.D. Mitchell, E. Stern and Y. Tepper, 'Dysentery in the Crusader Kingdom of Jerusalem: An ELISA Analysis of Two Medieval Latrines in the City of Acre (Israel)', *Journal of Archeological Science* Vol 35, issue 7, July 2008, pp. 1849–53.

9. Maalouf, *The Crusades*, p. 210, quoting Baha al-Din.

10. Benedict of Peterborough, *Gesta Henrici*, Vol 2, pp. 170–1; also Runciman, *A History of the Crusades*, p. 49.

11. Benedict of Peterborough, *Gesta Henrici*, Vol 2, p. 172.

12. Ambroise, *Estoire de la guerre sainte*, ed. G. Paris (Paris: Imprimerie Nationale, 1897), p. 386.

13. W. Stubbs, ed., *Itinerarium Peregrinarum et Gesta Regis Ricardi*, Rolls Series (London: Longmans, 1864), p. 223; Ambroise, *Estoire de la guerre sainte*, p. 386.

14. Benedict of Peterborough, *Gesta Henrici*, Vol 2, p. 174.

15. Some sources say 5,000 squires.

16. The numbers vary in different accounts.

17. Benedict of Peterborough, *Gesta Henrici*, Vol 2, p. 179.

18. Ibid, Vol 2, p. 181; Runciman, *A History of the Crusades*, p. 51.

19. Runciman, *A History of the Crusades*, p. 51.

20. Benedict of Peterborough, *Gesta Henrici*, Vol 2, p. 184.

21. Runciman, *A History of the Crusades*, p. 52.

22. J.W. Baldwin, *The Government of Philip Augustus: Foundations of French Royal Power in the Middle Ages* (Berkeley, CA: University of California Press, 1986), p. 80, quoted in Bradbury, *Philip Augustus*, p. 94. The Holy Land was also called Syria because it had formed part of the Roman province of Syria-Palestine.

23. William of Newburgh, *Historia Rerum Anglicarum*, Vol 1, p. 358.

24. Kelly, *Eleanor of Aquitaine*, p. 275.

25. Benedict of Peterborough, *Gesta Henrici*, Vol 2, p. 229.

26. Roger of Howden, *Chronica*, Vol 3, p. 167.

# 16

# Exit Philip Augustus

ichard, meanwhile, was receiving disturbing news with every despatch from Europe. In England, William Longchamp had made enemies at every level by his exactions to finance the absent king's distant enterprise. His fellow bishops had only one thought on hearing that Archbishop Baldwin of Canterbury had died on the crusade. Fearful that Longchamp's intimacy with King Richard would see him raised from the see of Ely to supreme status as the new primate of all England,[1] they found the moment to strike after Geoffrey the Bastard was consecrated at Tours and invested with the *pallium* of office.

The revenues of the see of York and all the other vacant sees had been coming to the Crown in Geoffrey's absence. So Longchamp peremptorily ordered the widowed countess of Flanders to prevent Geoffrey taking ship for England in any of her ports. His household was under no such embargo, and so were allowed to cross on 13 September, after which she shut her eyes to Geoffrey crossing alone and more discreetly on the following day. Landing at Dover in mid-morning, he was ordered by the water-guard to report to Longchamp's sister Richeut, who was the wife of the absent castellan. Instead, Geoffrey fled to Canterbury and sought sanctuary in St Martin's priory, where Longchamp's men tracked him down and dragged him outside by his legs, with his head banging on the ground while he screamed excommunications on those who dared lay hands on an invested archbishop.[2] Geoffrey was offered a horse to ride back to Dover, but refused to mount it on the technicality that it belonged to men he had excommunicated.

When news reached London that he had then been forced to walk 20 miles back to Dover under arrest, the bishops of England took this as an affront to their collective dignity. Prince John was hardly a friend of the Church, but took the opportunity at the council of Reading to side with them and the nobles who detested Longchamp's rapacious demands. Knowing her youngest son well, Eleanor had foreseen this or a similar situation, and prudently obtained from Pope Celestine III the authority for Archbishop Walter of Rouen to summon Longchamp to account for his acts. The miscreant bishop of Ely was therefore summoned to the council from Windsor, one day's ride to the east. Learning the strength of the forces arrayed against him, he turned tail in mid-journey and rode hell-for-leather to take refuge in the Tower of London.[3] For this defiance, Archbishop Walter of Rouen excommunicated him.

Longchamp had ordered that the gates of London be closed against his pursuers, but the citizens ignored this, several thousand of them gathering in open ground outside the walls east of the Tower next morning, calling on Longchamp to step outside and defend himself. This he did astutely enough, warning them all in French, which most could understand, against John's ambitions and the danger of treason if they supported him – for which they risked not only Richard's temporal justice but also the sanctions of the Church so long as their king was on crusade.

His arguments were in vain. Two days later, meeting at St Paul's, the Great Council listened as Archbishop Walter of Rouen and William the Marshal read letters brought back by Eleanor from Messina,[4] after which they banished Longchamp and replaced him as chancellor with Walter of Rouen. Exceeding their brief, the council also conferred on Prince John the fine sounding but legally meaningless title *summus rector totius regni* or 'supreme governor of the whole realm', which purported to give him precedence over even the chief justiciar. Longchamp's appointees were summarily dismissed so that new castellans, sheriffs and other officials could be sworn in. As its price for supporting the new administration, the increasingly powerful citizenry of London exacted a recognition of its status as a commune, entitled to elect its mayor, aldermen and other officers.

From the security of the Tower, Longchamp at first argued that surrendering his chancellor's seal and the castles Richard had bestowed on him would be treason. He eventually gave in after long negotiation and was allowed to keep the castles of Dover, Cambridge and Hereford because they were so far apart as to constitute no collective threat. After giving his word that he would not leave England without permission, he delivered up his brothers and chamberlain as sureties and was escorted on 12 October to the same castle at Dover where his sister had imprisoned Geoffrey the Bastard.

Five days later, he abandoned his brothers to their fate, scuttling out of the castle disguised as a woman in a long green gown, a hood pulled over his face. Although this was a disguise in which his small and unimposing stature was an asset, fortune had abandoned him. Waiting on the foreshore while his servants negotiated the hire of a boat to take them all across the Channel, he was accosted and groped by a curious fisherman. His sex revealed, Longchamp was rescued by his servants, but on being questioned in English by a local woman and being unable to reply in that language, he was hustled away by a suspicious crowd and locked up in a cellar.[5]

The universal ridicule that greeted this escape attempt was thought sufficient humiliation for the bishop who had arrogantly even used the royal 'we' on occasion. Before the end of the month, Prince John gave orders that Longchamp should be allowed to leave the country. Instead of heading back to Aquitaine in disgrace, Longchamp followed the same path as the Plantagenet

princes when they had fallen out with Henry: he travelled to
Paris, where he was acclaimed with all appropriate ecclesiastical
dignity – some said, in return for bribes.[6] Perhaps bribery also had
something to do with his ecclesiastical offices being confirmed
by cardinals Jordan and Octavian, in the city on papal business.[7]
But when these two gentlemen dared set foot near Gisors, which
Queen Eleanor still regarded as Plantagenet territory, she ordered
the seneschal of Normandy to inform the prelates that they could
travel no further without her safe conduct, which was not forthcoming. It was neatly done; in retreating towards Paris, Jordan
and Octavian excommunicated the seneschal and his garrison,
and placed the duchy of Normandy under interdict, but could
not excommunicate Eleanor, who had avoided putting her name
to any specific action for which she could be so punished.

Heartened by the cardinals' support, Longchamp denied his
own excommunication in England, excommunicating everyone there who had taken sides openly against him – with the
exception of Prince John. Geoffrey the Bastard, in turn, excommunicated his own suffragan, the bishop of Durham, and Walter
of Rouen escalated matters by placing Longchamp's diocese of
Ely under interdict. Even the bishops of England were unable
to agree unanimously as to who had the right to excommunicate whom in these circumstances, which would have been
comic if these religious spats were not taken seriously by the
mass of the population.

The period of Advent leading to Christmas of 1191 thus saw
entire counties in the Plantagenet domains on both sides of the
Channel denied the sacrament. Church bells had been removed
and laid on the ground and the statues laid on the floor of
churches; weddings could not be celebrated; the dead had to be
temporarily buried in unconsecrated ground, to be reburied in
churchyards after the eventual lifting of the sanctions. The man
at the centre of all this anguish had the nerve to attempt to enlist
Eleanor in his capacity as Richard's appointee, but without success. At Rouen, where she was staying at the time to govern

Normandy, she refused to meet Longchamp on the grounds that it was not permitted for a Christian to eat, drink or have any dealings with an excommunicate. Instead, she went straight to the top, appealing successfully to Pope Celestine to undo the chaos due to his cardinals' espousal of Longchamp's cause.[8] Visiting the diocese of Ely a few months later, she had Walter of Rouen lift the interdict under which the population was suffering.[9]

She was, however, still at Bures holding court for Richard's Norman vassals when Philip returned to Paris at the end of December. Holding his delayed Christmas court in Fontainebleau, he was hailed a hero of Christendom, much as his father had been after returning from Outremer in 1149. Since Eleanor knew all too well the true story of the failed Second Crusade, this hardly impressed her, although she may have been amused by an alibi dreamed up by Philip's spin-doctors on the Île de la Cité that the fall of Acre was down to him; and that his illness on crusade was caused by poison introduced into his food or drink by those enemies whose repeated treachery had eventually forced him to flee the Holy Land.[10] As to who might have engineered this, there was only one answer acceptable on the Île de la Cité: who would seek so to injure a Christian monarch dedicated to the salvation of the Holy Sepulchre, if not the 'crusading brother' responsible for so many other woes of the House of Capet?

It is hard to see what benefit Philip derived from his sufferings and humiliation on the crusade, apart from some kudos for having obeyed the pope's call to travel to the Holy Land and there risk his life. On his return to Paris on 27 December 1191 he prostrated himself before the altar of the royal abbey of St Denis, adding to the holy relics revered there a curious collection he had brought back with him, including a stone which was said to have been used in the lapidation of the martyred St Stephen by a mob egged on by St Paul when still Saul of Tarsus, an alleged sample of the three kings' incense, a reputed finger of John the Baptist and *the* manger from 'Judean Bethlehem'. One can only wonder whether people like Philip

– who was not a credulous believer like his father Louis – considered such objects to be genuine or whether they pretended to do so, either for the benefit of the unlettered hoi polloi and/ or as a quid pro quo for the political and military support of their bishops.

The manger is perhaps the most blatant fake, in that the time Philip had spent in the Holy Land should have given him sufficient knowledge of its geography to know that the founding prophet of Christianity would not have been born in Judea, but in *Galilean* Bethlehem. The place name *bet lechem* simply means 'house of bread' in Hebrew, and 5 miles to the west of Nazareth, where His family were known to have lived in Galilee, was a place with that name, which was possibly the home of Miriam, the mother of the prophet. Almost certainly, she would have gone there to give birth, because her own mother lived there and it was known from the gospels that the family was not well liked in Nazareth.[11]

Philip Augustus took to travelling with a reinforced bodyguard and ordered his vassals to reinforce their fortifications, as though under a real and present threat from Normandy and Anjou. Suspecting this might be his preparation for a pre-emptive strike, Eleanor in turn ordered similar precautions on her side of the unsettled frontier. On 20 January 1192 Philip met the constable of Normandy near Gisors, showed him the settlement with Richard brokered by the count of Flanders in Messina and demanded the return of Alais with the castles that constituted her dowry. The constable replied that he had no authority from Richard to do this, and Philip retired with the threat that he would be forced to gain by force of arms the legitimate entitlement he could not obtain by negotiation.[12] Elsewhere, the succession of Flanders gained him much of Artois, the Amiénois, Vermandois and Beauvais. Having lost so many of his father's chief vassals to disease and combat during the crusade, he was determined that their successors would see him as a strong suzerain when they came into possession of their lands.

It was about this time that Eleanor learned Prince John was intending to do homage to Philip Augustus and assembling a small army of mercenaries, with whom to invade Normandy alongside a Frankish force – and, with Philip's approval, be declared the new duke of Normandy after annulling the marriage to Isabel of Gloucester and marrying Alais.[13] Eleanor could have withdrawn to the safety of Poitou and Aquitaine, but her instinct was to attack fast. Prince John may have believed that Philip would install him as duke of Normandy and then quietly retire, but Eleanor had no illusions that Frankish incursions would stop there; having transgressed against the Peace of God once, Philip would have nothing to lose by moving against all the other Plantagenet possessions, province by province.

To nip the trouble in the bud, she moved with the same speed for which Henry II had been famous, defying the elements in yet another winter crossing of the Channel. Landing at Portsmouth, she did not head for nearby Southampton, where Prince John was assembling his forces, rightly reasoning that he was no threat at all, if deprived of the sources of his wealth. She therefore convened in Windsor, London, Oxford and Winchester a series of meetings of the Great Council.[14] The magnates had stood aloof from John's collusion with Philip after being promised by him that their own fiefs in Normandy would be safe. Showing that she had nothing to learn from the bishops when it came to arguing the dialectic, Eleanor invoked the Peace of God that protected Richard and his possessions while he was still on crusade and gave them a foretaste of his wrath when their rightful king returned and called them to account for their actions in his absence.

This redoubtable woman old enough to be their mother – in some cases, their grandmother – literally put 'the fear of God' into them, after which they agreed to threaten John with the confiscation of all his extensive English possessions, should he cross the Channel and join forces with Philip. Sulkily, he dismissed his mercenaries and retired to his castle at Wallingford. Eleanor's political coup was a masterly and bloodless solution to a situation that could have cost thousands of lives. Or so it seemed, until the game was changed by the reappearance on the board of a piece everyone had thought out of play: Longchamp crossed to Dover and, safe within its castle, declared himself still bishop of Ely and chancellor. Baffled, the magnates now sought to invoke Prince John's powers as the nominal 'supreme governor' to rid themselves of Longchamp once and for all, but Richard's frustrated and sulky brother demanded a higher price for his cooperation than the £700 in silver which – so he said – Longchamp had offered to pay for his support.[15]

In the Holy Land, many of the crusaders whom Richard had brought with him were dead from one cause or another, with the more prudent survivors already heading homeward, in many cases financially ruined and with their health broken. Enmeshment in the internecine politics of the Latin Kingdom weakened the military effect of those who remained, although both sides in the conflict had their fanatics. The *sufi* believed that dying in battle with the Christians gained them a ticket to paradise; what has been called 'the cult of martyrdom' in the Christian military orders likewise encouraged heroic, although militarily useless, self-sacrifice. By now even the Templars and Hospitallers, whose orders existed for no other reason than to protect pilgrims and fight the Saracen, were divided on the course to be followed.

The 10,000 troops left behind by Philip Augustus under the command of Duke Hugues III of Burgundy[16] were proving to be a mixed blessing because they had to be fed and equipped, for which Richard was relying on the arrival of the 200,000 *bezants* that had been demanded for the ransom of the garrison of Acre, and of which Philip had renounced his share for this purpose. Richard repeatedly pressured Conrad to hand over to him Philip's hostages, but Conrad refused to obey. On 11 August an instalment of one-third of the ransom and the exchange of prisoners was offered by Saladin, but Richard rejected this because a number of the named Christian nobles were not included in this first batch. On 13 August he threatened to behead all his hostages if the full ransom were not paid swiftly. To this, Saladin replied that he would then do the same and kill all his Christian captives.

In the third week of August Richard was again living in the camp outside Acre, the better to hustle preparations for the continuing campaign, but he was up against problems. As far as he was concerned, the whole army was now under his orders, but the rank-and-file protested that they had no clothes, arms, food or water, nor horses to ride and carry their baggage on the long trek south that he proposed as the next stage in the crusade. This forced him to purchase provisions and have them loaded onto the ships that were going to accompany the thousands of men on the march. He also had to hire all the archers locally available, who were not prepared to undertake another campaign without additional payment.

In between the negotiations over the prisoners, he and Saladin exchanged gifts and small courtesies, but tension was growing. According to the pro-Richard chroniclers, on 18 August it was rumoured that Saladin had summarily beheaded his Christian prisoners. That same day, Richard launched a savage assault on the Saracen force, in which his army suffered many casualties. On 20 August, suspecting that Saladin's delay in paying the ransom was a ploy to prevent the crusading army from moving on to its next objective, he gave orders for 2,700 of the captives to be executed outside the walls of Acre, sparing only 300 important persons for later ransom.[17] Acting for the departed king of France, the duke of Burgundy did the same with all the captives entrusted to him, so that the vast majority of the soldiers of the garrison and about 300 wives and children were roped together in groups and, in open ground in full view of the Saracen encampment, attacked with swords, lances, clubs and stones, their bellies slit open before the bodies were burned, in case gold or jewels had been swallowed.[18]

The scene is scarcely to be imagined: distraught parents forced to watch their children and friends killed before themselves being dragged forward to be slaughtered, the stink of blood, urine and excrement, the weeping and screams of terror and the blood-curdling groans of those not killed outright but beaten to death by executioners too exhausted to give them a clean end. Even for Richard's soldiers, hardened by years of combat, it was tough work under the midsummer sun. Eighteen years later the Cistercian abbot Arnaud Amaury, who was leading the Albigensian 'crusade', was approached at the siege of Beziers by the mercenaries given the task of executing thousands of prisoners, and who pleaded with him to order an end to the killing because they were exhausted by the sheer effort of hacking and stabbing victim after victim. The lack of compunction, or any feeling of humanity on the part of the soldiers killing the garrison and civilians of Acre is summed up by the chronicler Ambroise, who refers to them as 'these dogs who had shut themselves up in Acre and caused us so much harm'.[19] In despair, the Saracens attacked, hoping to stop the killing, but were beaten off.

## NOTES

1. W. Stubbs, *Historical Introduction to the Rolls Series* (London: Longmans, 1902), p. 227.
2. Gerald of Wales, *De Vita Galfredi*, pp. 382, 387–93.
3. Roger of Howden, *Chronica*, Vol 3, p. 144.
4. Benedict of Peterborough, *Gesta Henrici*, Vol 2, p. 212.
5. Gerald of Wales, *De Vita Galfredi*, pp. 410–11.
6. Benedict of Peterborough, *Gesta Henrici*, Vol 2, p. 221.
7. W. Stubbs, *Ralph of Diceto, Opera Historica*, Rolls Series No. 68 (London: 1876), Vol 1, p. 419.
8. Ibid, p. 420.
9. Ibid, p. 431–2.
10. William of Newburgh, *Historia Rerum Anglicarum*, Vol 1, pp. 266–7.
11. The story of Mary, heavily pregnant with twins, travelling 60-plus miles across difficult terrain to Judean Bethlehem, was introduced into the gospels in spurious fulfilment of a prophecy by Ezekiel that the Messiah would be born of the House of David, i.e. in Judea.
12. Kelly, *Eleanor of Aquitaine*, p. 297.
13. Benedict of Peterborough, *Gesta Henrici*, Vol 2, p. 236.
14. Ibid.
15. Ralph of Diceto, *Opera Historica*, Vol 1, p. 434.

16. A. Richard, *Histoire*, Vol 2, p. 214.

17. Ambroise, *Estoire de la guerre sainte*, p. 393.

18. Roger of Howden, *Chronica*, Vol 3, p. cxxxv.

19. Ambroise, *Estoire de la guerre sainte*, p. 394.

# Blood on the Sand, Blood in the Mud

On 22 August, when the work of disposing of those thousands of mutilated corpses must still been have ongoing, Richard handed responsibility for the reconstruction and defence of Acre to Bertram III of Verdun, who had faithfully served Henry II as sheriff and justiciar in England and also played an important part in Henry's conquest of Ireland. His co-castellan was Étienne de Longchamp, yet another brother of the bizarre bishop of Ely. Leaving them in charge of the city that had cost so many lives, he headed south towards Jaffa, the port he considered essential to a successful siege of Jerusalem and holding it afterwards – as did Saladin.

The progress of Richard's army of some 20,000 men followed the coast around the bay of Acre in the direction of Caiaphas. Scouts brought news that Saladin's main force was moving south further inland and no sooner had the long column of crusaders set out than Saracen skirmishers commanded by al-'Adil attacked the left flank and rear – riding in close at intervals on their nimble Arab and Turkmene mounts to loose arrows and throw spears before wheeling away out of bow-shot in the hope of luring the crusaders into a trap. For the marching men, the worst thing was the harassing fire of arrows. Unlike the wooden longbows of European archers, which were too long and unwieldy for combat use by the rider of a galloping horse, the Saracens used shorter recurved composite bone-and-sinew bows. Their range was somewhat less than that of the longbow, but they were far easier to manage in the saddle, the rider using both hands to knock an arrow to the string and fire it while controlling his mount by the pressure of his knees, even when heading away in the famous Parthian shot. The speed at which he kept moving throughout made him a difficult target for return fire.

Aware that the column could be attacked in force at any moment, Richard formed the mass of men and horses in such a way that it could swiftly turn left and face any attack, which was bound to be coming from the landward side. He divided his cavalry into twelve formations of 100 knights, positioning the Hospitallers, commanded by Brother Garnier of Nablus, in the rear and the Templars in the lead of the column under Robert de Sablé, who had been elected their Grand Master because of his record fighting the Muslims in Spain and Portugal. For linguistic reasons, the various contingents with a common language were kept intact, using their own tongues as the language of command, as was done in previous crusades: Poitevins and Gascons followed the Templars, the Bretons followed them; then came the Anglo-Norman knights, and the Flemings under Jacques d'Avesnes riding just in front of the Hospitallers. Commanding the vanguard was Guy de Lusignan; Richard placed Hugues III of Burgundy in command of the rearguard and positioned himself in the centre, from where he could most easily control the whole column. The vulnerable baggage train was placed on the right flank between the main column and the seashore.

The landward flank was composed of crossbowmen and archers, whose job was to break up the Muslim raids before they came too close. It was for a situation like this that all those thousands of arrows had been shipped out from England, for it would have been too dangerous to send men to recover undamaged arrows, as was often done after a battle in Europe. Keeping station just offshore was the crusader fleet, providing supplies at overnight stops and evacuation and a semblance of care for the daily quotas of wounded.

In this complicated military exercise Richard was in his element, controlling his large army on the march at battle-readiness. A recurring problem was restraining any impulse among the knights, unused to such strict discipline, to ride off in pursuit of the skirmishers, whose attacks were particularly difficult to bear in the early morning, when the sun was in the crusaders' eyes. Despite the legends of folk-hero archers like Robin Hood and William Tell, able to split a willow wand or transfix an apple at extreme range, the military use of longbows was to provide a barrage of simultaneously released arrows that came down on a closely packed body of advancing enemy troops, turning a heavy cavalry charge, for example, into a chaotic confusion of wounded, terrified, plunging horses. Hitting fast-moving individual Saracen riders with individual shots was far more difficult. Conversely, every Saracen arrow seemed to claim a victim in the close-packed ranks they were targeting.

The crusaders marched only in the relative cool between dawn and noon, before stopping at a source of clean water and setting up a well-guarded camp for the night so as to minimise the risk of heatstroke that claimed lives at Hattin. With the constant need to fend off raids by Al-'Adil's mounted archers, progress was slow: on some days they advanced barely a mile. At Caiaphas on the southern tip of the bay, they found the walls torn down and the inhabitants fled inland. From there onward, they travelled through a land of scorched earth, with fortresses and crops destroyed. One lightning attack by the Saracens in greater than usual force saw Hugues of Burgundy's rearguard briefly isolated from the main force until Richard's generalship and speed of reaction succeeded in hacking a way through to them. It was about this time that Guillaume des Barres so distinguished himself in combat that Richard forgave him their previous differences.[1] The constant

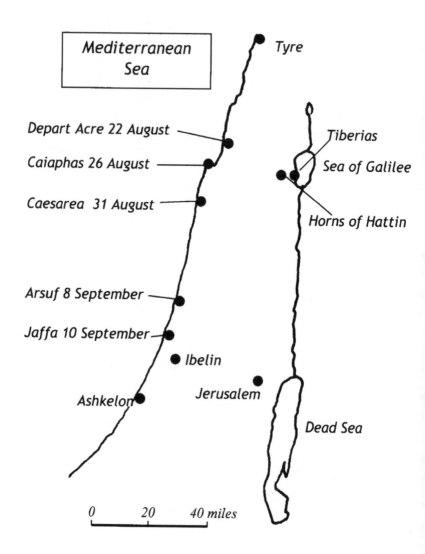

Principal cities and battles of the Third Crusade, with dates of the march from Acre to Arsuf and Jaffa

skirmishing attacks were not an end in themselves, but intended to wear down and, more importantly, slow down the army's progress while Saladin took a longer route inland to set a trap into which Richard must march. At one point, al-'Adil came under a flag of truce to parley, although whether this was a genuine negotiation or yet another delaying tactic is open to question.

On the last day of the month of August the army was nearing the ruins of Herod the Great's magnificent seaside palace, port and city of Caesarea Maritima, a small part of which near the port had been refortified by King Baldwin I in the First Crusade after slaughtering all the native inhabitants. This walled complex, less than a quarter the size of Herod's city, was currently occupied by the enemy. It was usual practice in medieval warfare to fill in or poison any wells that might be used by the enemy and Saladin had also chosen to encamp his army on the banks of a nearby river in the hope of denying to the Christian host its much-needed water. With his troops and their animals thus suffering severely from thirst, Richard divided the army into cohorts and despatched the first wave under Jacques d'Avesnes to attack the blocking party at a ford. The charge was successful, but in the carnage hundreds of men on both sides were killed.[2] Commanding the second wave, Richard then charged the centre of the enemy force and broke through to the river in a welter of blood and violence, so that his entire army was able to cross and replenish water supplies before moving on.[3]

However, the stress of the march was telling, especially on the infantry, so many of whom had to double as beasts of burden as more and more horses were killed: their duties were alternated, with men being moved from the exposed left flank to the baggage train for a few hours' respite as porters before being moved back. The 'armour' of most infantrymen consisted of leather caps and leather jerkins padded with multiple layers of cloth, worn despite the heat. On 2 September Baha al-Din noted how some of these men had up to ten Muslim arrows sticking in their jerkins and seemed untroubled by them.[4] Horses were the best targets for the Muslim archers because they had little protection and even a non-fatal arrow wound caused the animal that had been hit to plunge about desperately in an attempt to dislodge the arrow, panicking other horses nearby and knocking down any man who got in the way. So many horses were killed that their owners were selling the carcases to the sergeants-at-arms, who were butchering them and selling the meat on to the common soldiery. When Richard heard of this, he decreed that any knight *giving* a carcase for the men to consume would have his mount replaced by another of equal worth from his own string of remounts.[5]

Saladin made his next stand 10 miles north of Jaffa, 3 miles inland from the coast, near the sea-cliff fortress of Arsuf (modern Tel Arshuf) and the ruins of the town of Arsuf. His right flank was protected by a forest impenetrable to the crusader cavalry and his left flank by broken ground. Mounted scouts under Henry II of Champagne brought this news to Richard early in the morning of 7 September 1191. He sent heralds along the column, announcing an imminent major engagement. With the marching column looking left, the two armies were in clear view of each other, except that once again the sun was in the crusaders' eyes.

Saladin's plan was the traditional Saracen one of making repeated feigned advances and retreats to provoke the crusaders into breaking ranks and then sending in a massed cavalry charge to exploit the disorder. At about 9 a.m. his infantry began tormenting the crusader infantry screen with a hail of arrows and spears accompanied by psychological warfare, the clashing of brass instruments, the blowing of trumpets and screams of the attackers. At intervals, this was followed up by mounted archers passing through the Saracen infantry to harass the marching column of crusaders before rapidly wheeling away out of range.

As the column continued slowly to move south, some elements found themselves in hand-to-hand combat but Richard forbade any attempt by his cavalry to ride out in response to the Saracen attacks. Discipline was imposed by a mobile 'military police squadron' of knights under Hugues of Burgundy because waiting for the king's command to hit the enemy army when it had exhausted both energy and much weaponry went against the grain for knights who prided themselves on never receiving a blow without immediate retaliation. Having to watch increasing numbers of their horses falling victim to the rain of arrows made them reasonably question further delay that might leave them with too few surviving *destriers* to mount a heavy cavalry charge. Anything less would have been fatal.

After several hours of this, discipline was failing at the rear of the column among the infantry who had to stop, take aim and shoot each time an attack came in from the Saracen right wing that was curled around to attack them from the rear, then hasten to catch up with their comrades. Seeing this, the Hospitaller commander sent a messenger to Richard pleading for permission to go over to the attack. This was refused but, as often in combat, the 'man on the spot' decided to ignore orders from his commander-in-chief who was some distance away and appeared not to comprehend the local situation. When many of Saladin's mounted archers dismounted to step up the pressure on the broken ranks of the crusaders in the rear of the column, Brother Garnier seized the moment of their vulnerability and gave the order for the Hospitaller knights to charge. Whilst rare, this sort of insubordination was usually punished in the religious orders. The Templar commander of the palace at Acre, Jacques de Ravane was not only defrocked, his horse and accoutrement confiscated, he was also placed in irons for leading an unsanctioned and unsuccessful foray against the Muslims between Nazareth and Tiberias.[6] Lesser infringements of the Rule saw Hospitallers punished with *la septaine* or *la quarantaine* – seven or forty days of eating alone and being whipped in front of the other brothers twice weekly.[7]

Hearing the noise of the Hospitallers' charge – the thundering hooves, whinnying of horses and screams of wounded men – Richard realised that the Muslims would surround the knights with Brother Garnier and wipe them out. This was the moment

Saladin had been waiting for, but before the enemy could take advantage of the Hospitallers' impetuosity, Richard took an instant decision. If he threw the rest of his cavalry after the Hospitallers, it could be a fatal mistake, so he despatched the Breton and Angevin knights against Saladin's temporarily weakened right flank and himself led a third charge of the Anglo-Norman knights, wheeling around the right flank of the column and driving deep into the Saracen main force, sowing disorder and panic in its ranks that turned into a rout which not even the arrival in the field of Saladin's own elite mounted bodyguard, distinguished by a yellow silk sash worn over the breastplate, could halt.

The Muslim army broke and fled, pursued by Richard's cavalry, but warily and not too far into the hinterland. By nightfall, the Muslim camp was being looted and Richard's men were inside the fortress of Arsuf, putting all they found to the sword. The chroniclers claimed that 40,000 of the enemy were killed that day, but body counts, even in modern wars, are notoriously unreliable. Nevertheless, Arsuf was indubitably a major victory that cost Saladin dearly. Nor were Richard's losses negligible, however: Saracen scavengers visiting the battlefield after the Christians had moved on counted more than 100 dead Frankish warhorses.[8] Among the crusader dead was Jacques d'Avesnes, whose horse had been killed under him and whose body was said to be surrounded by the corpses of fifteen Saracens he had killed before being hacked to death.[9]

Saladin withdrew after this defeat from Caesarea, Jaffa and Ashkelon, with his garrisons literally demolishing the walls and every building of the fortress-cities before they left. Seeing the desolation of these defenceless cities, Richard rode back to Acre and – in the chroniclers' words – 'overturned the tables of the money-changers' to hire a reported 20,000 more Turcopole mercenaries and lead them south to rebuild the abandoned cities. Saladin had withdrawn inland to demolish Ramlah and continue to Jerusalem, whose defences, damaged during the siege of 1187, urgently needed repair. Had Richard been more flexible at this stage and moved fast, he might have reached Jerusalem and taken the city in a short, sharp attack. However, he was fixated on securing Jaffa first and let the opportunity slip.

In October 1191 morale plummeted in his army as he concentrated on refortifying the walls of Jaffa and the citadel on its hill overlooking the harbour. The arrival both by sea and by land of many of the whores from Acre to cater to the men's sexual needs must have raised a few spirits. This was noted disapprovingly by Muslim observers and Ambroise judged that the customers thereby forfeited the merit of the pilgrimage.[10]

Labouring is a task often imposed on soldiers, but rarely accepted with enthusiasm. While the rank-and-file could be coerced, the knights refused to participate because they considered physical labour beneath them, although on occasion the king himself was to be seen stripped to the waist and labouring among the men to inspire them to greater efforts. Scouting out the enemy on one occasion, Richard's small group was surprised by a squadron of Saracens while they were still asleep and his life was saved by Guillaume des Préaux yelling that he was *malik Rik* and drawing the attackers away after him.[11] It was about this time that al-'Adil, asked by Richard to provide some musical entertainment, arrived not with a young male singer but a woman, who sang and accompanied herself on the *oud* – a forerunner of the European lute, the name of which is probably derived from *al-oud*. Ambroise records that Richard greatly enjoyed the performance, and paid no heed to the general feeling in the army that it was wrong to have personal relationships with individual Saracens – an accusation among many others levelled at him during the captivity in Germany.

Once Jaffa was secured, Richard moved inland on 15 November to Ramlah, in the neighbourhood of which skirmishes were fought on 25 November and 3 December, but no major engagement, Saladin's main force being in Jerusalem. On 8 December, the crusader army retired into winter quarters to get its collective breath back, and Richard spent Christmas at Latrun in the shadow of the Judean hills, not moving against the enemy until 28 December. The crusaders from Europe had perhaps little idea of winter conditions in the Judean mountains, where the author has on occasion been stuck in a long queue of motor vehicles unable to move through thick snow on the outskirts of Jerusalem, but the *poulains* present – Templars, Hospitallers and others – must have warned them. They also warned Richard that in setting out to besiege the Holy City, he risked being caught in a pincer between the garrison and an Egyptian army that was encamped on the hills around the city.[12]

Even at lower altitude climbing up off the coastal plain, the army had to contend with Saladin's scorched earth tactics, leaving them with neither foraging for their animals nor shelter from the weather while fighting off harassing raids in torrential rain that made the muddy ground, churned up by thousands of hooves, into a slippery obstacle course for both foot soldiers and the knights who were obliged to dismount and lead their palfreys as they struggled through the mud. Incessant downpours made the basic rations of biscuit and pork inedible; the loss of many horses from malnutrition and cold made many knights worry that the army would soon be in no condition to advance, let alone attack a city. On 3 January they reached Beit Nuba, which they bowd-lerised to Bêtenoble – or 'noble animal' – some 12 miles from Jerusalem, where the castle built by William of Tyre in 1132 had been reduced to rubble.[13]

Sporadic negotiations in Arabic took place between Al-'Adil and Humphrey of Toron, but there was never any hope that Saladin would give up any more than the narrow strip of the littoral that could be defended by the cities and fortresses already taken and refortified by the crusaders. As the author of *Itinerarium Peregrinorum et Gesta Regis Ricardi* put it:

> For the Templars and the Hospitallers, as well as the *pullani* of that land, looking more acutely at what might happen in the future, dissuaded King Richard from going on to Jerusalem at that time.

> For, if the city were besieged and they pressed their attack with full strength against Saladin and those who were enclosed with him, the army of the Turks which was outside [the city] … would make sudden attacks on the besiegers … [and there would be] forays from those besieged within. Even if they succeeded in their desire and gained the city of Jerusalem … the people who were most keen to complete their pilgrimage would each without delay return home, for they were already wearied beyond measure by the pressures of everything.[14]

Perhaps Richard's most desperate ploy in this time was to offer al-'Adil the hand of his sister Joanna in marriage, with the idea that the couple could be crowned king and queen of Jerusalem, their progeny to found a new dynasty. Failing that, he offered him his niece Eleanor of Brittany, daughter of his brother Geoffrey, and therefore his chattel to dispose of as he wished. One wonders how Pope Celestine III could have given his blessing to either of these solutions. In any case, when Joanna heard of Richard's plan to get himself off the hook by marrying her to a Muslim prince, her rejoinder was a categorical *No!* Throughout all this time, the intrigue between the factions supporting Guy and Conrad continued, as illustrated by the day when Humphrey of Toron, representing Richard and Guy, was conducting talks with the Saracens and was surprised to observe Conrad's envoy Reynald of Sidon and Balian of Ibelin riding out from Jerusalem to go hawking with al-'Adil like the best of friends.[15]

By now there were problems with the remnants of the French contingent, who showed no interest in girding up their loins for an attack on Jerusalem when success would simply mean more kudos for the king of England. Even the locally born nobles and the Hospitallers and Templars, whose whole lives were dedicated to fighting in the Holy Land, had to admit that if they successfully besieged Jerusalem in the spring, they would be unable to hold it, since the slender supply and communication lines from Jaffa could be cut at any moment. It was known that few of the surviving crusaders had any intention of staying in Outremer when their overlords left, which meant that there would not be enough military presence to defend more than the handful of port cities on the coast. This meant in turn that it was out of the question to think of retaking the cordon of castles inland necessary for a defence in depth of the Latin states.

On 13 January 1192 the demoralised army turned tail and headed back to Ibelin. In the milder winter climate of the coastal plain, Richard led the army south to the razed fortress-city of Ashkelon, still an impressive ruin today. Aware of its strategic importance on the route to Egypt, he again incited the rank-and-file to labour on its reconstruction by the sight of their commander stripped off and apparently enjoying the unaccustomed exercise with them. No blandishments, however, nor Richard's bully-boy threats to declare forfeit all Conrad of Montferrat's possessions, could persuade the marquis to join the expedition to Ashkelon. This was probably because he knew from his own sources that the fortress would have to be razed again under the eventual agreement with Saladin – as indeed it was. Of all the energy and lives expended at Ashkelon the only benefit was the discovery of onion-like edible weeds growing in the surrounding countryside, christened shallots or échalottes in a corruption of the city's name and brought back to enrich European cuisine to this day.

With the coming of spring, interest in fighting the Saracens took second place to the renewed internecine dispute between Guy de Lusignan and Conrad of Montferrat over who was the rightful king of Jerusalem. So many of the barons of the Latin states now supported the marquis of Montferrat that Richard had to accept the claim of Conrad, by whom Queen Isabella was pregnant and thus likely soon to present the kingdom with a legitimate heir or heiress. It was to compensate Guy that he sold Cyprus to him for a nominal sum, enabling him to style himself 'king of Cyprus'. Count Henry of Champagne – who was Queen Eleanor's grandson by her Capetian daughter Marie of Champagne and therefore the son of Richard's half-sister – was despatched to Tyre to convey to Conrad of Montferrat the news that he was now the undisputed king of Jerusalem. A few days later, before he had been crowned, Conrad was attacked by two Hashashin and fatally stabbed in a street of Tyre. Conrad's bodyguards killed one of the assassins; the other, under torture, confessed that the murder had been commissioned from his master, known as the Old Man of the Mountains, by none other than the king of England.

This left young Henry of Champagne as the compromise candidate for the throne. Within seven days of the murder, the widowed and pregnant Isabella was forcibly married to him, all of which implies that Conrad was a victim of crusader politics and not killed by Saladin's orders, as was rumoured at the time. History, or at any rate the notoriously insular history taught in Britain, has been unkind to Conrad because he refused to knuckle under to Richard.

The latter, meanwhile, had been receiving, along with shipments of treasure for the campaign, news from the Plantagenet Empire to the effect that Philip's forces were encroaching on to his territory in western France and Prince John was inciting rebellion among the stay-at-home barons in England. However, a more immediate pressure came at a council in Ashkelon on 24 May of the Outremer nobility who were determined to make one last attempt to recover Jerusalem, a project on which Richard could not turn his back. On 7 June the army marched out of Ashkelon, heading north via Ramallah to Qalandiya, from where there was a clear view of the Holy City, only 10 miles distant.

However, too long had been spent in political squabbles and debating the various military possibilities, during which time Saladin's army had had the time to regroup. On 20 June at the wells of Kuwaifa in the barren land south-west of Jerusalem, crusader scouts observed a large Egyptian supply caravan en route to the city. Three days later, Richard attacked. With insufficient armed guards, the caravan was swiftly overcome and many of the

merchants killed, the army returning to Beit Nuba with a false
sense of triumph at the capture of so many supplies and some
thousands of horses and camels.[16] Otherwise, the expedition to
Qalandiya was a failure. On 4 July Richard led the army back
to Ramlah, rendezvousing there with Henry II of Champagne,
styling himself 'king of Jerusalem'. At this point, intelligence
reached them of renewed dissension among the various nation-
alities making up Saladin's garrison there. This seemed to indicate
a fresh opportunity to attack and take the city, but Richard still
held back.

Then, on 31 July came news that Saladin had outflanked the
crusaders by attacking Jaffa and breaking into the lower town.
Richard decided that the best course was not to attack from the
landward side, but to hire a task force of fifty Pisan and Genoese
galleys to transport eighty knights, 400 archers and some 2,000
Italian mercenaries with which to make a swift surprise attack
from the sea while the main army followed the land route to
rendezvous at Jaffa. Approaching land on 1 or 5 August in his
galley painted red with a red awning over the deck and red sails,
he saw Saracen banners fluttering from the ramparts of Jaffa and
despaired – until a courageous priest took the risk of swimming
out to the ships with the news that the survivors of the garrison
had retreated into the citadel, where they were still holding out
while representatives were negotiating with Saladin for a complete surrender.

Calling for a rapid decision and immediate action, this was
possibly Richard's finest hour. Giving the order to take advantage
of the onshore wind to beach the ships, he defied the thin line
of Saracen bowmen between the sea and the citadel by leaping
into the water without even donning his armoured boots and
physically led his knights into the attack under the cover of a
barrage of arrows that drove Saladin's men back from the beach.
Although the sultan tried to continue the negotiations, a sudden
flood of Saracens fleeing the city spoke louder than words and
the Christian spokesmen swiftly disengaged to join in the general

rout of the attackers, who fled en masse 5 miles inland to be safe from pursuit. They were right to flee. During the Muslim occupation of the lower town, all pigs had been slaughtered as unclean and thrown into pits. Richard ordered the Muslim rank-and-file prisoners to be slaughtered also and thrown in with the pig carcases as a final insult to their bodies.[17]

On the following morning Saladin's chancellor Abu-Bakr arrived to negotiate the ransom of noble captives and found the victorious king of England conversing jovially with some important Mamelukes taken prisoner at Acre. Abu-Bakr brought with him a message proposing new terms for a settlement: with Jaffa substantially damaged in the Muslim attack, Saladin considered that it would be acceptable for the crusader frontier to stop at the next city to the north, Kessariya. Without rejecting the offer, Richard said he would then hold Jaffa and Ashkelon as a vassal of Saladin. Not surprisingly, Abu-Bakr rejected this half-baked arrangement, which was bound to fail when Richard returned to Europe, if not before. Abu-Bakr was quite firm that Ashkelon must be given up. Richard refused. Once again, negotiations were broken off.[18]

Realising that the crusader army coming by land was still two or three days' march away, Saladin therefore launched a pre-emptive strike on 5 August, against the small force camped outside the damaged walls of the city. By lucky chance, a Genoese mercenary leaving the camp at dawn to answer a call of nature saw the rising sun reflected off many polished steel spearheads in the distance. The alarm was given. Richard had only fifty-four knights fit to fight, with fifteen horses between them, and the 2,000 mercenaries, whom he disposed in pairs with an archer between each pair, their shields and spears at an angle to impale incoming horses driven into the ground in front of them. In front of these a *frise* of tent pegs was set out to trip the Saracens' horses.

Saladin's cavalry charged in seven waves of 1,000 men, but were driven off each time. This continued for several hours – not continuously, as in a modern mechanised battle, but with intervals for horses and men to get their breath back and regroup, each side trying to grab an advantage by attacking again before the enemy was ready. Some time after noon, sensing that the Saracens were beginning to flag, Richard ordered the greatest barrage of arrows yet full on to an incoming cavalry charge, causing great havoc. At that point, he led the spearmen into the *mêlée*, where his horse was killed under him. Saladin, who was watching on a nearby hill that gave him a good view of the whole battlefield, sent a groom in the next lull, leading two remounts for his enemy. An act of gallantry or a diversion? At the same time he executed a flanking manoeuvre that drove back the Italian mercenaries at the walls, until Richard rode up on his new mount and rallied them.

Wisely, Saladin decided as evening drew on that nothing was to be gained by prolonging the slaughter, and retreated to Jerusalem, leaving Richard master of Jaffa. The Holy City, however, was still in Muslim hands, so the minor victory was irrelevant to the 'liberation' of the city to which Richard never came closer than twice glimpsing its towers in the distance, each time hiding his eyes behind his shield in order not to gaze upon the city he was fated never to capture. Lest that be thought mere play-acting, it must be remembered that one side of his confusing character was seemingly devout, as when he told the abbot of La Sauve Majeure, now an imposing ruin some 12 miles south-east of Bordeaux, that the abbey was 'dearer to me than my own eyeballs'.[19]

## NOTES

1. Ambroise, *Estoire de la guerre sainte*, p. 404.
2. Ibid, p. 399.
3. Benedict of Peterborough, *Gesta Henrici*, Vol 2, pp. 191–2.
4. Quoted in D. Nicolle and C. Hook, *The Third Crusade 1191: Richard the Lionheart, Saladin and the Struggle for Jerusalem* (Botley: Osprey, 2006), p. 59.
5. Ambroise, *Estoire de la guerre sainte*, p. 399.
6. H. de Curzon, *La Règle du Temple* (Paris: Renouard, 1886), rule 610, quoted in Hyland, *The Medieval Warhorse*, p. 159.

7. *The Rule, Statutes and Customs of the Hospitallers 1099–1310*, ed. E.J. King (London: Methuen, 1934), pp. 141, 160.

8. Hyland, p. 162, quoting Beha ed-Din Abu el-Mehasan Yusuf, *Saladin; Or What Befell Sultan Yusuf (Salah Ed-Din) (1137–1193 A.D.)*, Palestine Pilgrims Text Society 13 (London: Billing & Sons, 1897) Part I, p. 395.

9. Ambroise, *Estoire de la guerre sainte*, pp. 404–5.

10. Ibid, p. 408.

11. Ibid, p. 409.

12. Runciman, *A History of the Crusades*, Vol 4, p. 61.

13. For these dates, see Stubbs' footnote to p. 230 of Benedict of Peterborough, *Gesta Henrici*, Vol 2.

14. Benedict of Peterborough, *Gesta Henrici*, Vol 1, p. 70.

15. Runciman, *A History of the Crusades*, Vol 4, p. 63 avers that this was Stephen of Turnham, but he is not known to have spoken Arabic.

16 Runciman, *A History of the Crusades*, Vol 4, p. 68.

17. Ambroise, *Estoire de la guerre sainte*, pp. 228, 413–14.

18. Runciman, *A History of the Crusades*, Vol 4, p. 71.

19. See De la Ville, *La Sauve Majeure*.

# Part 4:

# Riding to a Fall

# The Cost of an Insult

Shortly after the battle, Richard fell ill with fever yet again. After an embassy from Saladin repeated the former offer of terms, he countered with a letter to the man he called 'my brother' – al-'Adil – pleading for his intercession so that Ashkelon might remain in crusader hands. Nothing came of this, partly because al-'Adil was also ill with fever somewhere outside Jerusalem. With his customary gallantry, Saladin sent fresh fruit and baskets containing snow from Mount Hermon to cool Richard's drinks, but would not yield over Ashkelon. Behind the pleasant gesture of respect for a worthy enemy was, as so often in warfare, the quest for intelligence. On this occasion, Saladin's gift-bearer returned to Jerusalem with the news that Jaffa was garrisoned by only 300 knights who were, it was subsequently learned, mostly mounted on mules, their highly trained *destriers* having long since succumbed to the climate, tick bites and disease.[1]

To Richard, the loss of Ashkelon seemed intolerable, for had he not personally laboured on the reconstruction of the walls there? Yet, among the *poulains* even the most fanatical Templars and Hospitallers had come to accept that his political and military problems at home demanded an early return. And what use was it, they asked, to have Ashkelon after Richard's army departed?

There would simply not be sufficient Christian knights in Outremer to hold one more fortress.

Richard had boasted that victory would be his within twenty days of Christmas 1191. It was not until 28 August 1192 that an emissary brought Saladin's final offer, which was enshrined in a treaty signed on 2 September 1192. The treaty declared Richard and Saladin to be allies, neither to raise the sword against the other for a period of three years, three months and three days.[2] As a monarch, Richard refused to swear to uphold the treaty, but ordered Henry of Champagne, Balian of Ibelin and the Templar and Hospitaller masters to swear on his behalf. After Saladin put his name to the treaty the following day, the Third Crusade was formally ended – with victory, in the shape of the Holy City, firmly in Saracen hands.

The terms allowed the Christians to keep the coastal strip, leaving Saladin to control the hinterland, with permission for unarmed travellers to pass through both Christian and Muslim territory and for pilgrims of any confession to travel to and from the holy places. A condition was that Ashkelon's newly rebuilt walls be razed to the ground, as well as the castle at Daron, so large that it was described as having seventeen towers, which threatened the main land routes between Egypt and Syria, essential to Saladin's dual realm both for political reasons and trade.[3]

Richard's prestige was at low ebb. He was widely suspected by the nobility of Outremer of Conrad's murder and despised by the more bellicose knights and barons for not making one last attempt to take Jerusalem. Perhaps, as so often in similar circumstances, some of them dreamed of 'a glorious death'. The works of the Roman poet Horace were well known in twelfth-century Europe, so many would have been able to quote his *dulce et decorum est pro patria mori* and, if it were sweet and proper to die for one's country, how much more so for a Christian knight to 'die for Jesus'?

Despite Saladin's gracious invitation for Richard to visit Jerusalem as his personal guest, the king of England considered that his crusading oath made it impossible for him to go there other than as liberator of the Holy City – a prospect that was now beyond the realms of possibility. The more important pilgrims who had no such inhibition were greeted personally by Saladin and invited to be his guests at table, the traditional sign of a Muslim lord's protection. Bishop Hubert Walter of Salisbury, who had replaced the dead Archbishop Baldwin of Canterbury as chief chaplain to the army and the principal negotiator with Saladin, and who had ably but hopelessly pressed the Christian claims in negotiation, went with Ambroise in one party of pilgrims. Received by Saladin, they discussed the absent king of England, dutifully praised by Hubert Walter but considered by Saladin to be lacking wisdom and moderation.[4]

On their return to Richard, the bishop and the poet described to their master how they had gazed with tears upon the hill of Calvary, the tomb of the Virgin and the Church of the Holy Sepulchre, restored by Saladin to the Syrian priests. These sites, some of them disputed, had been approved by the Emperor Constantine's mother St Helena when she visited Jerusalem in search of relics to bring back to Constantinople during the fourth century.

With the arrival of the prior of Hereford, new intelligence reached Richard of Prince John's plundering of the treasury and plotting with Philip Augustus' support to gain the throne of England. In France, the unrest stirred up by John and Philip had spread as far as Toulouse and caused Seneschal Bertin of Aquitaine to invade Toulousain territory with Richard's nephew Otto of Brunswick and Prince Sancho of Navarre, brother of Queen Berengaria. Their combined forces captured castles and towns, camping briefly just out of bowshot from the walls of Toulouse before heading north and west to 'pacify' the Auvergne and Angoulême.[5]

Finally, Richard could not pretend that he was accomplishing anything in Outremer. Ten days after despatching Joanna and Berengaria to reach Sicily before the winter storms, at nightfall on 9 October the king who had arrived with a fleet of 200 ships boarded a lone galley, having insulted so many of his allies that he had to beg a bodyguard of Templars to accompany him in return for the Saladin tithe that Henry had paid to the order. There are several partial accounts by the chroniclers of the mysterious return journey that was to cost Richard's subjects so dearly. In some it was alleged that Richard disguised himself as a Templar knight. According to Ralph of Coggeshall, Richard's chaplain Anselm said later that they set out for Marseilles with Baldwin of Béthune and the Templars. After stopping in Cyprus for a few days, Corfu was reached three weeks after leaving Acre.[6] Across the strait lay the friendly Norman port of Brindisi and the shortest overland route home, but this lay across territories of the German Emperor Henry Hohenstaufen, from whom no safe conduct was forthcoming for the king who had alienated him both by the treaty he had signed with Tancred in Messina and by the insult to his vassal Leopold of Austria at Acre.

As the autumn of 1192 became winter, the trickle of crusaders returning to Europe became a flood. From them, Eleanor heard tales of Richard's great valour in Outremer, mixed with accusatory alibis that only the machinations of the Franks and Germans and in-country factions had prevented the lionhearted king of England from triumphing over Saladin. But she was not fooled, having heard similar alibis after the undeniable failure of the Second Crusade that she had personally witnessed fifty years before. But where, she asked, was her son? No one had an answer. He was known to have left the Holy Land in a fast galley that should have overtaken the round ships transporting lesser travellers. After last being sighted making for Brindisi, all was mystery.[7]

On land, other crusaders had travelled by whatever means of fortune they could find. Able to purchase the best horses available, Richard should have made far better time. Yet Joanna and Berengaria's households waited in vain for him to join them in Rome and share what could have been spun into a triumphal return for the heroic king of England. The legal nicety that her constitutional status was undefined did not prevent Eleanor doing her best for him in the hope that he was still alive, so she returned to England to keep a beady eye on bishops Walter of Rouen and Hugh of Durham and the other justiciars, all the while aware that Prince John's partisans were not alone in spreading rumours of their king's death.

At Brindisi Richard had decided to avoid travelling the length of Italy, which entailed many miles across Hohenstaufen territory, by sailing on to make landfall in southern France. Putting in to an Italian harbour that may have been Pisa,[8] he learned that in avoiding one enemy, he was sailing into the trap set by another because his arrogance had made him the most hated man in Europe. To avenge himself on Richard for the invasion of 1187 and the more recent humiliation suffered at the hands of Richard's nephew Otto, Count Raymond of Toulouse, in concert with Philip Augustus, was defying the Peace of God by setting ambushes all along the French Mediterranean littoral. The alternative of landing on what is now the Costa Brava and gaining Aquitaine via Navarre meant first crossing the kingdom of Aragon – forbidden territory to the son-in-law of Sancho the Wise of Navarre. Richard therefore back-tracked all the way down the coast of Italy to Corfu, where he hired two Romanian pirate galleys for 200 silver marks to escort him northwards up the Adriatic.[9]

All three vessels were stranded by a storm on the coast of Istria, near modern Trieste, in territory held by vassals of Leopold of Austria. As returning crusaders, the small party – Richard, now posing as a merchant, with his chaplain Anselm, his clerk Philip, Baldwin of Béthune and the Templars – asked the local overlord Count Meinhard II of Görz for safe conducts under the Peace of God.[10] Most unwisely, Richard gave to the messenger a valuable ruby ring he had purchased in Outremer to use as a bribe. Meinhard was suspicious that a returning merchant should have so valuable a jewel but issued the safe conduct, at the same time advising his brother Frederik of Betestowe, through whose lands the travellers would have to pass next, to gather a sufficient force to arrest the group while on his territory.

Having in his employ a Norman named Roger who came
originally from Argentan, Frederik chose him to scout round
all the likely hostels and hospices in the area, promising a very
rich reward if he should track down Richard's party. Roger duly
did so. At first, Richard denied being the king, but then admitted his true identity, begging Roger, whose Norman French
betrayed his origins, to be merciful. To the surprise of the king's
party, this émigré Norman refused to betray the son of Henry
II, his erstwhile liege as duke of Normandy. Instead, he procured
fresh horses for the party to hasten on their way, and went back
to tell Frederik of Betestowe that the leader of the travellers
was Baldwin of Béthune. Frederik, however, had kept Roger
under surveillance, and set an ambush, which seized Baldwin
and some of the others, mistaking him for the king.[11] In later
ambushes Richard abandoned eight, and then six more, of his
Templar bodyguard. Still posing as a rich merchant, he continued with the reduced entourage, riding their horses into the
ground before replacing them en route until they took refuge
in a squalid tavern in the village of Ganina on the Danube, not
far from Vienna and roughly 200 miles from where they had
been shipwrecked.

It was a mammoth ride, worthy of Henry II at his best, but
Richard was ill with malaria and unable to ride on. Somewhere
along the way, he had picked up a German-speaking youth who
was sent into the marketplace to buy provisions, and there tried
to change a handful of gold *bezants* for the local currency and
succeeded only in unleashing a torrent of questions about the
mysterious group of foreign knights. Hastening back to the
tavern, the understandably alarmed youth tried to rouse Richard
and make him depart immediately, but found him too weak to
rise from his bed. Each day, the youth went back into the market
for more luxury provisions, arousing increasing curiosity about
his employer. There are several versions claiming to be the true
account of Richard's undoing, but it seems that disaster struck on
21 December, when the lad carelessly went out with a pair of the

king's monogrammed gloves stuck into his belt. Arrested, he was tortured by men who threatened to cut out his tongue if he did not tell the truth.

Still too weak from the malaria to mount a horse and flee yet again when the youth did not return, Richard was alarmed when the tavern was surrounded by a hostile crowd and men-at-arms. Discarding the disguise of the rich merchant, he endeavoured to disguise himself as a scullion, turning the spit on which a brace of spatchcocks was roasting. Sick he might be, but he still refused to surrender until Duke Leopold left his Christmas court in Vienna to accept Richard's sword and order his old enemy nursed back to health, well guarded, in the castle of Dürnstein on the banks of the Danube to the west of Vienna, intending to demand a ransom of 150,000 marks.[12]

Some news travelled fast, even then. Before the celebration of Twelfth Night, Eleanor learned that Philip Augustus had received a letter from Henry Hohenstaufen, according to which her son was a prisoner of the duke of Austria, whom he had so atrociously insulted at Acre. The letter ended:

> … inasmuch as he is now within our power, and has always done his utmost for your annoyance and disturbance … we have thought proper to notify your nobleness … knowing that the same is well pleasing to [you].[13]

Immediately Eleanor charged the abbots of Boxley in Kent and Robertsbridge in Sussex to travel to the Hohenstaufen court and ascertain where exactly Richard was being held and what were the terms for his release. On the same mission went Bishop Savaric of Bath, who was related to the emperor. En route between Rome and England, Bishop Hubert Walter changed course and also headed eastwards.[14] That indefatigable opportunist William Longchamp, who claimed to have seen the original letter at Philip's court in Paris, scuttled after them to see what he could find out.

Refraining from taking ship for Germany herself because she did not trust Prince John and Philip Augustus once her back was turned, Eleanor wrote to remind Celestine III that both Richard and his father had supported him when the pope was still a cardinal, and requested his help in the cause of a returning crusader who had been arrested in defiance of the Peace of God. That she was right to leave the on-the-ground quest to the bishops was proven when John sneaked across the Channel and demanded the fealty of the barons who held property in Normandy, arguing that Philip was their common overlord, and that Richard was as good as dead already.[15]

*Treason doth never prosper: what's the reason? For if it prosper, none dare call it treason.* Four centuries were to elapse before Sir John Harington penned this epigram, but Seneca had said more or less the same thing: *prosperum ac felix scelus virtus vocatur* – the favourable and fruitful crime is called virtue. The dilemma of the Anglo-Norman nobility on both sides of the Channel was as old as Babylon: if Richard were succeeded by John after dying in captivity, who would then be considered loyal by the new king, and who a traitor?

However, their reaction being a resounding vote of no-confidence in him, Prince John abandoned his court in Alençon and fled to the safety of Paris, where Philip Augustus humoured his pretensions to be duke of Normandy in return for an undertaking to marry Alais, still a prisoner in Rouen, after he had divorced his wife of three years, Isabelle of Gloucester, on the grounds of their widely known consanguinity.[16]

Deciding that this was a propitious moment to invade the Vexin, Philip took the castle of Gisors and demanded the surrender of Rouen and the release of his half-sister.[17] Unimpressed by the numbers and equipment of the small Frankish force, the earl of Leicester retorted from within the city that he had no orders from King Richard to hand over his hostage, but if the king of the Franks wished to sample Norman hospitality, he only had to cross the drawbridge alone. With no intention of being taken hostage and traded for Richard, Philip swore to exact revenge for this insult[18] and provided Prince John with the funds to hire a small army of Flemish mercenaries with whom to invade England at the end of Lent.

Eleanor's solution was not to pursue John, which might provoke open conflict with his supporters, but to order Crown officers in the English Channel ports – reinforced by a *fyrd* of local men who had good reason to remember the depredations of King Stephen's Flemings in south-east England – to arrest any of those mercenaries who set foot ashore and frighten the others away back to Flanders.[19]

During all this to-ing and fro-ing a political tug-of-war erupted in the Holy Roman Empire over who should hold the royal prisoner. Duke Leopold claimed the right both because it was he who had been insulted at Acre and who had taken Richard's sword. As his suzerain, the emperor reminded him that 'duke of Austria' was a courtesy title for a vassal whose true rank was that of count; for a count to hold a king prisoner was contrary to feudal custom, and therefore Richard must be handed over to him.[20] At a meeting in Würzburg during February 1193, Leopold and the emperor came to terms. Reducing his sights more than somewhat, the insulted duke of Austria accepted the promise of 20,000 marks from the eventual ransom in return for transferring his prisoner from Dürnstein into imperial custody at Ratisbon (modern Regensburg) and then Würzburg.

Less than three months after the emperor's letter had been received in Paris – on Palm Sunday 21 March 1193 – Eleanor's emissaries tracked Richard down at Ochsenfurt, on his way under escort to the emperor's Easter court at Speier (modern Speyer). Either Longchamp beat them to it or he arrived soon afterwards[21] to find Richard apparently in good health and high spirits, popular with his guards and their masters and assuming that, like any knight captured in a *mêlée*, he would shortly be ransomed for a sum commensurate with his high rank.

When given the news of Prince John's latest treason, he refused to take seriously the idea of his weakling younger brother usurping the throne, with or without Philip's help, and despatched Hubert Walter back to England with a handwritten letter, from which Eleanor learned on 20 April that her adored favourite son was alive and in good health. A second letter conferred on Hubert Walter the office of archbishop of Canterbury.

Gossip at the imperial court was that a sum of 100,000 marks would be demanded for Richard's ransom, but the royal prisoner had not been accorded an interview with the emperor to confirm this. Back in England, the population rejoiced that the king was not dead and the nobility had a second reason to celebrate on learning that Hubert Walter, and not William Longchamp, was the new primate of England. While Eleanor and the justiciars waited for confirmation of the ransom amount, they used the news that Richard was definitely alive to abate the unrest among the nobility that John had stirred up. Eleanor's constitutionally ambiguous position made her the ideal intermediary in this. John might have refused to surrender his castles peacefully to the justiciars, but agreed to hand over to her the castles at Windsor, Wallingford and the Peak – on the understanding that they were to be returned to him if Richard were not, for whatever reason, released.

At Speier, Emperor Henry Hohenstaufen was less impressed by Richard's Poitevin eloquence than his previous captors had been.[22] Before his principal vassals assembled for his Easter court, he charged Richard with a long list of crimes, including the murder of Conrad of Montferrat, who had been a close relative of Duke Leopold. Richard's entourage at the hearing consisted of Bishop Savaric of Bath, the abbots of Boxley and Robertsbridge, plus his chaplain and Longchamp. His competence in Latin had enabled him on more than one occasion to mock Hubert Walter, who was famous for his frequent grammatical errors in that language.[23] At the hearing, Richard did not use the bishops as spokesmen, but eloquently put his own case as being the epitome of knighthood on the greatest of all chivalric enterprises.

Many of Hohenstaufen's vassals were moved by this address,[24] and all the more impressed when, at the end of the speech, the king of England knelt in submission before the emperor and burst into tears – it was a habit of his at such moments. Bowing to the general mood, Henry Hohenstaufen raised his prisoner to his feet and led him to share the dais.

*Noblesse oblige*, but money was still money. The sum of 100,000 silver marks or £66,000 was now agreed as the price of Richard's freedom, with him to be released when 70,000 marks had been paid, with 200 nobles to be sent to Germany as hostages in surety for the balance. This global sum covered retribution for the failure of Richard's brother-in-law Henry the Lion of Saxony to support the imperial design and the compensation for the insult suffered by Leopold, which would provide a handsome dower on the marriage of his son to a bride who was a part of the price. She was to be Richard's niece Eleanor of Brittany, whom he had already offered to Al-'Adil after Joanna's refusal to marry him.[25] In addition, Hohenstaufen's relative Isaac Comnenus was to be released from captivity and his daughter, who had accompanied Joanna and Berengaria to Rome, was to be restored to him. Lastly, in compensation for the Treaty of Messina having prejudiced the Empress Constance's rights to Sicily, fifty galleys and 200 knights were to be furnished from Richard's domains for Hohenstaufen's war with Tancred.

On the day before Good Friday, Richard's chaplain departed for England with the ransom demand and a letter from Richard to Eleanor informing her that Longchamp had stage-managed the all-important interview with the emperor and that she should oversee collection of the ransom, noting carefully how much each baron contributed, so that Richard would know how much gratitude he owed each vassal, or otherwise. If they wished to continue in office, the justiciars were to give a good example by their own generosity.

To prevent his golden tongue gaining him too many supporters, the emperor placed his VIP prisoner in close confinement at the treasure fortress of Trifels for the first three weeks of April until Longchamp succeeded in obtaining his removal to more relaxed surroundings at Hagenau. He then departed with his master's blessing for England, to assemble the hostages who would be held surety.

Eleanor wasted no time in appointing five assessors to oversee the ransom collection from the kingdom already impoverished by Henry's Saladin tithe and Richard's crusading taxes.[26] They were Hubert Walter, formally installed as archbishop of Canterbury on 30 May 1193, Bishop Richard of London, the earl of Arundel, the earl of Surrey and Henry fitz Ailwin, the first mayor of London, from whom the citizens learned there was a price to pay for their enfranchisement: like the barons, they were to shell out a quarter of their annual rents and revenues. In the lesser nobility, each knight saw his fee assessed at 20 shillings, which was a considerable sum for many of them.

Hubert Walter informed the bishops of the realm that they were responsible for collecting the tax from the clergy in their dioceses, with priests who lived on tithes required to contribute a tenth of their income. The canons of Geoffrey the Bastard's cathedral at York refused to pay a quarter of their wealth, despite every abbey and cathedral being forced to empty its treasury of jewels and gold – in return for which promissory notes were given, payable after the king's return. The abbeys of the Gilbertians and St Bernard's Cistercians, who followed a rule of poverty, were obliged to give a whole year's clip of wool from their flocks.[27]

Even had he known the details, Richard would have been untroubled, assuming that it was the duty of his subjects to cough up whatever sum was demanded in the same way that knights defeated in tournaments were ransomed. He was overlooking the fact that this unjust practice had been made illegal by his father in 1177, since when the captured knight had had to find his own ransom. With spring giving way to summer, Richard was moved to Hagenau and treated more as guest than prisoner at the emperor's Pentecost court there. Sharing something of his prisoner's musical talent, Hohenstaufen even indulged him in some of the poetry contests that Richard had enjoyed in his youth at Eleanor's court in Poitiers.

The constant stream of prelates passing between the Plantagenet possessions on both sides of the Channel and Richard's various places of detention in Germany had given him more 'the prestige of an imperial statesman … than the forlorn dignity of a suppliant' in the eyes of the German nobility.[28] In consequence, the emperor's plan to conspire with Philip Augustus in June 1193 was therefore put on hold. Incensed by Hohenstaufen's failure to consult him since the original letter, Philip wanted to share in the ransom as compensation for the insults that he too had suffered at Richard's hands during the crusade. As a gesture, he offered the archbishop of Reims as mediator in the current dispute between Henry Hohenstaufen and his disaffected bishops, but on condition that Richard stayed right where he was. Meeting Philip at midsummer in Lotharingen (now Lorraine), the emperor weighed in the balance a better relationship with his neighbour the king of the Franks against the money represented by the ransom.[29]

Hoping to speed up his liberation, Richard was allowed to write to all and sundry, his captors having no objection if it would help to raise the ransom. Nor did they prevent the armour Richard had worn in the Holy Land from being taken by Stephen of Turnham to London for exhibition as an eloquent reproach to his subjects who had not yet paid their share.[30] No letter was sent to Berengaria, but Eleanor was greeted as 'dear mother' and also formally as 'by the Grace of God, queen of the English'. He even wrote to the Old Man of the Mountains in faraway Syria, requesting him as chief of the sect of the Assassins to confirm that it was not the king of England who had commanded the killing of Conrad of Montferrat.[31] Predictably, a mysterious reply was received, which Richard waved before the emperor, claiming complete exoneration on that charge. Whether or not the reply was genuine, other news did arrive from the Middle East. Saladin had died on 2 March 1193 at his home in Damascus aged only 55, his health broken by recurrent malaria. The efforts of the most famous doctor of the time, Musa ibn Maymun, also known as Maimonides, had failed to save his life.

In England, the ransom trickled in, slowed by the corruption of the unsupervised collectors working outside the normal Exchequer system, many of whom were afterwards accused of lining their own pockets. As and when each bullion train arrived in London, the gold and silver and precious objects were locked away in St Paul's Cathedral under heavy guard, in sacks sealed with Eleanor's own seal and that of Archbishop Hubert Walter. The first levies having proven insufficient, she ordered a second, and then a third, lambasting the tardy and the niggardly. Nor was it any easier to milk the impoverished continental possessions. Her sometime secretary Peter of Blois wrote to his friend the bishop of Mayence (modern Mainz) that:

> … the ransom would not be drawn from the royal Exchequer, but from … the pitiful substance of the poor, the tears of widows, the pittance of monks and nuns, the dowries of maidens, the substance of scholars, the spoils of the Church.[32]

An even more unpopular task was the selection of hostages to serve as surety until the entire ransom had been paid. Longchamp returned from Hagenau not as chancellor and justiciar, but as bishop of Ely and therefore a loyal servant of the Crown, whose duty was to agree with Eleanor the selection of the noble hostages. To her agile mind, this became a threat that could be used to scare families which had not declared their true wealth, for the less the amount raised, the greater the number of hostages who would have to be sent to Germany. While drawing up the list of hostages with Longchamp at St Albans – the citizens of London refused him access to the city – she excluded her own grandson William of Winchester, son of Matilda and Henry the Lion, for the same reason that many other noble families baulked at sending their sons. Since the pederast bishop of Ely was not a fit person to have the care of boys, they sent their daughters instead.

During all this time Queen Eleanor also had to keep her eye on Prince John, who was forbidden to leave England and had all his incoming mail from Paris intercepted. She was also haranguing the pope at a distance for what she considered his less than enthusiastic support. Her secretary Peter of Blois, now archdeacon of Bath, was famous for witty puns and epigrams. In accusing Celestine III of keeping the sword of St Peter in its sheath and failing, despite three requests, to send papal intermediaries to Germany in support of a wronged crusader, he punned that the papal legates had been *potius ligati quam legati* – they had been leashed rather than loosed upon the emperor.

Complaining that, if her son had been rich, prelates would have come running to be rewarded by his generosity, Eleanor signed herself not *Alianor regina gratia dei* – queen by the Grace of God – but *regina angliorum ira dei* – queen of the English by God's anger. As duchess of Aquitaine, she was also not above including a thinly veiled hint that the Cathar heresy so widespread in the south of France would be allowed to flourish in the duchy unchecked if the papacy did not do something to earn her gratitude.[33]

What more could the pope do? He had excommunicated Duke Leopold for laying hands on a crusader and threatened Philip Augustus with excommunication under the Peace of God for taking advantage of Richard's captivity. He had even waved the threat of interdict over England, should the ransom not be forthcoming. With vast Church possessions in Germany at risk of seizure by Henry Hohenstaufen, who also had large forces stationed on the Italian Peninsula, Celestine could not force the emperor to do anything.

In midsummer of 1193, Richard was moved yet again, to Worms on the Rhine, where his charm earned him the liberty to have his falconer and favourite birds sent out from England, with a consignment of clothes and utensils for his personal use. At a five-day plenary court, the emperor weighed all the

possibilities in the light of Philip's representations before confirming that the royal prisoner would be released against the
sureties when two-thirds of the ransom had arrived safely in
Germany. The bad news was that the amount had now been
increased by 50 per cent – the extra 50,000 marks being in
lieu of Richard's military help in the campaign against his
ally Tancred. The number of hostages to be supplied was also
increased accordingly.

Henry Hohenstaufen seems to have been in two minds about
Richard's claim that he had persuaded the German bishops to
end their long dispute with their emperor, but the change of epis-
copal policy was due to Celestine's urgings. However, Richard
was responsible for a reconciliation between the houses of
Hohenstaufen and Saxony. As a result, Henry the Lion mediated
between Richard and the emperor in some way unclear to the
chroniclers, and was offered Hohenstaufen's cousin Constance
as bride for his son Otto, who was a nephew of the royal captive, to cement the new *rapprochement*. The lady in question had
already been offered to Philip Augustus who, after years of widowhood, had arranged to marry Princess Ingeborg, the sister of
King Knut of Denmark, while allying himself with the Danes
against England.

It was probably at Worms, during another five-day plenary
session of the imperial court, that Richard composed a *sirventès*
addressed to his half-sister Marie de Champagne, expressing his
impatience with the pace at which his subjects were getting the
money together:

> Ja nuls hom pres non dira sa razon
> adrechament, si com hom dolens non
> mas per confort deu hom faire canson.
> Pro n'ay d'amis, mas paure son li don.
> Ancta lur es, si per ma resenzon
> soi sai dos yvers pres.

[No prisoner can put his case for long / without self-pity making it
sound wrong / but still for comfort he can pen a song. / My many
friends offer little, I hear. / Shame on them all if they leave me here /
unransomed for a second long year.]

On 20 December the emperor wrote to the magnates of England:

Henry, by the grace of God, emperor of the Romans, and ever
august, to his dearly beloved friends, the archbishops, earls, barons,
knights, and all the faithful subjects of Richard, illustrious king of
England, his favour and every blessing. We have thought proper to
intimate to all and every one of you that we have appointed a certain day for the liberation of our dearly beloved friend, your lord
Richard, the illustrious king of the English, being the second day
of the week next ensuing after the expiration of three weeks from
the day of the nativity of Our Lord, at Speier or else at Worms, and
we have appointed seven days after that as the day of his coronation as king of Provence, which we have promised him; and this
you are to consider certain and undoubted. For it is our purpose
and our will to exalt and most highly honour your aforesaid lord,
as being our special friend. Given at Thealluse on the vigil of
St Thomas the Apostle.[34]

Provence, although lying within modern France, was then
German territory under Hohenstaufen, with the Catalan Count
Alfonso II as its titular ruler. The province had not had a king since
the year 933, so presumably the title to be conferred on Richard
was a courtesy only. The important thing in Hohenstaufen's letter
was that it translated as setting 17 January 1194 as the date for
Richard's release.

## NOTES

1. Hyland, *The Medieval Warhorse*, p. 148.
2. Runciman says five years.

3. R. Ellenblum, *Crusader Castles and Modern Histories* (Cambridge: Cambridge University Press, 2009, p. 180.

4. Runciman, *A History of the Crusades*, Vol 4, p. 73.

5. A. Richard, *Histoire*, Vol 2, p. 280.

6. Ralph of Diceto, *Opera Historica*, Vol 2, p. 106.

7. Roger of Howden, *Chronica*, Vol 3, p. 194.

8. Benedict of Peterborough, *Gesta Henrici*, Vol 2, p. 221.

9. Roger of Howden, *Chronica*, Vol 3, p. 185.

10. Ralph of Coggeshall, *Chronicon Anglicanum*, ed. J. Stevenson, Rolls Series No 66 (London: Longmans, 1875), p. 54.

11. Ibid, pp. 54–5.

12. Ibid, p. 56.

13. Roger of Howden, *Chronica*, Vol 3, p. 195.

14. Ibid, pp. 196, 198; William of Newburgh, *Historia Rerum Anglicarum*, Vol I, p. 388.

15. Roger of Howden, *Chronica*, Vol 3, p. 204.

16. Stubbs, *Gervase of Canterbury*, Vol I, pp. 514–15.

17. Benedict of Peterborough, *Gesta Henrici*, Vol 2, p. 236.

18. Roger of Howden, *Chronica*, Vol 3, p. 207.

19. Stubbs, *Gervase of Canterbury*, Vol I, pp. 514–15.

20. William of Newburgh, *Historia Rerum Anglicarum*, Vol I, pp. 286–7.

21. Roger of Howden, *Chronica*, Vol 3, p. 198.

22. Ibid, p. 199.

23. Bartlett, *England under the Norman and Angevin Kings*, p. 485.

24. William of Newburgh, *Historia Rerum Anglicarum*, Vol I, p. 388.

25. Roger of Howden, *Chronica*, Vol 2, pp. 214–15.

26. Roger of Howden, *Chronica*, Vol 3, p. 210.

27. Stubbs, *Gervase of Canterbury*, Vol 2, p. 110.

28. M. Powicke, *The Loss of Normandy* (Manchester: Manchester University Press, 1999), p. 93.

29. Kelly, *Eleanor of Aquitaine*, p. 307.

30. Roger of Howden, *Chronica*, Vol 2, p. 288.

31. Roger of Howden, *Chronica*, Vol 2, p. 127.

32. Peter of Blois, *Epistolae* in Patrologia Latina Vol 207, ed. J.-P. Migne (Paris: Garnier, 1890), Vol 207, Col 341.

33. A. Richard, *Histoire*, Vol 2, p. 283.

34. Kelly, *Eleanor of Aquitaine*, pp. 314–15, quoting Roger of Howden, *Chronica*, Vol 3, p. 227.

# 19

# Richard and Robin Hood? Maybe

On 6 January 1194 there arrived in Cologne a considerable host of Richard's religious and lay vassals, some of them designated as hostages to remain in Germany until the ransom was paid in full, plus the armed guards for the chests of treasure, those nobles who were to attend Richard at the coronation and the usual household of chaplains, clerks, stewards, grooms, squires and cooks. Archbishop Walter of Rouen and Eleanor accompanied the vast treasure to Germany in order to record in person the delivery of the treasure and ensure that the first selected hostages were handed over in return. Ever one to dress up for a special occasion, Richard had also charged them to bring along his royal regalia with a suitable retinue to impress the emperor's court.

Before leaving England, Eleanor appointed Archbishop Hubert Walter chief justiciar on Richard's instructions, which made him effectively the regent in her absence or, should anything happen to her, until the king should return. On 17 January at Speier she was informed that her son's release was to be delayed because an alternative offer had been received from Philip Augustus at a meeting with the emperor in Vaucouleurs, where he had bid 50,000 marks, plus 30,000 marks from Prince John, if Richard were kept prisoner until Michaelmas – by which time they hoped to have taken control of the continental Plantagenet possessions. Alternatively, they offered monthly instalments of £1,000 so long as Richard was held captive in Germany. On learning of this treason, the Great Council of England deprived John of all his English possessions, in addition to which he and his chief partisans were excommunicated. Under Hubert Walter's guidance, the council also denounced Longchamp to the pope in a letter heavy with all their seals, which was to be shown first to Richard in Germany so that he would know what they thought of his ex-chancellor.

At Mainz on 2 February 1194, Eleanor's joy at seeing her son for the first time in three and a half years was tempered by an unpleasant surprise: Philip had raised the French offer to 100,000 marks, with another 50,000 from John, if Richard were handed over to them or held in Germany for another year. This was equivalent to the whole ransom from England.[1]

Seeking a counter-counter-offer, the emperor showed the letter from Paris to Eleanor and to Richard. Whatever the barons and bishops of England thought of William Longchamp, he was still an able advocate when addressing the imperial court at the castle of Mayence in Eleanor's presence that day. His argument was simple, but to the point: Philip and John had no chance of amassing the colossal sums being bandied about, and which totalled many times the annual taxation income of the whole of France, even if they did manage to conquer and plunder Normandy and the other Plantagenet possessions. Their offer was therefore invalid, whereas Richard's vastly greater territory could certainly assemble the agreed ransom.

The political complication for Henry Hohenstaufen was that in allowing Richard to walk free he would lose French support in the dispute with his bishops. The *quid pro quo* was that Richard pay homage, admitting that he held England as a vassal of the emperor.[2] Eleanor's retinue may have been horrified, but to her flexible mind, it mattered little if Richard thus denied his feudal allegiance to the House of Capet, which, in the person of Philip Augustus, had shown itself to be unworthy of it, and doffed his bonnet to place it in the emperor's hands, signifying that he was henceforth a vassal of the House of Hohenstaufen. As to the annual tribute of £5,000 demanded by the emperor, what was a promise like that worth in the mouth of a son of Henry of Anjou?

After swearing fealty to Henry and declaring with his customary eloquence that he held his possessions on both sides of the Channel as a vassal of the emperor, Richard was at last released on 4 February after agreeing to one last requirement: that the archbishop of Rouen, who had played a leading part in the negotiations, should be left behind as a hostage.

Philip managed to get a message to Prince John in England, warning him, 'The devil has broken his chains.' Terrified, John fled the country and took refuge in Paris.[3] Given the widespread unrest and disaffection in England during the Third Crusade and the long captivity in Germany, one would think that Richard would hurry home to punish those who had committed treason. Was it Eleanor's influence that persuaded him to take the leisurely but statesmanlike route they followed, spending a weekend as guests of the bishop of Cologne and stopping in Brussels and other cities to make alliances that might one day be useful on this, the eastern flank of Philip's realm? Six weeks after leaving Mayence, they were guests of the duke of Louvain in his castle at Antwerp, and may have been feeling a certain uneasiness at spending so long on Hohenstaufen territory.

In the port of Antwerp, the faithful Stephen of Turnham welcomed Eleanor and the king aboard the *Trenchemer*. It is unlikely that this was the same vessel that had taken part in the naval action off Tyre, and there was a shipmaster in Richard's service named Alan Trenchemer, so this might be the name not of the vessel but of its master. From this they trans-shipped to a larger vessel at the mouth of the Schelde for safety during the night and then moved back to the swifter *Trenchemer* for the Channel crossing the next day.[4] In case Philip had set naval patrols to intercept the royal party, they weighed anchor in the evening under cover of darkness. With 100 miles to row – possibly with a following wind and favourable tides – they are reported as landing at Sandwich 'at the ninth hour of the day' – meaning after noon – on 12 March. Six weeks after leaving Speyer, they rode 12 miles to give thanks at Becket's tomb in Canterbury Cathedral. Somewhere near Rochester, Archbishop Hubert Walter met the royal party and dismounted to kneel before the king. Richard too dismounted, knelt and embraced his fellow crusader with tears in his eyes, showing more emotion and gratitude than to all his other subjects. That night was spent in the keep of Rochester Castle, which still stands, bleak and grim beside the cathedral.

The news of Richard's return had preceded them, giving the citizens of London time to deck with banners and bunting the city that had contributed a sizeable share of the ransom. To the ringing of all the bells within the walls, Richard was led in procession to St Paul's, now emptied of the treasure hoard. Agents of Henry Hohenstaufen present to oversee payment of the balance outstanding had expected to find a country on its knees after all the exactions.[7] In the countryside there was visible hardship, but the pace of business in London made them comment that the ransom had been set far too low.

Richard's gratitude to the jubilant Londoners was limited to a stay of a few hours only. On 18 March he was at Bury St Edmunds – giving thanks at the shrine of one of his favourite saints, the eponymous martyred king of East Anglia. Eleanor travelled with him because he knew nothing of England or its customs and she feared that the arrogance which had caused all his problems in Outremer might otherwise alienate Anglo-Norman vassals who had still to make good their pledges for the unpaid part of the ransom.

After the Great Council meeting that dispossessed John, Archbishop Hubert Walter departed at the head of an army equipped to reduce his castles with copious supplies of arrows, armour and shields as well as pitch and sulphur to make

Greek fire – the formula of which must have been brought to England by returning crusaders – plus a battery of mangonels. Marlborough surrendered in a few days, as did Lancaster. John's castle at St Michael's Mount in Cornwall did not require a siege: its castellan dropped dead from a heart attack when he heard Richard was back in England,[5] but when the garrison at Tickhill Castle offered to surrender if he would guarantee their lives, he refused – in exactly the intransigent mood that Eleanor had feared. Fortunately, Bishop Hugh of Durham, commanding the loyalist besiegers, took it upon himself to agree terms.

Nottingham held out until Richard arrived there on 25 March, the garrison not believing who he was, even when he donned his armour and led the assault, taking the outerworks and many prisoners, whom he hanged on a gallows erected in full view of the castle. Hubert Walter arrived with reinforcements for the besiegers' ranks. Two days later, Hugh of Durham arrived with the prisoners he had taken at Tickhill, but Nottingham continued to hold out until two knights of the garrison had been given a safe conduct to see for themselves that the commander of the besiegers was indeed their lawful king.

When Nottingham surrendered, the rebellion was over. A Great Council was summoned there, in the heart of the territory that had been loyal to John. While its members were assembling, Richard amused himself for a few days at one of Henry II's old haunts, Clipstone on the fringes of Sherwood Forest, where the hunting of stag and boar so pleased him that he compared it favourably with his own forest of Talmont in far-off Poitou. This was the stuff of the triumphal return at the end of every Robin Hood film, although whether a meeting in some greenwood glade between a loyal outlaw and the returned crusader king – as described in the fourteenth-century *Ballad of Robin Hood* – actually took place, is anyone's guess.

On Wednesday 30 March in the hastily repaired great hall of Nottingham Castle, 72-year-old Eleanor in all her majesty as dowager queen surveyed with understandable cynicism the

assembled earls of the realm and the bishops and archbishops
doing homage to Richard, whose safe return she had done more
than anyone else to secure. Unfortunately, his current mood cut
short the national elation and thanksgiving for his return. Furious
with his English subjects who had paid the lion's share of the
ransom too slowly, in his view, and blaming them and not himself
for the fifteen months' imprisonment, he cared nothing for their
acclamations, wanting from them only more money to hire mercenaries and buy materiel with which to fulfil his main priority:
to repulse Philip's incursions into Normandy. To raise this money,
all the offices and privileges bought five years earlier at such high
prices to finance the abortive crusade now had to be bought
anew. To the few office-holders who dared protest, he replied that
whilst he and his heroic crusaders had faced death, all the stay-
at-homes had been growing fat on the profits of war, which they
could now cough up in his new hour of need.

As always, some took advantage of the situation. Henry
Longchamp, imprisoned after William's flight to France from
Dover Castle, bought the office of sheriff of Worcestershire,
while his brother Osbert was named sheriff of Norfolk and
Suffolk. The hated bishop of Ely offered 1,500 marks down and
500 marks annually per county to be named sheriff of Yorkshire,
Lincolnshire and Northamptonshire, but was outbid for Yorkshire
by Geoffrey the Bastard, who offered 3,000 marks for that county
alone to ensure that William Longchamp had no authority in
his see. Even Prince John's unhappy wife, Isabel or Hawise of
Gloucester, had to pay £200 to keep her dowry lands and marriage portion.

Teams of clerks laboured day and night keeping the accounts.
On the third day of the council, Richard moved on to the
question of taxation, in particular the arrears in payment of
the ransom contribution levies, for which final demands were
issued – with the implication that failure to pay could indeed
prove final. In addition, he announced his requirement that every
knight in the realm should perform one-third of his annual forty

days' knight service by crossing to Normandy with him, to confront Philip Augustus.[6] This would have produced a total cavalry force of around 2,000 knights, but the demand was more probably intended to raise the scutage paid in lieu of knight service, so that he could hire mercenaries. Here he was on thin ice for, as Bishop Hugh of Lincoln had ruled in 1197, knight service was owed by Anglo-Norman vassals for warfare on English soil – in other words, to suppress a rebellion, but not for wars the king wished to wage abroad.

To squeeze the last drops of wealth out of a country exhausted by the ransom, Richard named William Longchamp chancellor once more, because he knew more than anyone else alive about milking England down to its last penny, jewel and fleece. In addition to some new taxes, the pre-conquest land tax last levied in 1162 was reintroduced. Known as Danegeld, its rate was set at 2 shillings for every hide of cultivated land recorded in the Domesday Book, with none of the traditional exemptions for Church lands, so the moneyless monasteries that had no rents or precious objects to sell were ordered to surrender their wool-clip for the second year running in settlement of their assessments. The Pipe Rolls show the cost of hauling wool from the Cistercian foundations in Yorkshire to Holme in Norfolk and hiring ships to transport it to Germany.[7] Among the many individual victims was William the Marshal, required to pay 4 shillings for his wife's estates in Sussex.[8]

The last debate of the council concerned Richard's oath of fealty to Henry Hohenstaufen and his undertaking to pay an annual fee to the emperor. To the assembled barons this was a shameful act, unworthy of the dignity of their king, to reaffirm which it was decided that Richard should be re-crowned at Winchester. Although Richard adored ceremonial for which he could dress up and in which he was the central figure, matters of state bored him, so it is possible that the idea came from Eleanor. Either way, there was a problem. It was almost forty years since she and Henry II had held a ceremonial crown-wearing and nobody could remember the proper ritual. So messengers posted to Canterbury Cathedral, to consult the records of the ceremonial used when Stephen of Blois had been re-crowned there in 1141 to reaffirm his sovereignty after release from imprisonment by Empress Matilda.[9]

It seems that Eleanor stayed close to prevent Richard's impatience causing further problems. On 8 April she was one of the witnesses to his charter setting out the honours due to King William of Scotland when called to the English court. At Winchester on 17 April, which was either just before or just after her seventy-third birthday, she sat in state on a specially built dais in the cathedral surrounded by a bevy of noble heiresses waiting to be bestowed as rewards upon those who had served the Crown well in the recent troubled times while he took communion in preparation for his coronation.[10]

Although the official queen of England, poor Berengaria was far away in Poitiers. So, fittingly, it was Eleanor who played the role of queen in Winchester Cathedral on that morning when her son processed with William Longchamp on his right side from nearby St Swithin's priory and up the aisle beneath a canopy borne by a count and three earls, one of whom was one of Henry II's bastards named William Longsword,[11] to the altar where Archbishop Hubert Walter was waiting.

Business after the ceremony included setting the ransoms for the most important prisoners taken at Tickhill and Nottingham, the lesser rebels being freed against a surety of 100 marks each, to stand trial later. Fetters and chains costing the considerable sum of 29 shillings and 9 pence were purchased to ensure that the conditions in which the prisoners were confined would be as distressing as possible. The large number of estates confiscated were not sold, but administered for the Exchequer.[12] Almost as an afterthought, 10,000 marks were despatched to Germany to ransom Archbishop Walter of Rouen and a few others, but no provision was made for obtaining the release of the many other hostages kept there against payment of the outstanding balance of his ransom. Richard was chafing at the bit, his normal impatience not helped by more bad news from France that made him regard every pound raised for the hostages' ransom as better applied to financing his war against Philip Augustus. Just one week after the coronation, on 24 April he and Eleanor arrived at the walled city of Portsmouth, where he planned to construct a fortified harbour for a fleet of galleys – whose manoeuvrability, especially against unfavourable winds, had impressed him in the Mediterranean – and use them to blockade Philip Augustus' ports.

With his customary enthusiasm for everything martial, Richard threw himself into this enterprise, but spared the time to go hunting in the New Forest, interrupting his sport when riots broke out between his Welsh and Flemish mercenaries, who turned the streets of Portsmouth into a battleground. No sooner was he ready to cross to France than the weather changed. Ignoring the advice of his captains, he ordered men and horses to embark on Monday 2 May. For a whole day and night his fleet of 100 vessels was driven everywhere except towards France, the horses cooped up in their stalls suffering more and more. At last, he abandoned the crossing and returned to land, to everyone's great relief. The prolonged stay cost over £100 in lodgings and lasted until 12 May when his small army of levied English knights and the mercenaries weighed anchor and set course for the port of Barfleur, to resume his favourite occupation: warfare.[13]

Richard's second visit to England as monarch had lasted barely two months and he was never to set foot in the island realm again. Eleanor's reappearance on French soil had, for his continental vassals, something of the characteristics of a return from the dead: she seemed almost supernatural by virtue of her great age, her legendary travels, her imperiousness and her extraordinary physical vitality as she rode with Richard through Normandy. The squire of William the Marshal reported that church bells greeted them everywhere and the common people sang hymns of thanksgiving while the turncoats among the marcher lords changed sides yet again as Eleanor and her son progressed in state from Barfleur to Caen and Bayeux. Many Norman nobles had believed Richard dead long since and thus given their support to Prince John during the long years he had been absent from his continental domains. They now hastened to reaffirm their loyalty, those who delayed suffering the penalty as Richard's levied knights and the mercenaries under Mercadier embarked on three months of bloody reprisals.

Yet the greatest traitor went unpunished. On the third or fourth night after disembarking at Barfleur, Richard was staying at Lisieux in the house of Archdeacon John of Alençon, one of the messengers whom Eleanor had despatched to the Holy Land with the news that finally set her son on his disastrous voyage homeward. Richard was not resting, but was attempting to persuade his household knights to ride through the night to relieve a fortress besieged by Philip's forces, when he received a visitor under cover of darkness. Abandoned by Philip Augustus as nothing but a liability and dispossessed of his English properties and revenues by the Great Council, John Lackland now merited the sobriquet 'John Lack-all'. Desperate to enlist, if not an ally, at least a mediator before the confrontation with the elder brother who could reasonably have ordered his execution for treason or alternatively sentenced him to life imprisonment, John begged an interview with Eleanor beforehand.[14]

Subsequently sounded out by John of Alençon, Richard said he bore no animosity against his brother. Although having frequently employed floods of crocodile tears on similar occasions himself, he was nevertheless moved by others' penitential weeping – even John's. Echoing their father's words when his sons repented of their treason, he pardoned John and blamed instead the evil advisers who had led his 'little brother' astray, never mind that John was 26 years old at the time.[15] Sitting down to dine on a freshly cooked salmon that had been presented to Richard for his own dinner, John must have been immensely relieved when given a chance to prove on whose side he now was by providing a retinue of knights and men-at-arms with whom to relieve the garrison at Évreux by cutting Philip's lines of communication.[16]

Philip's betrayal of a vassal protected, as a crusader, by the Peace of God already had him excommunicated. If taken prisoner in that condition, no protection or assistance would be forthcoming from the Church to secure him the feudal kiss of peace;[17] if killed, his soul would go straight to hell. Unquestionably in the right this time, Richard excelled himself in this campaign. His ability to weigh up military priorities and drive horses and machines to destruction and men to their limits of endurance had Philip beating his retreat within days. Freshly arrived from Germany, Archbishop Walter of Rouen and William Longchamp joined Richard in Normandy, leaving the governance of England in the hands of Archbishop Hubert Walter of Canterbury, who ruled the kingdom wisely and well for the rest of Richard's reign, and was made a cardinal the following March.

Attempting to relieve the siege of Aumale during the Norman campaign, Richard narrowly escaped capture by Guillaume des Barres, his old enemy from the winter on Sicily who had fought alongside him on the crusade, and who now abandoned three other captives in the attempt, thereby losing their ransoms. Another of Philip's men, Alain de Dinan, unhorsed Richard, who managed to remount in the skirmish and make good his escape. At Gaillon on the Seine, which he was besieging in order to get money for the construction of a new castle to replace Gisors, now in Philip's hands, Richard was wounded in the knee by a crossbow bolt fired by Cadoc, Philip's mercenary castellan. His equally stricken horse falling on top of him, Richard's injuries took a month to heal.

Such was the devastation from fire and sword that the Church once again called for a halt to the violence, resulting in a truce signed by Richard and Philip Augustus on 23 July. A month later, by a letter dated 22 August 1194, Richard made tournaments legal at five named places in England,[18] ignoring his father's ban on such events because they enabled several hundred knights, fully armed and accoutred, to assemble legally, and could thus mask preparations for rebellion. To counter the Church's condemnation of the bloodshed, sin and widespread damage to property caused by *mêlées*, promulgated by Lateran councils in 1139 and 1179, Richard argued that the less than enthusiastic response of Anglo-Norman knights to the call for the Third Crusade justified the new tournaments to prepare them for what they would experience when he led them back to the Holy Land. Uppermost in his mind, of course, was the income he could expect from sales of licences to promote tournaments in England and the fees due from every participant, ranging from 20 marks for an earl down to 2 marks for a landless knight.[19]

After dealing rough justice to his Norman vassals, Richard swung south towards the Loire Valley to recover the castles handed over by John and those at Châteaudun and Loches, which he himself had yielded. The army now consisted of his Flemish mercenaries under Mercadier and a Navarrese force commanded by Berengaria's brother Prince Sancho. It also included 150 artillerymen with trebuchets and other missile launchers, which were used to batter the refortified château of Taillebourg into submission, this time razing it to the ground shortly after Geoffroy de Rancon's death so that hardly a trace of the substantial twelfth-century walls remains.

Each time Richard's speed of advance caught him at a disadvantage, Philip fled. Near Vendôme, the latter abandoned all his siege engines and personal chapel fittings, as well as the Capetian treasury and the top-secret list of Richard's vassals who had sworn allegiance to the House of Capet.[20] This was given into William the Marshal's safekeeping as Richard pressed onwards, at one point, after the Battle of Fréteval in July 1194, coming within minutes of capturing Philip and his personal escort. Told by a Flemish straggler met by the roadside that his prey was far ahead, Richard's haste took him galloping straight past the humble country church in which his enemy was hiding. With Philip now behind his pursuers, Richard's party was far into Frankish territory when his horse dropped dead from exhaustion and one of Mercadier's men gave up his mount for the king, leaving him to ride back on the withers of a comrade's horse. The saddles used had a high pommel and high cantle, like a modern western saddle, so this was no comfortable ride.[21]

Richard next rampaged into his own duchy of Aquitaine where the traditional internecine feuding had flourished unchecked during his long absence. There was little hope for the rebels holding out against him as all their fortresses were as familiar to his military mind as a sibling's face, every strongpoint and every weakness known by heart. His forces ravaged the countryside throughout July. After taking the count of Angoulême's fortress-city in a single evening, he wrote to Archbishop Hubert Walter that they had captured 40,000 men-at-arms and 300 ransomable knights. Like most modern battle statistics, that claim was probably exaggerated, but Richard's generalship and ruthlessness in this brilliant campaign succeeded in restoring the *pax ricardi* throughout his continental possessions from the Channel to the Pyrenees.[22]

By now the hostages remaining as sureties in the hands of Leopold of Austria were becoming uneasy at his threats to execute some of them to speed up the final payment and the liberation of his kinswoman, the maid of Cyprus, who was still a captive in England. A group of the hostages were given permission to send Baldwin of Béthune – one of the small band of knights that had been captured with Richard in Austria – back to Britain to fetch her. Hearing on the return journey that Leopold had died in December 1194, Baldwin turned back with his charge and returned to England, whence she subsequently reappeared in southern France.[23] Richard's tardiness in paying off the ransom bore fruit when the German emperor waived the last 17,000 marks as a contribution to Richard's war against their common enemy, Philip Augustus.

## NOTES

1. William of Newburgh, *Historia Rerum Anglicarum*, Vol 1, p. 402.
2. Roger of Howden, *Chronica*, Vol 2, p. 202.

3. *L'Histoire de Guillaume le Maréchal*, ed. P. Meyer (Paris: Société de l'histoire de France, 1901), Vol 3, p. 134.

4. J. Choffel, *Richard Coeur de Lion ... et l'Angleterre cessa d'être normande* (Paris: Lanore/Sorlot, 1985), p. 237.

5. Roger of Howden, *Chronica*, Vol 3, p. 203.

6. Ibid, Vol 3, p. 202.

7. Pipe Roll 5 Richard I, pp. 44, 69.

8. Pipe Roll 7 Richard I, pp. 261–2.

9. J.H. Round, *Geoffrey de Mandeville* (London: Longmans, 1892), p. 138.

10. Roger of Howden, *Chronica*, Vol 3, p. 248.

11. Also known as Longuespée. Some of his charters recorded in the cartulary of Bradenstoke Priory mention *comitissa Ida, mater mea*, which confirmed his birth to Countess Ida of Norfolk.

12. Pipe Roll 6 Richard I, pp. 1–27, 213.

13. Roger of Howden, *Chronica*, Vol 3, p. 251.

14. Meyer, *Guillaume le Maréchal*, Vol 3, p.134.

15. Ibid, Vol 3, p. 137.

16. J. Gillingham, 'William the Bastard at War', in *Anglo-Norman Warfare*, ed. M. Strickland (Woodbridge: Boydell, 1994), p. 204.

17. Ralph of Diceto, *Opera Historica*, Vol 2, p. 117.

18. Ibid, Vol 2, p. 120.

19. Bartlett, *England under the Norman and Angevin Kings*, p. 206.

20. Richard, A., *Histoire*, Vol 2, p. 293.

21. Powicke, *The Loss of Normandy*, p. 102.

22. Ralph of Diceto, *Opera Historica*, Vol 2, p. 119.

23. Roger of Howden, *Chronica*, Vol 3, p. 257.

# Good King Richard

leanor's court at Poitiers had never recovered from Henry's purge of 1174, and she no longer had the energy to revive the great audience hall beside the Maubergeonne Tower where Berengaria held her lonely and inconsequential court when not in her own territory further north in Maine.[1] The haven to which Eleanor retired in order to distance herself from the turmoil of the world was the monastery/convent to which Henry had sought to consign her. As her first father-in-law Louis VI had installed his chancery and war office in St Denis, so she betook her modest court to Fontevraud, midway between the Channel coast and the Pyrenees. On her way to Mass each morning, she walked over the permanent inhabitants of the abbey church and past Henry's tomb with its effigy showing his restless hands stilled at last and quietly holding the sceptre of state.

Fontevraud's several thousand religious and lay inhabitants of both sexes, ruled by the abbess, included an upper stratum of noble ladies whose husbands had tired of them or found a more advantageous match, plus those who had chosen to put the Peace of God between themselves and a society that used their bodies, titles and possessions as the disposable filling in the sandwiches of treaties and alliances. To this elegant society Eleanor came as a natural queen regardless of the worldly titles she claimed.

She remained at Fontevraud while Richard held his Christmas court in Rouen, but she was kept up to date by a stream of clerical and lay visitors from all over Europe.

It is said that not long after that, while hunting in Normandy, Richard was recognised by a hermit who lived in the forest, who reminded him of the destruction of Sodom and warned him to give up his forbidden pleasures before the hand of God struck him down.[2] Shortly after, at Easter 1195 he fell seriously ill and took this as a divine warning to change his lifestyle and acquire some merit in the afterlife, the crusader's absolution being only retroactive. Although still as avid for taxes as ever, and as brutal against those he considered to have transgressed against him, he also started to perform good works like feeding the starving poor and compensating some religious communities for the treasures that had been seized to pay his ransom.[3]

Hostilities broke out again when Philip Augustus defied a truce and advanced within 12 miles of Rouen, forcing a swift removal of Princess Alais to Caen and thence from one fortress to another as the tide of battle ebbed and flowed. She was now 34, an age by which most women of the time were dead. Having been handed over to Henry as Richard's betrothed when a 9-year-old girl, she had never known freedom and was a stranger to her own family. Under the Treaty of Louviers, signed in January 1196, Philip gave back all the territory recently gained from Richard in return for the Vexin.[4] He also recovered Alais and married her off to Guillaume de Ponthieu, whose strategically important domains lay between Normandy and the territory of Richard's ally Baldwin of Flanders. With that, Alais disappeared from history, after spending a lifetime captive in the gilded cage of a family that despised her as she was used and abused in turn by Henry, Eleanor and Richard.

In keeping with the clause in the Treaty of Messina that had caused so much trouble, Richard confirmed his nephew Arthur of Brittany as his heir, but when he ordered Geoffrey's widow Countess Constance to bring her son to Rouen, she was imprisoned by the second husband Henry II had imposed on her, Earl Ranulf of Chester. Hastening to his nephew's rescue, Richard found that he had been spirited away to Paris and was being brought up in Philip Augustus' household with crown prince Louis. For Prince John, this seemed to augur well and gave him hope that he must now be recognised as heir to the whole Plantagenet Empire by default. He kept a low profile nonetheless – as well he might, having had his estates restored to him the previous year on condition of good behaviour.

The widespread misery and suffering north of the Channel was made worse by Archbishop Hubert Walter attempting to satisfy the insatiable king by imposing a scutage on tenants-in-chivalry, or knightly tenants. He also introduced a new tax of 2 shillings per carucate for the *socage* or civil tenants, which translates as a swingeing imposition, a carucate being the extent of land a team of oxen can plough each season. Every freeman was also assessed as owing a quarter of the value of his personal property. The moneyless Cistercian and Gilbertian monasteries forfeited wool-clippings from their flocks of sheep, and the great churches had to surrender the treasures that had not already been seized for payment of the ransom. A *tallage* tax was also levied on towns and the royal demesnes, as assessed by Hubert Walter's travelling justices.[5] This was the third time in his brief reign that Richard squeezed the fiscal resources of his island realm 'until the pips squeaked': first for the failed Third Crusade, second for his ransom and now to finance his wars in France.

One inbuilt problem, as in many countries today, was the corruption of the officials collecting the taxes. Abbot Robert of Caen persuaded Richard that something like half the tax money was never handed over by the collectors, and that a strict audit of their accounts would double the revenue without further legislation being required. Sent to London in April 1196, he set about his task by summoning the sheriffs of every county to suffer a complete audit of their accounts. This was an open insult to Archbishop Hubert Walter's authority and the zeal with which

he had been serving the king. It may be coincidence that the
abbot was taken ill while dining with Hubert Walter and died
five days later. William of Newburgh drily commented that 'those
persons who had dreaded his coming sorrowed not at his going'.[6]

It was not only in the country that dissent was growing. The
emerging class of tradesmen and artisans in London also thought
that they had to bear an unfair share of the burden of taxation and
were seething with discontent. Life for them had become so grim
that a charismatic crusader knight and London magistrate named
William fitz Osbert took it upon himself to champion their cause,
preaching passive resistance to the excessive impositions placed
upon them, all the while protesting his loyalty to the king, so that
he could not be accused of treason. In the fifth book of William
of Newburgh's *Historia Rerum Anglicarum* the chronicler treads a
delicate path, disparaging fitz Osbert to demonstrate his own loyalty to the Crown. A sort of bourgeois Robin Hood, fitz Osbert
claimed to be the saviour of the poor and declared that he would
'divide the humble from the haughty and treacherous … and the
elect from the reprobate, as light from darkness'.[7] Drawn by this
rhetoric, his supporters were said to number 52,000 in London
alone and rumour had it that they had accumulated secret caches
of weapons, and intended breaking into and robbing the houses
of the rich to compensate themselves for the burden of taxation.

Aware that he had made himself vulnerable, fitz Osbert went
about surrounded by a bodyguard of followers. That spring,
he travelled to Normandy to lay before Richard the plight of
the urban poor who were bearing an unfair share of the crippling burden of taxes, and also to protest his personal loyalty. He
pleaded his case so well that Richard let him depart the court
freely but, to seasoned courtiers who had served under Henry II,
there was an odour of Becket's demise in the air. Richard's hands
were seen to be clean but, after fitz Osbert's return to England,
Hubert Walter as chief justiciar ordered his arrest one day in
mid-Lent when the former crusader's self-appointed bodyguard
was elsewhere.

After one of the archbishop's officers was killed in the arrest, fitz Osbert and some followers took refuge in the London church of St Mary le Bow, claiming sanctuary but also prepared to defend themselves vigorously. To force them out, Hubert Walter ordered the church to be set on fire. When fitz Osbert emerged, choking from the smoke, he was stabbed in the belly and arrested. Within days, he was convicted, 'drawn asunder by four horses'[8] and hanged at Tyburn with nine companions, his followers subsequently digging out so much ground beneath the gallows for souvenirs that they had to be kept at bay by armed soldiers.

The bishops of the realm were horrified at Hubert Walter's excess. His own chapter, whose property the church in question was, had long voiced disapproval of him and placed this act of sacrilege at the head of the list of his other misdoings to be attached to an indictment they were preparing for the pope requesting that the archbishop be divested of his ecclesiastical offices.

The main reason why Richard's avarice had spiralled out of control was his decision to replace the castle of Gisors, forfeited to Philip Augustus. Under the terms of the Treaty of Louviers in January 1196, both monarchs agreed that neither would fortify a limestone spur dominating the Seine Valley above the town of Andely, but Richard had no intention of respecting that undertaking. He tried to buy the spur and adjoining land, which belonged to the see of Rouen, from its Archbishop Walter. Well understanding the strategic importance of the site, two-thirds of the way from Paris to Rouen, where an impregnable castle could blockade river traffic between Paris and the sea and effectively deter any drive by Philip Augustus along the Seine Valley into Normandy, the archbishop held out for a high price in compensation for the revenues that would be lost and the damage that had been sustained to ecclesiastical property in the recent fighting.

Castle building almost always displaced existing populations and disrupted the economic life of the area, such as food production and markets. Throughout the construction, quarries had to be opened up and operated; masons and other skilled artisans had to be hired from elsewhere; a local labour force had to be impressed; the new chapel might disturb existing parish demarcations; vineyards and fields were ruined and forests cleared – as at Bures, where Henry's rebuilding had required the felling of 1,000 mature oaks. So, the archbishop's demands were not unreasonable.

As usual in any prolonged negotiation, Richard's patience ran out before an agreement was reached and he began construction anyway atop the limestone spur standing almost 300ft above the river. The Pipe Rolls recording the expenditure for the work list all sums disbursed to quarrymen, masons, carpenters, smiths, diggers who hacked out the rock-cut ditches by hand, carters who transported the supplies to the castle and all the other skilled and unskilled workers. Since the rolls contain no mention of an architect or master mason being paid, it is possible that Richard laid out the ground plan and directed the work himself. Certainly he paid many visits to hurry the work along, in case Philip made a surprise attack before it was completed. Inevitably, many workers died in accidents during construction; the first deliberate spilling of blood occurred when three of Philip Augustus' soldiers who had been taken prisoner were thrown to their deaths from the top of the walls in retaliation for a massacre of Welsh mercenaries in which they had taken part.

In an attempt to win Pope Celestine III's intercession in his negotiations with Richard, Walter of Rouen set out for Rome in November 1196, obliging Richard to despatch a delegation led by William Longchamp to plead his case at the papal court. Longchamp died en route while passing through Poitou early in February 1197 – unmourned by anyone in England except his brothers and his close friend, Richard's chaplain Milo.[9] This left Bishop Philip of Durham and Bishop Guillaume of Lisieux to continue to Rome and make Richard's case there. Walter of Rouen had meanwhile issued an interdict against the duchy of Normandy which prohibited church services from being performed; contemporary chroniclers described unburied  corpses lying in the streets of Norman towns. Richard defied the interdict, which was not lifted until April 1197 after he had done a deal with Walter of Rouen, ceding to him two manors and the port of Dieppe as part of the purchase price for the land.

Letters signed by Richard when at his new castle bore the mention *apud bellum castrum de rupe* – at the fine castle on the rock. In *la langue d'oïl* or northern French it was called Château Gaillard or Bold Castle. At the same time, the walled town of Petit Andely was built on the riverbank below. Because of complications in the work and Richard's haste, costs rocketed, and were eventually said to have totalled something in the region of £20,000, spent in less than two years. This was more than twice the total expended on castles in England during his reign.

The design of Richard's 'Bold Castle' is similar in some respects to the Angevin treasure castle at Chinon, built by Henry II half a century earlier, which also stands on a promontory overlooking a riverside town, but this one was far more ambitious. It had three *enceintes* or walled baileys separated by dry moats. In the outer baileys were the stables, blacksmiths and armourers' forges, carpenters' workshops and storage space to stock all the food and other supplies necessary to withstand a prolonged siege.

The castle incorporated all the latest improvements in fortifications that Richard had seen on the crusade and in Germany, especially the concept of concentric fortifications that had impressed him in the east. The gates were protected by towers on either side, from which attackers could be enfiladed, thus eradicating the blind spot immediately outside each gate. Earlier castles in Europe had *hourdes* or temporary wooden shielded platforms erected, jutting out from the top of the walls in time of war, from which archers could shoot down on attackers approaching the walls. These were vulnerable to missiles fired by siege engines. Château Gaillard was among the first to improve on this idea: its towers had a projecting top floor provided with machicolations or gaps in the masonry floor through which the defenders could shoot more safely. Virtually all the walls were curved so that the missiles fired by siege engines would tend to ricochet off instead of shattering the masonry, as happened with flat walls.

The plan of Château Gaillard drawn by the nineteenth-century architect Viollet-le-Duc (plate 33) shows the innermost bailey and keep at the top or north-western end with the outer bailey at the bottom or south-eastern end. It is pentagonal and has five towers spaced along the wall, three of which are at the corners. The middle bailey is an irregular polygon whose walls are protected with many towers, the idea being to enfilade any attackers at the base of the walls. After little more than a year, the castle was nearly finished, causing Richard to boast of his 'beautiful 1-year-old daughter', which he swore could never be taken, even if its walls were made of butter.

In England, Hubert Walter had resigned his temporal offices in humiliation after the abbott of Caen's audit, but was not long absent from the corridors of power, introducing a law establishing one uniform system of weights and measures throughout England, which was to last 800 years until Britain went metric in the last years of the twentieth century. For many years, Richard was credited with being a great lawgiver on account of some excellent and long-lasting legislation enacted during his reign, but these laws were enacted in his absence from the country, largely by Hubert Walter. Among his other laws was a requirement that, on his fifteenth birthday, every male must swear to uphold the law, to neither commit crime nor be accessory to it, and must join the 'hue and cry' pursuing malefactors in support of sheriffs and their officers. In their absence, every citizen was entitled to make 'citizens' arrests'.

In 1197 Hubert Walter found the time to travel to Normandy to serve as Richard's peripatetic envoy, settling disputes with prelates and even arranging a truce with Philip Augustus. In November he was back in England, charged by his king to send 300 knights for twelve months' service in the continental possessions or money sufficient to purchase the services of 300 mercenaries for twelve months. At a Great Council held in

Oxford early in December he proposed to the assembled Anglo-Norman barons and bishops that they should furnish these men from their own resources, but the scheme foundered on the old argument that the obligations of the English vassals were to support the king of England in England and not across the Channel.

Shortly afterwards, Hubert Walter forced a reassessment of all the arable land in England for the purpose of taxation using his newly standardised land measurements. Before the commission charged with enforcing that had concluded its task, however, the youngest cardinal ever to be elected pope began a rule of nearly two decades in Rome under the name of Innocent III. This vigorous and intelligent 37-year-old started as he meant to go on. Among the first of his acts was the restoration of the old prohibition on members of religious orders holding secular office. Hubert Walter immediately resigned the title and functions of justiciar and remained without secular responsibility until, after Richard's death, he accepted the post of chancellor under John, to the general relief of the barons, since he alone could restrain the new monarch's excesses. In this, he succeeded so well that, on hearing of the archbishop's death in 1205, John was to say, 'Now at last I am truly king.'[10]

The confinement in Germany had slightly moderated Richard's arrogance that had made him so many enemies before and during the crusade. It was there too that he first became Good King Richard,[11] winning the hearts of most of the emperor's vassals who met him. For this reason, they approached him now to resolve the knotty problem of succession when Henry Hohenstaufen died suddenly in Messina on 28 September 1197, shortly after releasing Richard from the oath of fealty given under duress at Mainz.

Of the two contenders for the imperial throne, the infant son of Constance of Sicily was unacceptable to the German electors by virtue of his minority. Although Philip of Swabia, the late emperor's brother, had much support in the south, he was not well thought of in the north or by the bishops of the empire. In this dilemma the hero of Christendom seemed an ideal compromise candidate to many of the northern barons and bishops of the empire, who had come to know him personally.[12] Henry II must have turned in his tomb at Fontevraud when Richard failed to leap at this chance to close a vice around Philip by constructing the greatest empire since Rome, comprising England, Wales, Ireland, most of France and the German empire north and south of the Alps.

Richard lacked the strategic vision, but looking after his friends and protégés was another matter. As he had used his influence in the Holy Land in favour of his nephew Henry of Champagne, so he now proposed Matilda's son Otto of Brunswick as candidate. Otto had served Richard loyally after remaining in France when his father returned to Germany. He had even been named count of Poitou – a post for which his youth and haughty disregard for local customs and laws made him a disastrous appointment, despite Eleanor's attempts at tutelage.[13]

That apart, he was now a knight of proven valour, schooled in the arts of warfare by his famous uncle, and well thought of by the Church, to capitalise on which Richard borrowed 2,125 marks from a Lombard banker to grease palms that could be influential on Otto's behalf at the papal court.[14] He also outfitted his nephew in considerable splendour for his return to Saxony. Endowed with a liberal supply of money for bribes and presents to the German electors, Otto departed with Richard's blessing en route to Liège, then on German soil. Unwelcome there, he continued with the archbishop of Cologne to that city before leading the archbishop's knights at the assault of Aachen, which surrendered on 10 July 1198. Within twenty-four hours he was married to the infant daughter of the duke of Lorraine, whose head was too small and whose neck too weak to wear a crown at the coronation next day.[15]

To Philip Augustus, the Otto–Richard alliance was a new menace. In addition, the Church had forgiven neither his invasion of a crusader's lands nor his violent rejection of his Danish wife

Ingeborg immediately after their wedding night on 14 August 1193. Contemporaries hypothesised that he had discovered she was not a virgin, or that she was deformed 'in her parts' or had bad breath. Unable to plead consanguinity for an annulment, Philip eventually advanced the superficially humiliating argument that she had unmanned him. It was a clever move because admitting impotence enabled him to plead non-consummation, always grounds for annulment. Whatever the truth, she remained confined in the convent of Soissons so that he could live in sin on the Île de la Cité with his German mistress Agnès de Méranie and their children.[16]

With the whole world and Heaven too against him, it seemed, Philip Augustus decided that he had nothing to lose by invading Normandy at its weakest point, adjacent to Ponthieu, the county allied to his cause by poor Alais' body. Before they were driven back by Mercadier and William the Marshal, Philip's forces took several castles, which he refused to return. Once again, he came within minutes of capture when a bridge collapsed under the weight of too many men and horses fleeing from their pursuers close behind. The collapse dumped him in the river, and drowned twenty of the armoured knights in his entourage.[17]

Richard had taken a calculated risk in leaving his main force far behind in the heat of battle. The confusion of the skirmish at the bridge is evident from these lines in the 'life' of William the Marshal:

> And in that place we unhorsed Mathieu de Montmorency and Alain de Ronci and Fulk de Gilerval with a single lance and kept them captive. Of the Frankish force there were captured at least 100 knights. We send you the names of the more important ones, and you shall have the names of others when we know them, for Mercadier took about thirty whom we have not seen.[18]

Three knights unhorsed with one lance! The Marshal was not boasting, for it was not the first time he had achieved such a hat-trick. It is interesting also to note that the Flemings under Mercadier kept their own captives for ransom in addition to their pay. Or was Richard letting them loot and take hostages for ransom in lieu of payment from him? The record is mute.

From Rome at Christmas 1197 came Cardinal Peter of Capua on a mission to bring peace to France. William the Marshal's squire described the man as having been to a school where he had learned to prove black was white,[19] but all the dialectic in the world could not have reconciled Richard with the suzerain who had betrayed him during his exile. Nor was he amused when the cardinal changed tack and argued that under canon law a bishop could not be imprisoned. His point was that Richard should immediately release the battling bishop of Beauvais, who had the misfortune to be captured by Mercadier in May 1197 and was currently held in the tower of Caen. For the mercenaries who took him prisoner, the bishop represented a source of ransom, but Richard refused to let them accept the 10,000 silver marks offered by the cardinal. The reason was not just that the prisoner was a cousin of Philip Augustus, but that he was one of the many lay and religious in the Frankish host with whom Richard had fallen out personally in the Holy Land. A war of words between them saw each blistering *sirventès* from Richard answered by an equally well-composed poem from the bishop.

To Peter of Capua's pleading that he should release this cleric who had the effrontery to confront him on crusade, Richard furiously compared the futility of the Church when he was a prisoner in Germany with its lively interest in the bishop's predicament,[20] which had nothing to do with his religious office. He had been captured in armed combat with his helm closed, so that he was unidentifiable.[21] The cardinal was dismissed with a warning that, had he not been protected by his status as a papal envoy, he would have been castrated, as a warning to the pope not to meddle in affairs that had nothing to do with him. In a fit of rage reminiscent of Henry II, Richard locked himself in his bedchamber in a foul sulk.[22]

On a visit to Caen, Eleanor tried to pour oil on troubled waters by asking to have the captive bishop brought before her during one of Richard's many absences on campaign – a command that his gaolers dared not refuse. On his way to the audience, the battling bishop managed to break away from his guards, despite being fettered hand and foot, and hurled himself at the door of a church, to claim sanctuary. The door was locked, so he clung to the ring handle of the latch desperately invoking the Peace of God at the top of his voice. Eleanor's plan came to naught when Richard refused to recognise the bishop's right to sanctuary, after which he was transferred to stricter confinement in Chinon Castle.

## NOTES

1. *The Autobiography of Gerald of Wales* (Giraldus Cambrensis De Rebus a se Gestis), ed. and trans. H.E. Butler (London: Jonathan Cape, 1937), p. 153.
2. *Recueil*, Vol 17, pp. 573–4.
3. Roger of Howden, *Chronica*, Vol 3, p. 290.
4. Ibid, Vol 4, p. 3.
5. Biography of Hubert Walter by Kaye Norgate in *Dictionary of National Biography* (Oxford: OUP), Vol 28 (online version).
6. William of Newburgh, *Historia Rerum Anglicarum*, Vol 2, pp. 464–5.
7. Boyd, *Eleanor*, p.307; Stubbs, *Roger of Howden*, Vol 3, pp. 18, 42; Vol 4 pp. 5, 6, 48 (fully quoted in note 6, above); also entry in *Oxford Dictionary of National Biography* (Oxford: OUP, 2004–13).
8. Ibid.
9. Richard, A., *Histoire*, Vol 2, p. 305.
10. Matthew Paris, *Historia Anglorum*, ed. F. Madden (London: Longmans, 1869), Vol 2, p. 104.
11. Benedict of Peterborough, *Gesta Henrici*, Vol 2, p. 146.
12. Roger of Howden, *Chronica*, Vol 4, p. 37.
13. Richard, A., *Histoire*, Vol 2, p. 313.
14. Ibid.
15. *Flores Historiarum*, ed. H.R. Luard, Rolls Series No 95 (London: Eyre & Spottiswoode, 1890), Vol 2, p. 117.
16. Kelly, *Eleanor of Aquitaine*, pp. 313–14, 337.
17. Roger of Howden, *Chronica*, Vol 4, p. 56.

18. Powicke, *The Loss of Normandy*, p. 122.

19. Meyer, *Guillaume le Maréchal*, Vol 3, p. 152.

20. Ibid, p. 156.

21. Ibid, Vol 2, pp. 52–3.

22. J.R. Crosland, *William the Marshal* (London: Owen, 1962), pp. 78–81.

# Death in Agony

We owe the knowledge that many medieval diplomatic marriages of noble and royal daughters were arranged by their mothers or other noblewomen largely to academics working in women's studies. Eleanor now turned to a traditional method of bridging rifts between royal houses and cast around for a suitable granddaughter who could be married off to Philip's son Prince Louis. On the same wavelength, it seemed to her that her 31-year-old daughter Joanna was serving no purpose. Joanna's dowry, clawed back from Tancred by Richard during the winter on Sicily, had all been spent to pay the expenses of the crusade, so a match would not make her new husband rich, though she had, like Henry II's mother the Empress Matilda, kept her title as queen of Sicily.

When Count Raymond V of Toulouse died early in January 1195, his son Raymond VI decided to confirm allegiance to Philip Augustus, whose cousin he was. Since neither her father, either of her husbands nor Richard had solved the long-term problem of the breakaway county by force of arms, Eleanor's pragmatic mind began exploring a different solution. She dangled before Raymond VI the idea of rejecting his second wife Bourguigne de Lusignan and becoming the husband of a titular queen by a marriage that would safeguard the eastern frontier of Aquitaine. With Navarre already on-side through Berengaria, it was a brilliant idea.

Raymond was still excommunicate for the repudiation of his first wife and the Church would not look kindly on him sending away his second spouse, but there was always a complaisant churchman to sort out that kind of problem, so the marriage duly took place in Rouen during October 1196.[1] Among the witnesses was Richard's neglected wife, who otherwise lived quietly in her dower lands. Eleanor insisted that the marriage contract include a provision for Joanna's offspring by Raymond to inherit the county of Toulouse on his death – and could afford to feel pleased that, after three generations, the county of Toulouse was reattached to Aquitaine. Joanna, of course, had no more say in the matter than when Henry despatched her as a child bride to William II in Sicily. But what was love, except a game of *What If?* played by poets, maidens and married women yearning for an emotionally richer life? Even that great romantic Bernat de Ventadorn, who had sworn to be true to Eleanor until death, wrote before he died, probably in 1195:

> Estat ai com om esperdutz
> per amor un long estatge
> mas era'm reconogutz
> qu'ieu avia faih folatge.

[I was a man by love destroyed. / It ruled my mind for far too long. / But now at last I've understood / that I have lived my life all wrong.]

Another loveless arranged marriage of that year ensured Richard the gratitude of his bastard half-brother William Longsword, who was awarded the daughter of the count of Salisbury.[2] A hint of satisfaction can be read on the eroded features of Longsword's effigy in Salisbury Cathedral, despite the year in question being recorded as one of famine and disease so rampant in England that corpses of the rural poor were dumped en masse into communal graves because there was no time to bury them individually.

In July 1198 large stones fell from the sky in and around Paris, presumably from an asteroid that had fragmented in the upper atmosphere. At the same time, terrible thunderstorms ravaged crops in England, with hailstones so large that they killed many birds. In November a bright comet was sighted on fifteen consecutive nights. Like all unusual meteorological phenomena, these events were considered evil omens, although it is hard to imagine what could have been more feared in France than the bloodshed and the famine that came from the ceaseless laying waste of vast tracts of land as first Philip's and then Richard's forces advanced and retreated. At long last, during a meeting on 13 January 1199 conducted between Richard, shouting his terms from a boat in the middle of the Seine a few miles upriver from Les Andelys, and Philip on horseback on the bank, a five-year truce was agreed, motivated on both sides not so much by the approach of Lent as financial exhaustion. Despite twice capturing the Capetian treasury, Richard had spent every penny of the scutage levies in England in three consecutive years starting in 1194 on paying his mercenaries and building and strengthening fortresses. This compared with only seven scutages in the thirty-five years of Henry II's reign. Neither he nor Philip Augustus then knew that before the expiration of the five years, one of them would be dead and Normandy would be lost to the English Crown forever.

In Kipling's phrase, the captains and the kings departed. So did the mercenaries; on the way home to Flanders, Mercadier and his men awarded themselves a bonus by plundering the great fair held outside the walls of Abbeville and robbing all the merchants assembled there. But Richard's empty purse could not be filled so easily. He was always bemoaning the lot of a sovereign whose vassals did not hear his summons when his purse was empty. In a *sirventès* addressed to the count of Auvergne, who was once again exploring the possibilities of reaffirming allegiance to Philip Augustus, Richard included these reproachful lines:

> Vos me laïstes aidier per treive de guierdon
> e car saviès qu'a Chinon non a argent ni denier.
>
> [You no longer support me since my pay ceased to flow. /
> My treasury's empty, as you very well know.]

It seemed like a temporary answer to Richard's prayers when he heard that a hoard of Roman gold had been unearthed on the land of Viscount Aymar of Limoges shortly before Easter 1199.[3] The most valuable piece – a ceremonial shield or breastplate – was said to depict a king or chieftain seated at table surrounded by courtiers or members of his family. When he demanded that this treasure trove be handed over to him, Aymar offered to go halves – a reply that incensed Richard, coming as it did from a vavasour who should have been eager to ingratiate himself, in Richard's opinion at least. The gold had been taken for safekeeping to the castle of Châlus. Although a castle might be manned by 1,000 soldiers or more during periods of hostilities, at other times a handful of men sufficed so long as the drawbridge was up and the portcullis down. Châlus was held by two sergeants-at-arms. Being lowborn, their names were never certainly recorded, but they were probably Pierre Brun and Pierre Basile. With them inside the walls were a total of thirty-eight men, women and children.[4]

An alternative explanation of the siege is that Richard had his sights on capturing the largest gold mine in France, which was situated not far from Châlus. Whichever is true, he defied the Lenten truce by sending Mercadier to besiege the nearby castles of Nontron and Piégut, and thus ensure that his retreat from Châlus, if it became necessary because Viscount Aymar arrived with a superior force, would be unhindered. He himself then headed for Châlus with a force of about 100 mercenaries. At their approach on 25 March, the defenders were desperate because he had announced in advance that he would give no quarter.

It says much for the construction of the castle that the paltry force of defenders held out through three days of determined assault. What happened after its fall is a good example of the level of violence and bloodshed in the routine siege of a relatively unimportant castle. On the evening of 26 March, Richard was checking the progress of the sappers undermining the outer wall. With the tunnel entrance shielded by wattle fences to protect them from the defenders' missiles, they had dug a huge cavern in the hillside. The roof was propped up with tree trunks copiously packed with pig carcases smeared with pitch and other combustible material which, when fired, would consume the props and bring down the wall above, making a breach through which the attackers could swarm.

Richard was wearing a helmet but no body armour. Instead, he was carrying a buckler to fend off stray missiles fired from the arrow slits high up in the walls of the keep. Their own supplies of arrows long since exhausted, the men of the garrison were reduced to scrambling about at risk to life and limb in the outer bailey, collecting missiles fired by the attackers that had not broken or been deformed on impact. Pierre Basile had spent the day doing this and dodging the incoming fire under the shelter of a huge frying pan from the castle kitchen, which he used as a shield. He was now on watch at the arrow slit, which is still visible in the wall of the circular keep, and waiting for a target of opportunity before daylight failed.

There are two versions of what happened next. In the first, Richard let his shield drop at the very second a reused arrow from his own armoury flew through the air to pierce his shoulder. The more credible version is that the missile that struck him was a reused crossbow quarrel. The accuracy of a crossbow was greater than that of a bow and the quarrel travelled faster than an arrow, so that a peasant might deliberately kill a king, which is why the weapon had been outlawed by the Lateran Council of 1139 as being unchivalrous. Ironically, Richard was one of the kings who had defied the ban; his troops had used this weapon both in Cyprus against Isaac Comnenus' forces and against the Saracens in the Holy Land. He was also credited by William le

Breton with having introduced the weapon into France when hiring mercenary Genoese crossbowmen.[5]

Caught literally off-guard, Richard was hit by the quarrel at the junction of the neck and left shoulder.[6] Giving no sign to the mercenaries around him of the pain he was suffering, he mounted his horse and rode back to the house commandeered for his use. While it would have been difficult to conceal an arrow nearly 3ft long sticking out of his shoulder, a far shorter quarrel could have been hidden in the poor light in order not to affect the mercenaries' morale. Richard had been wounded many times, and this was not the first crossbow bolt to pierce his skin. Back in his quarters, he was laid on a couch, where Mercadier's medic attempted to pull out the missile in the flickering light of resinous torches. The wooden shaft broke off, as it was designed to do, and revealed the mark of the Angevin armoury at Chinon, leaving the pointed metal head still deep in the wound. Fortified with alcohol, the only analgesic available, Richard had to grit his teeth and bear the medic's clumsy efforts to cut deeper and deeper into the shoulder muscles, hampered by a layer of fat: his patient had been putting on weight for some time.[7]

With a bandage to hold in place a poultice, Richard carried on directing the siege next day, unaware that infection had entered his tissues, whether on the quarrel itself or on the hands and knife of the medic. By the morning of 28 March the stench of gas gangrene and steadily increasing pain told him that an agonising death lay ahead. In his years of campaigning he had seen thousands of men, women and children dying at his command or in his cause. He therefore had no illusions about his condition and despatched to Eleanor at the abbey in Fontevraud a sealed letter written by his chaplain Milo, instructing her to hasten with all possible speed to Châlus.

Receiving the missive, Eleanor despatched the most discreet of messengers, Abbess Matilda of Bohemia, to fetch Berengaria from Maine. Once that duty had been discharged, Matilda's orders were to seek out Prince John, wherever in the north he might be.

Eleanor's choice of a nun for the second part of this errand suggests that she had reason to suspect John of being in territory where an Angevin knight, or even a cleric from Fontevraud, might not be welcome.

Setting out herself with the abbot of Turpenay and a small escort, she covered the distance of more than 100 miles separating Fontevraud from Châlus by travelling day and night.[8] Despite her speed, on her arrival at the siege the stink of the gases formed by bacteria in the wound and the discoloration of the necrotised tissue told her that her beloved son was beyond any help, apart from spiritual consolation from Pierre Milo, his chaplain and erstwhile crusading comrade.[9]

Ever the stateswoman, Eleanor had come not to give way to her feelings, but to safeguard the succession by recording discreetly the last wishes of the dying king of England. Who else was present is unknown. If a formal testament was dictated to Milo or the abbot of Turpenay, it was never to see the light of day, although Richard's nephew Otto of Brunswick was afterwards said to have been generously remembered with the bequest of all Richard's personal jewels and three-quarters of his treasure. What that was worth at this stage is a mystery. Bequests also went to Richard's favourite religious foundations like the abbey of La Sauve Majeure. As to the succession to all Richard's many titles, there is no record that the clause in the Treaty of Messina naming Arthur of Brittany was rescinded. Had Richard changed his mind and named John instead, Eleanor would almost certainly have acted differently in the immediate future.

The dying king had not confessed and been given absolution since 1194, before his second coronation at Winchester. This awkward fact was glossed over by the chroniclers pretending that the soul of the crusader king had been labouring under an un-Christian hatred for Philip Augustus, which he had not been prepared to renounce, and could therefore not make an act of contrition and receive absolution.[10] The more likely reason is his refusal to pretend contrition for the forbidden practices against which the

Norman hermit had warned him in order to take the sacrament. Only on his deathbed could he sincerely say that he would not sin again.

After the sap was fired and the wall breached – there is still a hollow in the hillside marking the spot – Richard told the mercenaries, who had slaughtered all the other defenders, to haul Pierre Basile before him in chains. As an act of charity before meeting his Maker, he then pardoned the sergeant-at-arms as being an instrument of God's displeasure at the defiance of the Lenten truce constituted by the siege of Châlus.[11] He ordered Basile to be given a purse of gold coins and released. Notwithstanding, the wretched sergeant-at-arms was later flayed alive by the mercenaries and hanged from the battlements of the castle he had defended, literally, to his last breath.[12]

As was the custom, Richard then ordered the disposal of the parts of his own body. His heart was to go to Rouen Cathedral, where Young Henry lay among the former dukes of Normandy. The rest of his body was to be buried in Fontevraud Abbey at the feet of Henry II, in symbolic atonement for a son's betrayal of his father. To England he gave not a thought. In the early evening of 6 April, eleven days after suffering the fatal wound, he received absolution and communion from Milo the chaplain.

Thus, Eleanor's favourite son died in agony at the age of 42, having bequeathed his genes only to one bastard, Philip of Cognac, who was alleged to be aged about 15 at this time. What happened to the treasure of Châlus, the greed for which had caused Richard's death, is not recorded. Was the flaying alive of Pierre Basile an act of vengeance for daring to kill the king who pardoned him, or torture to make him betray the whereabouts of the treasure? Since it was never heard of again, either it never existed or else it was hacked up and shared out among the mercenaries, later being melted down as bullion.

In Normandy on 7 April William the Marshal received a letter dictated by Richard after his injury, appointing William castellan of the castle of Rouen and guardian of its treasure. Staying at the

priory of Notre Dame du Pré across the river was Archbishop
Hubert Walter. Guessing that the wound must be serious, they
discussed the succession. With William supporting John and the
archbishop's vote going to Arthur of Brittany, these two men,
who both knew Richard's last surviving brother well, mirrored
Eleanor's dilemma.[13] On 10 April another messenger brought
them the news of Richard's death. When this reached Paris,
Philip proclaimed as suzerain of the continental possessions that
Arthur of Brittany took precedence over Prince John as the son
of his elder brother Geoffrey.

Eleanor knew that the succession must be settled before the
news of Richard's death sparked disaffection among his vassals,
inciting Philip Augustus to profit from the death of his great
enemy. For the second time, a king's death had left her the only
figure of regal authority in England and the continental possessions. Torn between the unsuitability of both Prince John and
Arthur of Brittany, now a 14-year-old puppet of Philip Augustus,
as successor to all Richard's titles, she rode back to Fontevraud
at the slow pace of the funeral cortège, hoping to find a way to
ensure that the empire she and Henry II had built would not
crumble to dust one short decade after his death.

Soon after the cortège reached Fontevraud, Berengaria arrived
to officially mourn the husband she had hardly known, and
whom she was to survive by a celibate widowhood of thirty-one
years devoted to good works, including the foundation of the
Cistercian convent of L'Épau near Le Mans, where her effigy can
still be seen in the chapter house. With her came Matilda of La
Perche, daughter of Matilda of Saxony, to press the case of a third
contender for the succession: her brother Otto of Brunswick. Of
the three, he had been the nearest to Richard, and for a while had
acted as duke of Aquitaine, but Eleanor had found his performance sadly lacking in statecraft. The pendulum swung towards
John, who at least spoke the language of England that Richard
had never learned and even Henry had never properly mastered,
using an interpreter for any important conversation.

Tracking John down, Abbess Matilda encountered Bishop Hugh of Lincoln on the road and took him into her confidence,[14] which caused him to hurry south to Fontevraud, where he took precedence over the bishops of Agen, Poitiers, Angers and a host of lesser clergy swarming to the royal funeral like bees to honey. With them were the seneschals who had served Richard and now waited anxiously to know who was their new master: Arthur, John or Otto?[15]

The news of his brother's death reached John as he dallied in treason yet again, attempting to form a new power bloc by exploiting Constance of Brittany and the Breton lords' mistrust of Richard, Philip and anyone else who was not a Breton. Hurrying south, he first stopped at the castle at Chinon to find the treasury empty. Meeting Bishop Hugh returning from the funeral, he attempted to enlist the venerable churchman-diplomat's support in his cause as Richard's successor.[16] Although he had enjoyed a relationship of mutual respect with Henry, the bishop disapproved of all the king's sons and especially of John, whose experience as an oblate made him hostile to the Church. Despite John's offer of bribes, Hugh consented only to return to Fontevraud with him and see how matters lay.

On arrival, John hammered on the abbey door demanding to be shown his brother's tomb[17] until restrained by the bishop, who diplomatically obtained permission for them to enter. On 18 April, Easter Sunday, Bishop Hugh gave a sermon in the abbey church on the duties of kingship. It was normal for the noble congregation to fidget and chatter among themselves – except at the three great feasts of Easter, Whitsun and Christmas, they did not take communion, but only attended the service – but John's behaviour exceeded normal bounds. He twice yelled at the bishop to cut his sermon short, and was taken aback the third time when ordered to leave the sanctuary.[18] It was an inauspicious beginning for a prince who needed all the support he could get from the Church.

He also needed Eleanor, as dowager queen and witness to Richard's last wishes, to rebut Philip's announcement that Arthur was the legitimate successor, but she withdrew into retreat instead. Was that to hide her grief? Given her six decades in political life, it is more probable that she was still wrestling with the problem of the succession. On 21 April, three days after John's angry exchanges with Bishop Hugh, she resumed her public duties, granting to the abbey of Turpenay a fish farm at Langeais in consideration of its abbot's help at Châlus. John was one of the witnesses to this charter, but is described in it only as her 'very dear son' and 'count of Mortain'.[19] Why was the abbot being rewarded at this fraught time, when there were matters of great import in abeyance? Had he been present when Richard dictated a will naming Arthur of Brittany or Otto of Brunswick to succeed him? Was the gift a reward for silence? Three months later, on 21 July, Richard's confidant the chaplain Milo was also rewarded by gifts to his abbey of Le Pin. Was this for his silence too?

At Fontevraud, the time for mourning Richard was curtailed by news that a consortium of Breton vassals under Arthur and his mother Constance had been reinforced by barons from Maine and Anjou. Marching against Angers, only a day's ride from Fontevraud, they took it without opposition.[20] Le Mans and several other cities went over to them and Viscount Aymar of Limoges took revenge for Richard's unjustified siege of Châlus by lining up too on Arthur's side. Reluctantly, Eleanor gave her backing to John, who hurried north to be invested on 25 April by Archbishop Walter of Rouen with the ritual sword and golden crown of the dukes of Normandy. The ceremonial was a farce, John joking with his cronies throughout and even dropping the sword but, once officially duke of Normandy, he sent the ever-loyal William the Marshal and Archbishop Hubert Walter across the Channel with orders to see every royal castle in England prepared for civil war[21] and to force all free men to swear an oath of fealty to Henry II's last surviving son.

Apart from John's few partisans, the Anglo-Norman magnates gathered in council at Nottingham could find little good in him, deciding to accept him on conditions that laid the foundation for Magna Carta sixteen years later. In Normandy, so little confidence did his vassals have in John's ability to keep Philip at bay that many barons and knights avoided taking sides before the political-military situation had stabilised by going on pilgrimage or taking the Cross for the Fourth Crusade.[22]

So John had Normandy and was king-designate of England, but Eleanor was not prepared to give him Poitou and Aquitaine. Luckily she had Mercadier, who ordered his mercenaries back from the Limousin and led them against the coalition forces invading from the north in the rare phenomenon of two medieval armies confronting each other, each in the service of a woman. Constance's forces fell back on Le Mans, leaving Angers to be sacked by Eleanor's men under Mercadier, whose reward was to hold its principal citizens for ransom.

Meanwhile, John, as duke of Normandy, was leading a force of Normans into Maine. In retaking Le Mans, fire and sword were again the order of the day, but Constance had slipped away with Arthur to Tours, where Philip Augustus again took charge of the boy as an important piece to be saved for later in the game. The immediate danger over, Eleanor wheeled south to make a regal progress through her own domains of Poitou and Aquitaine accompanied by an impressive retinue of bishops and barons. She did not solicit her vassals' loyalty to John, who was to them a distant figure who had spent much of his life on the wrong side of the Channel and had neither Richard's valour nor his poetic prowess to commend him. Instead, she reintroduced herself to her vassals – most of whom had not been born when she inherited the duchy in 1137 – as mother of one legendary dead hero and granddaughter of the great crusading troubadour-duke William IX.

Maintaining that Richard's title to the duchy had been valid for his lifetime only and was not therefore part of his inheritable estate to be claimed by John, she reasserted plenary powers for herself on the grounds that she had never actually renounced her titles as countess of Poitou and duchess of Aquitaine, even during the fifteen agonising years when Henry used every trick to force her to do so. She then ceded Poitou and Aquitaine to John on condition that he swear fealty to her and renounce all his rights for the duration of her lifetime or until such earlier time as might suit her. Her price was that he confirm all her prerogatives as queen of England, which kept her still the richest woman in the world. That was the best she could do; after that, she retired to Fontevraud for the rest of her days. There, although she did not seek the world, it came to her in the persons of nobles and churchmen who brought her news – none of it good.

## NOTES

1. J. Vaissete, *Abrégé de l'histoire générale de Languedoc* (Paris, 1799), Vol 3, pp. 219–40.
2. A. Richard, *Histoire*, Vol 2, p. 299.
3. Ralph of Coggeshall, *Chronicon Anglicarum*, p. 96.
4. A. Richard, *Histoire*, Vol 2, p. 324.
5. J. Bradbury, *The Medieval Archer* (Woodbridge: Boydell, 2002), p. 77.
6. Ibid.
7. Roger of Howden, *Chronica*, Vol 4, p. 83.
8. Ralph of Coggeshall, *Chronicon Anglicarum*, p. 96.
9. Ibid, p. 98.
10. Ibid, p. 96.
11. Roger of Howden, *Chronica*, Vol 4, p. 83.
12. Ibid, p. 84.
13. Meyer, *Guillaume le Maréchal*, Vol 3, pp. 159–60.
14. *Magna Vita Sancti Hugonis Episcopi Lincolniensis*, ed. J.F. Dimock, Rolls Series No. 37 (London: Longmans, 1864), pp. 282–3.
15. A. Richard, *Histoire*, Vol 2, p. 332–3.
16. Dimock, *Vita*, pp. 286–7.
17. Ibid, p. 288.
18. Ibid, pp. 290–3.
19. A. Richard, *Histoire*, Vol 2, p. 333.
20. *Recueil*, Vol 18, p. 325.
21. Roger of Howden, *Chronica*, Vol 4, p. 88.
22. Powicke, *The Loss of Normandy*, p. 128.

# Of a Siege, Sex and Saddles

The troubadour Gaucelm Faidit composed a *planh* lamenting the death of Richard. The first verse runs:

> Fortz chausa es car cel q'era de valor caps e paire
> lo rics valens Richartz, reis dels Engles
> es mortz. Ai Dieus, cals perd'e cals dan es!
> Cant estrains motz e cant greus ad ausir.
> Ben a dur còr totz hom qu'o pot sofrir.

[It is an awful thing, for the very father-figure of valour, /
brave Richard, king of the English, / is dead.
God knows, 'tis terrible news to hear. / Only the hardest-hearted
man can learn such cruel news without shedding a tear.]

That was conventional lip service on the lines of the lament on the death of the Young King composed by Bertran de Born. There were many who recalled instead Richard's arrogance and the heedless avarice that had caused his death. As to his boast that the most costly castle in the world was impregnable, over the winter of 1203/04 a six-month siege of Château Gaillard by Philip Augustus forced the capitulation of the castellan Roger de Lacy. About 2,000 civilians took refuge inside the walls at the start of the siege when their homes in the village below were destroyed by the invaders. Twice de Lacy evicted groups of 500 of these 'useless mouths' to economise food stocks and these people were allowed to pass through the siege lines. After Philip Augustus learned of this, he forbade any further clemency, so when de Lacy evicted the remaining 1,000 civilians – mainly old men, women and children – the besiegers opened fire on them, driving them back to the castle walls, where they were trapped with the gates firmly closed against them. Hundreds died in the midwinter cold, including at least one woman in childbirth, and the others from starvation and exposure, until Philip took mercy on the few gaunt survivors and allowed them to leave.

The castle was finally taken after the wall of the outer bailey was undermined through the solid limestone bedrock. One of Philip's men then led a storming party through the breach into the second bailey through an unguarded latrine chute associated with a chapel, said to be a modification by John of Richard's original design. The small group of attackers lit fires once inside, which panicked the garrison into thinking the whole building was on fire. This enabled the invaders to lower the drawbridge over the dry moat. De Lacy's force retreated into the inner bailey. When the wall of this was also breached, they withdrew into the *donjon* itself. There, running out of food and everything else, de Lacy and twenty knights with 120 men-at-arms surrendered on 6 March 1204.

The fall of Château Gaillard was followed, a fortnight later, by the death of Eleanor of Aquitaine, which spared her the sight of the Plantagenet Empire she had made with Henry II subsiding into the quicksands of time.

How is one to sum up Richard's life? It is impossible to use modern criteria to assess a prince living in a period that more resembled the Dark Ages than, say, the time of Henry V or VIII. In his time, each lord and baron may have inherited title to his land and the people on that land, but he was only master of it and of them so long as he could dominate his vassals, fight off his neighbours and take part in greater struggles, aligning himself with this or that powerful suzerain. On that score, Richard comes out well. He spent his whole adolescence and adult life in warfare. Lacking Henry II's statesmanship, he did not expand the Plantagenet Empire, but neither did he directly contribute to its demise.

But in one significant duty he failed – by not begetting a warrior prince to defend the empire by force of arms after his death. He must have been aware that his brother John would never be able to hold together the empire assembled by their parents, so why, whatever his sexual preferences, did he not sire a legitimate son or daughter as a duty to the state? Homosexuals have had children for all sorts of reasons, and what more important reason was there than to provide an heir for an empire?

But was he homosexual, as some historians have inferred? Was his bastard Philip of Cognac the result of possibly a single aberration from his normal preference? 'The love that dare not speak its name', as Oscar Wilde termed it, was a taboo subject for the Victorian divines who translated from Latin the chronicles and charters that continue to illuminate twelfth-century history for modern readers – and this prudery continued for the first half of the twentieth century. Yet, Ralph of Diceto and Gervase are among the chroniclers who commented on Richard's treatment of women. Roger of Howden went so far as to write, 'He carried off his subjects' wives, daughters and kinswomen by force and made them his concubines. When he had sated his own lust on them, he handed them down for his soldiers to enjoy.'[1] Alfred Richard, among others, lent credence to this allegation.

In the latter half of the twentieth century, when the media search for scandal made celebrities' sex lives a fertile field for journalists to plough, historians reflected that trend by attributing to homosexuality Richard's lack of legitimate progeny, his tolerance of, and closeness to, pederast William Longchamp, his preference for male company and especially his period of intense intimacy with Philip Augustus. The pendulum effect has recently seen some biographers leaning the other way, pointing out that hand-holding between men – normal conduct in many Arab countries today – and even sharing bed and board with Philip Augustus did not at the time necessarily indicate sexual congress any more than the symbolic kiss of peace implied genuine affection.

Infertile marriages have often been, and remarkably often still are, blamed on the wife, so some have switched the blame for Richard's lack of progeny on to Berengaria by suggesting that she was sterile. She may have been, but Richard spent so little time with her that it would be hard to test that argument. In any case, the remedy for a sterile wife was simple for a king, who could always have the marriage annulled by a complaisant primate and take a new wife known to be fertile – as indeed Alais was.

Even fertile unions failed very often in the Middle Ages to produce more than one or two offspring. There are exceptions, like William the Conqueror, whose ten children fought over the inheritance, and Henry II, whose five sons and three daughters with Eleanor constituted a large family for the time. But knights and nobles so often died leaving only one living infant or no heir at all that feudal practice allowed the overlord to allocate their fiefs to favoured vassals.

This leads to another possible explanation for Richard's failure to leave an heir: infertility due to low sex drive and/or low sperm count. Of the pre-testicular causes, the most common is hypogonadism or low testosterone secretion, but that usually shows up in other ways: low energy levels, low bone density, low aggression and low muscle strength and mass. None of these apply to Richard. He was unusually tall for the time, or even for today, standing well over 6ft tall. He was also very heavily built. His numerous injuries, except the last, at Châlus, seem not to have produced lingering effects and he suffered no broken limbs on the many occasions when he was unhorsed, so we can write off low bone density. When in good health, he was very strong, controlling powerful, spirited *destriers* with heels and left arm while wielding heavy weapons to terrifying effect in combat with the right arm and hand, so his muscle strength and mass must have been well above the norms for healthy, active men. As to aggression, anyone reading this book knows that he was extremely aggressive.

Malaria was endemic in Europe at the time. Richard was known to suffer from it, both on the crusade and at home. Whilst the disease is extremely debilitating during crises, it is not generally blamed for lowering sperm production; modern complications in this direction are usually attributed to the drugs used in the treatment of the disease.

So much for pre-testicular causes of infertility. There is however another, more likely possible explanation for his lack of issue.

Two and a half thousand years ago, the Greeks noted that the Scythian nomads and other Asiatic peoples then arriving in Europe tended to have low fertility. Hippocrates (460–370 BCE) imputed this to the fact that the males spent most of every day astride their horses, with the testicles compressed by their body weight and kept constantly too warm, with the perineum suffering repeated trauma when thumped against the horse's spine or saddlecloth in rough riding and combat. Both Plato (424–348 BCE) and Herodotus (484–425 BCE) agreed with this finding.

The scrotum is, after all, an adaptation of the female labia expressly designed by nature to contain the testes outside the body because sperm production is severely reduced or non-existent at body temperature. The Greeks worked out the connection philosophically and by observation, but modern fertility clinics using more scientific methods find exactly the same thing happens with men who, for example, habitually wear tight underpants or trousers, or sit for hours in school and offices and cars – and especially those who practise long-distance cycle racing or mountain biking, or … regularly ride horses.

But even regular indulgence in modern equestrian sports like polo and endurance trials are nowhere near as punishing to a male rider's perineum and testicles as the lifestyle of a medieval knight. Richard was an archetypical horseback warrior who, throughout his adolescent sexual development and for the whole of his adult life, spent many hours every day in the saddle. This was frequently a war saddle with high pommel and high cantle, designed like a western saddle to lock the rider tightly in place so that he could not easily be unseated in the heat of combat. The modern equestrian custom is to have the stirrup leathers short, which enables the rider to rise out of the saddle on broken ground and avoid the worst shocks to the perineum. In Richard's day the leathers were long to keep the centre of gravity low. Since the rider could not easily lift himself by standing on the stirrups, the pounding hooves of his mount transferred into a sustained series of shocks to the crotch from banging up and down against the hard leather saddle. Such repeated punishment frequently produced haemorrhoids, from which Henry II suffered greatly. More seriously, it also caused chronic prostatitis and/or blocked the sperm ducts or the epididymis, where semen is stored. Richard was known to ride his horses so hard that many foundered under him, so it would be strange indeed if he suffered no trauma to his reproductive organs.

Richard's maternal grandfather Duke William X of Aquitaine had produced only three children. Similarly, Richard's paternal grandfather Geoffrey the Fair of Anjou had only three legitimate offspring. But by no means all knights inherited a fief like them and married to found a family early in life. Indeed, the typical landless knight spent many years' riding in the service of his lord before winning a noble wife as reward for some great feat of arms, by which time his ability to inseminate his spouse was in many cases severely reduced. The statute *de donis conditionalibus* – concerning conditional gifts – was passed into English law in 1285. It provided for the entailment of property through the male line so that, in the event of its owner dying without leaving a son, title would go to his nearest male relative, effectively disinheriting female progeny. So long as the horse was the principle means of travel, damage to 'male parts' from horse riding continued to bedevil inheritance in the aristocracy. Entailment to the male line was therefore very common in equestrian society and this is reflected in books by authors such as Jane Austen, where it is an important element in the plot of novels such as *Pride and Prejudice* and *Sense and Sensibility*.

So, was Richard gay, as some historians have concluded? Or was he heterosexual or bisexual, but rendered infertile by the saddle? DNA analysis might have given an answer, but although his effigy still lies in the Cistercian simplicity of Fontevraud abbey, the remains originally beneath it were scattered, no one knows where, when the Plantagenet tombs were despoiled during the French Revolution. The greatest of his many failings as monarch – the lack of progeny – must therefore remain a mystery.

## NOTES

1. Quoted in Gillingham, J., *Richard I* (Yale: Yale University Press, 1999), p. 66.

# On the Trail of the Lionheart
## – Places to Visit

British Museum medieval rooms: floor tiles from Clarendon Palace, Limoges enamel work, chess sets and other twelfth-century artefacts.

Worcester Cathedral: tomb of John.

The castle and cathedral of Rochester.

Pilgrims' hospice at Ospringe, Kent.

Canterbury Westgate and Canterbury Cathedral.

Portchester Castle.

Rouen Cathedral: effigy above the tomb of Richard's heart.

Le Mans: Abbey of l'Épau: effigy of Berengaria.

Chinon: Sainte Radegonde chapel and Chinon Castle.

Fontevraud Abbey: effigies of Richard, Eleanor, Henry II and Isabelle of Angoulême.

Taillebourg Castle ruins.

Poitiers: the great hall (now the law court), the Tour Maubergeonne and cathedral.

Saintes: Roman triumphal arch used as town gate (re-sited); cathedral and cloisters; Abbaye aux Dames.

Bordeaux: Musée d'Aquitaine for enamelled cross given to La Sauve Abbey by Richard or Eleanor; tiles and other artefacts.

Créon: La Sauve-Majeure Abbey.

Châlus Castle.

# Index

If you enjoyed this book, you may also be interested in …

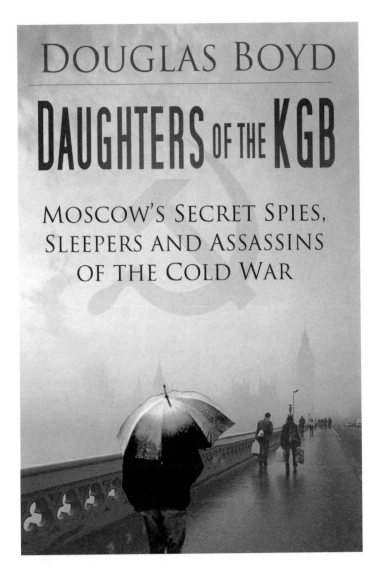

DOUGLAS BOYD

# DAUGHTERS OF THE KGB

## MOSCOW'S SECRET SPIES, SLEEPERS AND ASSASSINS OF THE COLD WAR

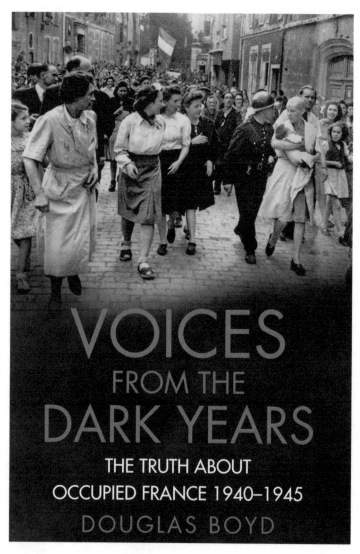

# VOICES
## FROM THE
# DARK YEARS
### THE TRUTH ABOUT
### OCCUPIED FRANCE 1940–1945
DOUGLAS BOYD

9780750961790

# THE KREMLIN CONSPIRACY

## 1,000 YEARS OF RUSSIAN EXPANSIONISM

## DOUGLAS BOYD

REVISED AND UPDATED

9780750961394

# THE OTHER FIRST WORLD WAR

## THE BLOOD-SOAKED RUSSIAN FRONTS 1914-1922

# DOUGLAS BOYD

9780752493589